Contents

Contents

Editorial introduction

This aim of this book is to give you as clear a picture as possible of the events and developments in the period you are studying. You may well be using this book to prepare for an examination and the book has several special features, listed below, to help you in this. Most of all, we hope it will help you to develop a critical awareness about, and a continuing interest in, the past.

FOCUS: Each chapter has a main focus, listed in the contents. These are the main issues and 'concepts', like cause and consequence, the evaluation of evidence, the role of the individual, key themes, historical controversies or interpretations and so on. All of these are important in studying and understanding history. Identifying a focus does not mean that the chapter only looks at the past in one way; rather that you are encouraged to find out about topics from a different slant.

TIME CHARTS: Most chapters begin with a time chart. It helps you follow the chronology. Some time charts develop a basic point which is not in the main text. You should also find that the charts provide you with a handy reference point.

KEY TERMS: There are some words or phrases which it is important to know in order to understand a wider topic. These have been highlighted in the text so that you can easily look up what they mean. Sometimes quite simple ideas appear in unfamiliar form or in jargon. Decoding these should help you to make sense of the wider ideas to which the terms relate. Towards the end of the book you will find a separate index of the key terms.

PROfiLES: There is not space in a book like this to provide full biographies of the people you will meet. The profiles give you the information you need to understand why an individual is important and what his or her main achievements were. Like the time charts, you might want to use these for reference. As with 'key terms', there is a separate index of people who are the subject of profiles.

TASKS and ACTIVITIES: Nearly all the chapters end with some suggestions for follow-up work and further study. These include:

- guidance on how, and why, to take notes
- suggestions for class discussion and debate

- help on how to use historical evidence of different types
- tips on answering source questions
- hints on planning and writing essays
- speciment examination questions so that you can prepare for assessment.

FURTHER READING: You will find that you need more help on certain topics than can be provided in a book like this. The further reading guides you to some more detailed or specialist texts. The reading is listed with the most immediately obvious supporting texts placed first, followed by others – some of which may be considerably more detailed.

INDEX: Many individuals, issues and themes are mentioned in more than one chapter. The main index is designed to help you find what you are looking for quickly and easily by showing you how to collect together information which is spread about. Get practice in using an index; it will save you a lot of time.

The historian's job is to recreate the past. On one level, this is obviously an impossible task. There is far too much of it to put into one book while at the same time much of the information we need has been long since lost. Most of it can never be recovered. It is because there is so much of it that the historian has to impose his or her priorities by selecting. It is because so much more has been lost that he or she has to try to fill in the gaps and supply answers which other people can challenge. The processes of Selection and Interpretation are the key tasks of the historian and they help to make the subject endlessly fascinating. Every time a historian makes a decision about what to put in and what to leave out that decision implies a judgement which others might challenge. Historians try to get as close to the truth as they can, in the knowledge that others may disagree with what they say. Don't be surprised, then, to find a number of personal views or 'interpretations'. Some of these will make comparisons between the present and the period you are studying. These personal views have not been included in order to persuade you to agree with them. We aim to make you think about what you are reading and not always to accept everything at face value. If this book helps you to tell the difference between fact and opinion while keeping up your interest in the past, it will have served its purpose.

Christopher Culpin
Eric Evans
Series Editors

Part One   The war and interwar years, 1914–39

1 Introduction: Britain in and after 1914

Many writers in the interwar period looked back nostalgically to the years before 1914 as Paradise Lost. Britain had then been great: Britannia ruled the waves and the sun would surely never set on its empire. It seemed to be a time of unparalleled stability, prosperity and optimism. But there are few things as fallible, or as subject to emotional distortion, as human memory. It was only after the mass slaughter of the Great War that the charms of prewar Britain seemed so attractive, only in comparison with the carnage on the Western Front that Edwardian England seemed idyllic. In the years immediately preceding 1914 – when, ironically, *The Times* noted that nowadays people 'place the golden age behind them' – Britain faced problems in plenty. Indeed many observers believed that their society was fast disintegrating.

In 1914 the United Kingdom embraced England, Scotland, Wales and the whole of Ireland, containing approximately 46 million people, three-quarters of whom lived in England. Of these roughly 75 per cent can be classified as working class, the rest comprising the middle and upper classes. The birth rate had been falling for several decades but average life expectancy was rising and so the population was larger than ever before.

The British Empire

Britain was also the centre of the largest empire the world had ever known, containing 400 million people and covering about a quarter of the world's land surface. It was a source of immense pride to people of all classes: Britons were able to glory in being a great governing race, able to lord it over those whom Kipling dismissed as 'lesser breeds without the law'. But the Empire was more a symbol of prestige than an engine of power. British strength was not proportionate to the size of the area coloured imperial red on the big maps in every school classroom.

As well as the largest, it was also the most diverse and scattered empire in history, containing land in every continent. The main distinction was between the **Dominions** and **colonies**.

Of the dependent Empire, India, with a population of 300 million, was not only the 'greatest jewel' in the imperial crown, it was the country's

KEY TERMS:

Dominions and colonies

The settlers who had gone to Australia, Canada, New Zealand and South Africa had all, by 1910, been granted internal self-government, though retaining the British monarch as head of state. Britain, however, was still responsible for their foreign policy and defence, at no inconsiderable cost. In the interwar period they became generally known as **Dominions** – autonomous countries but freely associated with Great Britain.

Colonies were governed by the British, who made their laws and levied taxation, and did not have self-government. At the most, local people had seats in the local parliament.

largest export market. Britain insisted it was a 'trustee' or guardian, governing in the interests of the Indian wards; but imperial rhetoric could not disguise the fact that British rule in India was essentially autocratic, and nor could it prevent the growth of nationalist movements in the subcontinent.

British politics

Britain was a kingdom. George V had been monarch since 1910, and there was no organised republican movement, but real political power lay with the House of Commons – 670 Members of Parliament (MPs) elected by about two-thirds of the adult male population. This is not to say that Britain was a democracy. Out of 45 million inhabitants, only 8 million men could vote and no women, though some women were allowed to vote in local government contests. The House of Lords, containing hereditary peers and the bishops and archbishops of the Church of England, was far more important then than now. In 1911 the Parliament Act had clipped its wings: henceforth it did not have the power to reject a budget and it could only delay other bills for a maximum of two years, rather than veto them altogether. But even so, the peers were still vitally important in Parliament and generally occupied a sizeable minority of ministerial and cabinet positions. The government in 1914, a Liberal administration headed by Herbert Asquith, contained half-a-dozen lords, and several other ministers were landowners related to the aristocracy. MPs had been paid since 1911, but politics was still largely a rich man's game.

Over the previous decades a strong party system had grown up. The Liberals and the Conservatives, national parties with local constituency organisations, tended to alternate in office. The electoral system almost seemed to guarantee political stability. There was no system of proportional representation, whereby the number of seats allotted to a party would be in direct proportion to the number of votes it polled: instead, then as now, Britain used the 'first-past-the-post' system. Whoever received the largest number of votes in a constituency was elected its Member of Parliament. Such a system of winner takes all, loser takes nothing, had the advantage of simplicity; but the disadvantage was that a government with a majority of seats in the Commons was not necessarily supported by a majority of the electorate. Indeed sometimes the opposition actually received more votes than the government. Another problem was that whereas this system seemed ideally adapted to two parties, it was very uncertain how well it would function if there were three or more strong parties. The political future was obscure. Certainly no one could predict with any certainty that the Labour Party, formed in 1900, would become a major force in politics.

The economy and decline

Economically, Britain was one of the richest countries in the world. Its production was rising significantly, so that by 1914 it had never been more prosperous. It was producing perhaps one-quarter of the world's manufactured goods, and although it was in fact importing goods worth more than those it was exporting, there was no overall 'balance of payments' deficit because of so-called '**invisible exports**'.

The British economy was therefore highly prosperous around 1914. There was no 'decline' in the sense of an actual fall in economic output. Nevertheless, some contemporaries were acutely conscious of a **relative decline**. Britain had been the world's foremost economic power 40 years earlier. Now the Americans and Germans were in the lead, and Britain's share of world output had fallen significantly, even since the start of the century. A trend of relative decline had been established: the question was, where would it end? Pessimists could see no end at all. They were alarmed because foreign goods were penetrating the domestic market and because Britain was no longer at the forefront of technical innovation. Increased output arose more from the employment of extra workers rather than the use of more powerful machinery: productivity (output per worker) scarcely seemed to be increasing at all in 1900–14. In particular, Britain seemed over-reliant on its **staple industries**, and their products were now no longer in such demand.

There were further causes for concern. Surveys in York and London established that real poverty existed. Around 30 per cent of the urban working classes seemed to be living in poverty. Here was a scandal at the heart of the British Empire, and one moreover that seemed likely, in a competitive age, to add to British decline. Recruitment for the Boer War (1899–1902) exposed the poor physical condition of many who volunteered to fight, while the difficulty experienced in winning against the Dutch settlers in southern Africa further undermined British morale. Britain was victorious in the end, but the contest had been far too close for comfort. Many observers decided that the imperial race was deteriorating. Might Britain go the way of ancient Rome, experiencing first decline and then fall?

Prewar Liberal governments

The Liberals had been in power from 1905 onwards. The reform measures they passed were motivated as much by a sense of national peril as by humanitarianism. As well as reducing the powers of the House

'Invisible exports'

'Invisible exports' were the profits derived from British investments abroad and from the financial services offered to other countries by the City of London. These were usually substantial, since London was the financial capital of the world, acting as banker and money-lender on a large scale. The pound sterling was the world's standard currency.

Relative decline

Britain's output was not falling in absolute terms: indeed industrial production was growing. But since the 1880s the United States and Germany had been growing at a much faster rate. Therefore Britain was experiencing economic decline compared to (or relative to) its rivals. Many historians see **relative decline** as one of the key themes of British history in the twentieth century.

Staple industries

Staple industries were industries which, before 1914, produced the bulk of Britain's exports and on which the country substantially relied for its prosperity. They included textiles, iron and steel, shipbuilding and mining; and they were concentrated in particular parts of Britain – notably South Wales, the Clyde Valley of Central Scotland, north-east England, Lancashire and parts of Yorkshire.

of Lords, they introduced old age pensions in 1908, free at the point of need for those aged 70 and over, and compulsory health and unemployment insurance for selected numbers of workers. They were laying the foundations for what later became the 'welfare state'; but many judged that Asquith and his Chancellor, Lloyd George, might be overstepping the bounds of what a government ought to do. Traditionally, governments had pursued a policy of *laissez-faire*, contenting themselves with keeping the peace at home and defending the realm as economically as possible. There was a philosophical unease, therefore, at so much interference with the lives of British citizens. Economists also insisted that high government spending would inhibit economic growth. The economy, they believed, was a gigantic self-regulating mechanism whereby supply and demand would always balance – but only if government stood aside and refused to interfere. On the other hand, there was a growing number who believed that government should intervene much more to solve society's problems.

There were other difficulties too for the Liberals. Industrially there was a wave of unrest, especially from 1908 to 1913. There were 4 million trade union members by 1914, twice as many as in 1900, and some believed that they were intent on using their industrial muscle to bring about a revolution. Certainly national strikes in the mines and on the railways seemed menacing, and in April 1914 the 'triple alliance' of miners, railwaymen and transport workers appeared to threaten a general strike. Scarcely less intimidating were the activities of the suffragettes, who were prepared to take direct action to secure the vote for women. The cabinet was divided on the issue. Some ministers were implacably opposed, believing that a woman's place was in the home; others were more sympathetic. The result was stalemate and an escalation of suffragette violence. Cabinet ministers were assaulted, windows smashed, works of art slashed, and some women courted arrest in order to have the opportunity to go on hunger strike.

Most menacing of all was the situation in Ireland. The majority Catholic population wanted control of their own local affairs, but they were opposed by the Protestants of Ulster, who wished to continue as an integral part of the United Kingdom. An impasse had been reached. The Liberals recognised the rights of the majority while wishing to safeguard those of the minority. The Conservatives (or 'Unionists' as they were beginning to call themselves) were less philosophical about it: 'Ulster will fight, and Ulster will be right'. They believed that the union with Ireland had to be maintained: otherwise Home Rule for Ireland would encourage Indian nationalists and other troublemakers in the Empire. Civil war looked a distinct possibility by the start of 1914. Both the South and the North were armed, organised and implacable. What is more,

5

Conservative support for Ulster gunmen seemed to imply that peaceful, parliamentary government might be breaking down not only in Ireland but in the United Kingdom as a whole. 'There can no longer be the slightest doubt,' insisted *The Times* on 28 June 1914, 'that the country is now confronted with one of the greatest crises in the history of the British race.'

Foreign affairs

Newspapers made little of the news from far-off Bosnia on 28 June that the heir to the Austro-Hungarian Empire had been assassinated. But in fact the bullets of the assassin ricocheted all round Europe and set off a chain reaction that resulted in the First World War. The British were indeed confronted with one of the greatest crises in their history, but not the one they expected.

Traditionally Britain had kept aloof from the continent of Europe. Lord Salisbury, Prime Minister at the start of the century, insisted that 'We are fish', more concerned with the seas – and the navy – than with the nearby continental land mass. But when Kaiser William II began to construct a great fleet, Britain reacted. Nothing so soured Anglo-German relations as the naval race. Britain emerged victorious, but anti-German feeling led the Liberals to move closer to France and its ally Russia. The ententes signed with France and Russia before 1914 were not alliances, they were merely settlements of disputes; but the heavy-handed diplomacy of the Kaiser and his ministers seemed almost calculated to push Britain into Franco-Russian arms.

The assassination in June 1914 led to confrontation between Germany and Russia. Britain's reaction was uncertain. There was a chance that Asquith's government would stand aside. France had made no decision whether or not to aid its Russian ally, but the German chiefs of staff decided they could not proceed in a war against Russia and leave their western flank exposed. They were committed to the Schlieffen Plan, whereby they would deliver an immediate and overwhelmingly strong knockout blow against France before moving eastward against the larger, but more slowly mobilising, Russian army. In order to avoid a war on two fronts, they therefore attacked France, violating Belgian neutrality in the process. The British cabinet had been split down the middle, a division that ruled out action, but now there was consensus for joining in. Britain declared war on Germany on 6 August 1914.

The Foreign Secretary predicted that the lamps which were going out all over Europe would not be 'lit again in our lifetime'. Others too thought that civilisation might be coming to an end. But such doubts and fears were exceptional. Most people rejoiced. They had been so conditioned by propaganda over the previous decades that they believed the war would be a glorious, fulfilling adventure. Poems were written celebrating the conflict. Over a million men volunteered to join the army over the next few months, far more than the authorities expected. Trade unions urged that existing strikes should be hastily ended. The suffragettes ceased their activities. Instead of seeing the war as yet another example of male stupidity, and one moreover that made even more vital the immediate enfranchisement of women, they urged the menfolk to volunteer. Even the Irish conflict was calmed. Existing problems simply dissolved in a welter of patriotism.

People expected that the war would be all over by Christmas. It is hard to understand why. The conflict against the Boers had lasted two and a half years; and now Britain, with its French and Russian allies, faced not only Germany but also Austria-Hungary and, by early in 1915, Turkey and Bulgaria. The war that began in August 1914 was soon known as the Great War and, later, as the First World War. It was a titanic struggle, the like of which had never been seen before, a war not just between armed forces but between whole nations. The 'Home Front' became as important as the 'fronts' where the fighting took place. The war lasted for over four years and claimed approximately 8–9 million lives.

Britain after 1914

The agenda for the next 25 years, and possibly for the rest of the twentieth century, was being set around 1914:

1 How would Great Britain cope with the war, and what would be its consequences? Long conscious of being a great power, Britain now had to make good its pretensions. But having entered what was in essence a European civil war, would Britain be able to disengage itself at its close, or would it be permanently entangled in European affairs? Britain's world role was in the melting pot.

2 How would the British economy cope with a major war making virtually limitless demands for munitions? Would the overall effects of the war be negative, or might there perhaps be positive benefits? It certainly seemed unlikely that the prewar pattern of world trade, in which Britain was so vitally involved, would be resumed after the conflict. Perhaps the most fundamental question was whether the prewar trend towards relative decline would continue, and if so, at what pace? And what of industrial relations? The outbreak of war produced industrial harmony, but it was far from certain whether this would continue.

3 What of the Irish issue? There seemed no reason to believe that a crisis had been more than postponed. On a larger scale, how would Britain's relations with its empire be affected? The whole of the British Empire went to war in 1914. Might the common imperial war effort boost a movement towards unity or, on the contrary, emphasise tendencies towards separatism?

4 What of politics? Would representative government be able to cope with the demands of the war? Not all Britons, by any means, were convinced democrats. It was also possible that the monarchy might topple: after all, the war ended dynastic rule in Russia, Germany and Austria. Would the conflict accelerate votes for women, and for unenfranchised men as well? Many believed that the participation of so many 'ordinary' people in the war almost guaranteed that, at its close, the franchise would be extended more widely. But, if so, would a truly democratic Britain be able to survive in the new world of change and upheaval? Some suspected that universal suffrage would simply open the door to demagogues. Could democracy work, or would Britain fall victim to two ideologies which were tremendously boosted by the war – communism and fascism?

5 How would ideas be affected? The war might be expected to leave as many psychological, as economic or social, scars. Would attitudes and expectations be the same? Might there be a slow, gradual modification or, perhaps, a radical transformation that would affect the way Britons perceived the world and themselves?

The remaining chapters in Part One will explore these vital issues.

Task: note-taking

Why take notes? There is a simple answer to this question: imagine tackling an essay or an exam without having first made any! It would be quite impossible, unless we possessed brilliant memories. As well as encouraging concentration and comprehension, making notes will also increase your skill in distinguishing between what is important and what is less important.

How to take notes? Unfortunately, there is no simple answer to this one. No method of note-taking is perfect. Everyone is different, and therefore everyone must find the best method for himself or herself. Why not experiment with different styles? For instance, can you summarise the main points of this chapter in a diagram? Or would a chronological table help? Most people, however, use written notes, grouped under convenient headings and subheadings. The chapters in this book have such divisions, which you can use as the basic structure for your own notes. A few minor but useful hints include the following:

- Use your own convenient abbreviations.
- Make a real effort to write legibly, since you may have to use your notes a year or 18 months hence.
- Spread out your notes, so that you can add extra material at a later date.

Occasionally, however, it may be best to adopt a different approach. Take this chapter, for instance: if you fully understand the issues raised, and have summarised them in brief notes, you could then attempt to list the 'strengths' and 'weaknesses' of Britain around 1914. Such restructuring will test your understanding of a chapter. Tips for doing this will be given in later chapters.

Above all, perhaps, you should bear in mind the uses to which you are likely to put your notes. If you are working for a particular essay, you can judge on which issues you need to be particularly detailed. For the present chapter, however, which introduces half-a-dozen themes in a fairly general way, you may wish to be relatively brief. Try to grasp the main issues (like the meaning of 'relative decline' and the 'staple industries') rather than copy down very many precise details. Always think about the purpose and the best means of taking notes, and never allow note-making to become a mechanical exercise.

It is also important to realise that the notes for a single chapter may not cover all you need to know about a particular issue. Therefore do use the index. The index in this book gives you page references to the main issues and events, as well as to key terms and the key people. Remember that a good index can give you numerous shortcuts to valuable information.

Further reading

A. J. P. Taylor, *The First World War: An Illustrated History* (Penguin, 1966) – a witty and provocative account; Taylor's captions are sometimes brilliant.

J. M. Bourne, *Britain and the Great War 1914–18* (Edward Arnold, 1989) – an excellent, up-to-date account, especially useful for political and military themes.

2 The First World War – a turning-point?

Time chart

1914: August
Start of First World War

1915: April
Unsuccessful Gallipoli campaign
May
Coalition government formed

1916: July
Battle of the Somme begins
December
Lloyd George becomes Prime Minister

1917: March
Russian Tsar abdicates
April
USA enters the war
October–November
Battle of Passchendaele
November
Lenin pulls Russia out of the war

1918: Vote extended in Britain (to men aged 21 and women aged 30)
April
Last German offensive
11 November
The end of the war
December
British general election

In entering the war in 1914, wrote Lloyd George, ministers 'pulled a lever which might land us on a star or lead us into chaos'. Whatever the results of the war, they were expected to be momentous – and most historians have agreed that they were. The 1914–18 war has been generally interpreted as producing fundamental historical changes. There seems to be a wider chasm separating prewar and postwar Britain than a mere four and a half years could possibly span, so that the war marks a massive discontinuity in history. The period after November 1918 seemed to be a new era: 'Modern Times' had begun. The theme of this chapter is therefore the issue of change and continuity. Was the war a major turning-point in British history?

The war

The 1914–18 conflict was not 'just another war'. Its like had not been seen before. The generals of the belligerent countries were themselves taken by surprise. Most had cut their military teeth in colonial wars and knew more about cavalry than trenches, let alone the tanks and aeroplanes that marked the closing stages of the war.

There were several theatres of war. On the Eastern Front, the Russians (the allies of Britain and France) did reasonably well against the Austrians but poorly against the more efficient German units. The war further destabilised an already weak and unpopular regime in Russia, so that the autocratic Tsar, Nicholas II, abdicated in March 1917. In November Lenin and the Bolsheviks came to power and pulled Russia out of the war. This withdrawal was a blow for Britain and France, but in April 1917 President Woodrow Wilson had brought the United States into the conflict after German unrestricted submarine warfare had wrought havoc with American shipping. The presence of the USA seemed to guarantee eventual victory for the Anglo-French side. It was also useful for propaganda purposes. The substitution of a democratic for an autocratic ally meant that Britain could claim it was fighting not merely to win but for the cause of freedom and democracy.

Britain's own part in the war involved colonial conflicts in Africa and elsewhere and an important campaign against Turkey. In the Middle East, partly by encouraging Arabs to revolt against Turkish rule, Britain and France gained control of most of the Turkish Empire, including Palestine and Mesopotamia. This was some compensation for earlier failures against Turkey, including an unsuccessful attempt to gain control of Gallipoli in April 1915, which resulted in 4,000 deaths. The Gallipoli campaign had itself been an attempt to break the deadlock in the main theatre of war, the Western Front.

The Western Front

The German plan to knock France out of the war in six weeks failed, narrowly. The French army, supported by the small British Expeditionary Force, halted the Germans at the river Marne in September 1914. Both sides then dug trenches and a long war of attrition began. The 'front line' between the enemies was not to change by more than a few miles over the next three years – but hundreds of thousands of men were killed in gaining these few miles of territory. The great battles of the war achieved remarkably little.

Casualty figures

1 July 1916 (first day of Battle of the Somme): 20,000 British soldiers killed

July–November 1916 (the Somme): over 400,000 Britons killed in total

October–November 1917 (Passchendaele): 300,000 British and Canadian soldiers killed

---

Critics complained that Britain's western strategy was misconceived and its generals criminally incompetent. Ordinary soldiers were 'lions led by donkeys'. Apologists insisted that the Germans were more weakened by such encounters than the British and French allies. The issue is still hotly debated. But it was the Germans who seized the initiative in April 1918. Their spring offensive was a last-ditch attempt to end the war before the United States entered in force and the British blockade of Germany caused further hardship. Again they reached the Marne, but by August it was the Anglo-French forces that were advancing in all sectors. German troops retreated eastwards – committing unspeakable barbarities in the process, according to allied propaganda – and on 11 November, a few days after the Kaiser abdicated, the new German government signed an armistice. It had seemed to many that the war would go on forever; now it came to an abrupt end.

Perhaps 750,000 Britons had been killed (30 per cent of all men aged 20–24), and 1.6 million wounded. These were large totals, and people spoke of a 'lost generation'. But altogether over 8 million people died in the war, so Britain had escaped relatively lightly. London had been bombed by German Zeppelins, but there had been no fighting on British soil. Certainly many other combatant states suffered much more. Yet the war on the Western Front was indelibly etched on the consciousness of those who fought. The great battles on the Western Front were not glorious adventures, they were Armageddon – destructive, wasteful, hideous and brutal. After this, could the survivors pick themselves up, dust themselves off and start their lives all over again? Could Britain ever be the same?

The consequences of war

Political results

At first it had seemed that the war would have few political consequences. It was 'Business as usual'. The soldiers would get on with winning the war; the Liberal government, augmented now by the imperial hero Lord Kitchener as Secretary for War, would administer the country. But early victory failed to materialise, and a shortage of weapons for British troops together with the Gallipoli failures produced a political crisis in May 1915. Asquith survived as Prime Minister but had to accept an all-party coalition, in which Lloyd George held the key position of Minister of Munitions. In December 1916 continuing stalemate in the war produced another crisis: **Lloyd George**, the one undoubted political success of the war years, overthrew his former boss with the help of Conservative leaders and became Prime Minister himself.

PROFILE: *David Lloyd George*

Brought up in north Wales, **Lloyd George** trained as a solicitor before being elected to Parliament in 1890. In 1905 he began 17 continuous years in office, serving first as President of the Board of Trade and then as Chancellor of the Exchequer. A dynamic executive, he was responsible for inaugurating old age pensions and national insurance, and it was he who took the lead in limiting the powers of the House of Lords. During the war he was successful as Minister of Munitions and then as Prime Minister, and at the end of 1918 he was widely regarded as 'the man who won the war'. He seemed secure in office for years to come, and A. J. P. Taylor considers him the greatest ruler of Britain since Oliver Cromwell. But he could not throw off a reputation for unorthodoxy and immorality, and in 1922 the Conservatives left his coalition government. Lloyd George never held office again. He died in 1945.

The first general election for a decade was held in December 1918. It reveals the impact of the war on politics. Most important of all, the electorate had virtually trebled. In 1918 the vote had been extended to all men aged 21 and over and to women of 30 and above. In 1910 there had been 7.5 million men eligible to vote; now there were 21 million electors, 8 million of whom were women. We may therefore, for the first time, talk of something approaching real democracy in Britain. It was also decided that henceforth elections should be held on a single day, instead of being spread over several weeks. In many ways politics had taken a distinctively 'modern' form.

No one, before the war, would have been so eccentric as to predict the results achieved in 1918. A government was formed by Lloyd George, supported by a relatively small number of Liberals and a much larger number of Conservatives. The 1916 coalition was thus carried on in peacetime, and so the breach between Lloyd George and Asquith was not healed. The war had thus split the Liberals virtually down the middle, and they ceased to be a major force in British politics. The Conservatives were the main beneficiaries, and the First World War heralded their domination of politics until 1945.

The rise of the Labour Party was almost as rapid as the decline of the Liberals. Labour had won 42 seats at the end of 1910; but its success was in large measure due to an electoral pact with the Liberals. In the 1918 election Labour won 63 seats. This may not seem a dramatic increase, but in fact Labour's share of the poll had increased by a massive 2 million votes (from 7 to 22 per cent of all votes cast). The party had gained valuable ministerial experience and had also used the war years to draw up a new and more effective party constitution, giving it a distinctive, 'socialist' position. Clause 4 pledged it to bring about 'the common ownership of the Means of Production'. Labour's collectivism had been far more suited to the wartime era than the Liberals' traditional emphasis on individualism; Labour was far more united than the Liberals; and in 1918 Labour won more votes and more seats than the official Liberal Party led by Asquith. Over the next years Labour's growth continued.

Clearly the First World War produced major political changes. The extension of the franchise stemmed from the participation of previously unenfranchised men and women in the war effort. Similarly, the rise of Labour and the decline of the Liberals are directly connected to the war. So is the ascendancy of Lloyd George.

However, there are several reasons for thinking that politics might have developed in a broadly similar direction even without the war. These include the following:

- Many historians have argued that the decline of the Liberals and the rise of Labour were deep-seated historical trends, stemming from fundamental changes in British society, including the emergence of a self-conscious working class. Perhaps, therefore, the war merely speeded up these developments.

- Might not the widening of the franchise have come about even earlier than 1918, but for the war? Certainly many Liberal politicians favoured universal suffrage.

- Similarly, Lloyd George's dynamic political talents seemed destined, sooner or later, to earn him the premiership. But for the war, he would certainly not have ended up as Prime Minister of a predominantly Conservative government, but that government lasted only until 1922.

Clearly, the war did not change everything. There was no political revolution. The authority of Parliament remained intact, and the monarchy did not fall.

Economic results

The Great War put massive strains on the British economy. By 1918, 5.7 million men had been mobilised, so that nearly half of all workers were in the army – and yet industry had to cope with an insatiable appetite for weapons and shells. In total, British workers produced 187 million shells; in 1918 alone they constructed 120,000 machine-guns. Small wonder that women had to enter industry or that government had to take the trade unions 'into partnership'. In return for improved pay and conditions of work, unions agreed to suspend strike action and to allow skilled work to be 'diluted' into simpler tasks that the unskilled could perform. Union membership increased from 4 million to 6 million during the war, and many union leaders worked closely with government; but often their authority in the factories diminished, and they were powerless to prevent unofficial, and often bitter, strikes, for instance those on Clydeside, in the Glasgow shipyards, in 1915.

The war enforced the abandonment of *laissez-faire*. War was too serious a business to be left to the operation of free market forces. The government introduced conscription in 1916; ministers had to try to keep price and wage levels in equilibrium; the mines and railways passed under state control. Indeed the government soon controlled virtually the whole of the economy.

In 1913 the government had spent a total of almost £200 million, all of which had been raised in taxation; but in 1918 it spent £2,500 million, only one-third of which came from taxes. Not only did more people than ever before now pay tax (7 million as against 1 million), and at much higher rates, but government had to sell off overseas investments and borrow on a massive scale. By the end of the war, Britain owed the United States £1,000 million and the National Debt had increased twelve-fold.

Clearly 1914–18 saw momentous economic changes. The economy was radically reoriented for the efficient prosecution of the war: there could, therefore, be no easy or quick return to satisfying peacetime needs. The staple industries (iron and steel, coal, shipbuilding and textiles) had been given a great boost, their products being needed in massive quantities; but after the war they were almost bound to experience a slump, and consequent unemployment. In addition, overseas markets had been lost. Nor would London ever again be the centre of the world's financial markets.

Yet there were also advantages stemming from the war. The productivity of British industry increased rapidly owing to state-sponsored mechanisation. There was a greater standardisation of engineering products, and electric power was being used much more in the factories, just as more tractors were working on the land. In addition, the new aircraft industry was basically a wartime creation.

So great was the degree of change experienced that the First World War must be considered an economic turning-point. But this does not mean that the subsequent course of history was predetermined. How Britain would cope with the economic and financial problems caused by the war was as uncertain as how well it would exploit the new opportunities provided. A similar uncertainty surrounded industrial relations. Might wartime arbitration herald a more fruitful means of settling disputes, or were the strikes organised by the shop stewards a better foretaste of things to come?

Imperial and foreign results

The First World War saw the expansion of the Empire to its maximum territorial extent, as territory was taken from the German and Turkish Empires and added to the British. The war also testified to a new sense of imperial unity. Troops from the Dominions served in several theatres of war, including Gallipoli, and Lloyd George inaugurated an imperial war cabinet. Might this lead to a new postwar integration of the empire; or might the Dominions claim, as reward for their loyalty, still greater powers to control their own destiny? And what of the dependent empire? In 1917 Britain pledged that India would eventually be given 'responsible government ... as an integral part of the British Empire'. But this was a wartime promise calculated to rally the Indian intelligentsia and calm nationalist agitation. It did not necessarily prescribe the policy Britain intended to pursue.

In foreign affairs, Britain became uncomfortably enmeshed with Europe. The war ended in 1918, but the peace treaties had still to be written, a task not completed until 1923. Whether Britain would then be able to withdraw from Europe, as its politicians undoubtedly wanted, was at first an open question. What was not in doubt, however, was that European power and prestige on the world stage would not be as great again. The United States and Japan, two merely nominal combatants, were the real victors in the war. Everyone else, whether victors or vanquished, had in reality lost. In fact, we see in the postwar world Britain vainly trying to retreat into semi-isolation until, in 1939, a Second World War followed the First. The decision to enter the war back in August 1914 had thus been a greater turning-point than the politicians realised.

Social results

The war affected the psychology of the whole nation in some degree, the combatants most of all but also their families at home. In particular, ideas about war changed. The First World War undoubtedly produced a more realistic understanding among the British people of what modern warfare involved. It helped to produce not only a pacifist movement in the following decades but a conviction among the great mass of Britons that another war should be fought only as a last resort. But the war had other effects too. The term 'lost generation' applies not only to those who perished in the war but to those who were permanently alienated and disoriented by it. Nevertheless, many combatants were resilient, and some even managed to enjoy the conflict and to remember it fondly. The mass of the people drew the lesson that British society had to be reconstructed. 'A country fit for heroes' was one of the slogans on which Lloyd George won the 1918 election. Improvements had to be made which, somehow, would compensate for the lives lost in 1914–18, so that their sacrifice would not have been entirely in vain. It was a conviction which lasted until the first postwar slump, in 1921, after which many people simply wanted to forget the war and get back to some sort of normality. But there could be no return to the past. After the war, British society was never quite the same again.

Conclusion

The war was vastly important in British history. A war on this unprecedented scale was bound to have momentous consequences. It therefore seems that the question with which this chapter started – was the war a *turning-point?* (generally defined as something like 'a crisis at which a decisive change occurs') – can be given a very simple answer: 'Yes'.

Yet we should not attribute every change that occurred to the influence of the war. As with the discussion of politics above, many of the developments of 1914–18 might have happened anyway, though perhaps at different times. We have therefore to distinguish between the war as a catalyst, speeding up or slowing down processes which were already under way, and the war as an originator. We must also be careful not to assume that any degree of change constitutes a turning-point. Just what is 'decisive change': how extensive or long-lasting does it have to be? Also, we must not forget that there are many elements of continuity spanning the years before, during and after the First World War. Many things stayed the same, or were merely modified. For example, those in authority after the war were those who had been in authority before. After all, it was the young who had died fighting, not the old.

Many things stayed more or less the same – necessarily so. There are elements of continuity even in the most revolutionary era. But the degree of change experienced during the First World War is surely remarkable and so justifies its description as a 'turning-point'. But the term is relative not absolute. Rather than being content to conclude that yes, the war was a turning-point, we should, ideally, try to determine the degree of 'turning' that occurred in particular aspects of British history. A full answer would involve a consideration of other issues besides the broad categories introduced above (the following three chapters examine some of these). It would also trace the influence of the war as far into the future as possible. Indeed a comprehensive answer to the simple question posed in this chapter is likely to develop into a full-scale history of Britain!

Task

Historians need to be able to recognise and measure change. They regularly employ the notions of 'change' and 'continuity', and measuring the degree of each is a sophisticated, and fascinating, problem.

Make a start in reaching your own conclusion about change and continuity following the First World War by carrying out the following tasks:

■ First, list the main changes brought about by the war.

■ Then decide which of these changes were the most important, giving reasons for your views.

■ Finally, having marshalled evidence about specific changes, you can now formulate a general view about whether the war was a turning-point in British history.

Further reading

Robert Pearce, *Britain: Industrial Relations and the Economy 1900–39* (Hodder and Stoughton, 1993) – in the 'Access to History' series; a coherent introduction.

John Stevenson, *British Society 1914–45* (Penguin, 1984) – scholarly and well written.

A. J. P. Taylor, *English History 1914–45* (Oxford University Press, 1965) – an excellent account, provocatively written.

3 The changing role of women, 1914–39

Time chart

1914: Start of First World War. An extra 1.5 million women were
employed during the war

1918: End of the war
Votes for most women at the age of 30
Married Love by Marie Stopes published

1919: Restoration of Prewar Practices Act

1923: Reform of the Divorce Laws (and in 1937)

1928: Votes for all women at 21

1929: First woman cabinet minister, Margaret Bondfield

Traditional roles

Before 1914 most Britons believed that men and women had sharply
contrasting natures. In the course of human evolution, man had evident-
ly developed his intelligence while woman had focused on beauty in
order to attract a mate and perpetuate the species. Men were therefore
the builders and constructors, the politicians and professionals; women
were good at having babies and keeping house. Man was the breadwinner, woman the home-maker. Tennyson described the unequal power
relationship between the sexes in a famous poem of 1847: 'Man to command and woman to obey'. It seemed (at least to men!) the perfect division of labour.

Men made the laws of the land; and, naturally, such laws tended to
recognise only men's rights. Adultery, for instance, was sufficient
grounds for a man to divorce his wife, but not for a wife to divorce her
husband, however blatant his infidelity. Furthermore, only boys were
worth the expense of educating properly: girls from poorer families were
scarcely worth educating at all, while those from wealthy families were
trained to be genteel. The 'natural' woman was a wife and mother, and
those who did not marry and have children were surplus to requirements. Ideally they should not exist; but, failing that, they should
emigrate to areas with a surplus of men or devote their lives to caring for
male relatives. It was as though only men had a right to exist for

themselves. Women's sole function in life was to serve men in various capacities.

Yet such ideas were wearing thin even before 1914. Some women were demanding the vote, and a large number of unmarried women were seeking paid employment outside their homes. There were, for instance, 1.6 million female domestic servants around 1911; and even when the traditional caring image was not broken by the transfer of her role from her own home to someone else's – or indeed to the hospital or school – women were also finding employment in factories and offices. There were 600,000 female textile workers and 200,000 office workers around this time. In total, about 35 per cent of women had paid employment, but only 10 per cent of married women. Most men expected that women would return to the traditional role of home-maker after marriage and most women too accepted this as the norm.

The impact of the First World War

As soon as the war began, the campaign for the franchise was put aside, and, significantly, the journal *Suffragette* was patriotically renamed *Britannia*. At first it was expected that women would have a minor role in the war effort; but when it became clear that the war would be a long slogging match, devouring men on the Western Front, women were drafted into industry. Female labour spread most quickly in those areas where women had previously been employed, such as the textile factories. But as the months passed, women were needed in new industries, like engineering, where skilled work was 'diluted' into simpler tasks which the unskilled could perform. One skilled engineering job was even broken down into 22 separate tasks performed by 22 women. Women workers were thus substitutes for men. About 1.5 million extra women took paid employment during the war, bringing the total to almost 7.5 million. Around 750,000 women took jobs in manufacturing, especially munitions production, and the same number took on clerical, transport and other jobs. For instance, Woolwich Arsenal, producing shells and weapons, employed 125 women in 1914 but 28,000 in 1917. Women built huts for the Western Front, they laboured on the surface of coal-mines, they became porters and bus-conductors and did other traditionally 'unfeminine' jobs. Consider, for instance, the photograph of women coke-heavers at a London gasworks during the war (Figure 3.1). This was not the typical male stereotype of women.

Far more married women were working in 1914–18 than ever before. Indeed married women now constituted about 40 per cent of the female workforce. The provision of nurseries in some industries, such as

Figure 3.1 *Women coke-heavers during the war: the unglamorous reality*

engineering, convinced many that the roles of wage-earner and mother were not irreconcilable. Nor could it be denied that in some jobs women performed better than men, and many employers were very happy with women workers, especially since, on average, they were paid only two-thirds of men's wages. At the close of hostilities, many women themselves rejected the old, prewar image of themselves. They wanted to be 'breadwinners not brides'. Would the war lead to permanent changes in the position of women in British society?

Postwar years

Women and politics

In politics there were permanent changes. In 1918 women aged 30 and over received the vote, providing that they were householders or married to local government electors. As a result, some 8 million women were eligible to vote, and women were also eligible to become Members of Parliament. In 1928 the Equal Franchise Act abolished the age difference between men and women, so that all citizens over the age of 21 could vote. At last women's right to equal political participation with men had been recognised. There were now more women than men on the electoral registers.

Yet it should not be imagined that male politicians had suddenly and spectacularly been converted to belief in human equality. To the Conservative Lord Birkenhead, women in politics were an 'intrusion', while Asquith considered that the female electorate was 'a dim, impenetrable, and for the most part ungetatable element'. It is probably true to say that women's suffrage was accepted by most male politicians with some reluctance, because it was popular with the electorate. But if women had the vote, they did not have equal political power with men. Prospective female candidates tended to meet with a cool reception from (male) selection committees. At the first general election of the interwar period, in 1918, there were only 17 female candidates, while in the last, in 1935, there were no more than 67. The largest number of women MPs was elected in 1931, 15 out of a total of 615 MPs. The only woman cabinet minister of the period was appointed in 1929, when Margaret Bondfield became Minister of Labour. It was in the less important sphere of local government that women made their most significant political mark. Small wonder, then, that issues of most concern to women, like birth control or equal pay, did not figure prominently on the political agenda. Many of the radical feminists of prewar days deplored the limited effects of the extension of the franchise and were dismayed that hopes for a specific women's party came to nothing.

Women's militancy had all but evaporated. To give one example, there was a world of difference between the old suffragette movements and the new Women's Institutes (WIs). These grew in numbers from 40 in 1916 to over 5,500 in 1937, by which time membership was over 300,000. Margaret Wintringham neatly summed up their philosophy (see quote in margin).

'The whole tendency of the Women's Institute outlook is to present the work of the Housekeeper, the Home-keeper, or better still, the Home-maker, in the light of a highly privileged, skilled and nationally important occupation.'

Margaret Wintringham MP

The WIs were concerned with women's welfare in the home, not their emancipation from it. Yet this is understandable enough, given the type of work, and the poor pay, available to women outside the home. Servants, for instance, often worked on a six-month contract and would be paid only at the end of that period, so that if they left early they would receive nothing. Dressmakers often served a two-year apprenticeship, for much of which time they would receive no pay at all. In addition, many women genuinely preferred the roles of wife and mother to that of wage-earner. But this was certainly not true of all women, especially those who did not marry or who were divorced or widowed. The WIs therefore helped to circumscribe the roles available to women. They endorsed male-prescribed boundaries between a man's world and a woman's.

A woman's place unaltered

Women had been admitted to the factories with some reluctance, as an exceptional measure during the wartime emergency. Trade unions had accepted women workers – and the dilution of skilled jobs – on the condition that, at the end of the war, there would be a return to traditional practices. This came about in 1919, with the Restoration of Prewar Practices Act. The traditional image of a woman's place had survived the war. The government offered women munitions workers two weeks' pay in lieu of notice and a free train journey home. Female civil servants were dismissed and unemployment benefit was denied to those who refused to accept domestic posts or laundry work. Women were expected to leave the factories in the same way as the men left the army – with a sense of relief. Most women did believe it was their duty to stand aside and return to their 'proper' sphere. By 1920, three-quarters of the extra 1.5 million women who had taken jobs in the war had left the labour market. Yet substantial numbers refused to leave their jobs voluntarily and were not attracted by the prospect of domestic service at slightly better pay and shorter hours than before 1914.

The attitudes of many men had not changed, but circumstances had. Even before the war there had been more women than men in the British population: now the death toll from 1914 to 1918 meant that there were 2 million more women than men. As many as one in three women were unmarried – 'Our Surplus Girls' as the *Daily Mail* patronisingly called them. Most of these wished to find work to support themselves, but they faced a hostile employment market.

Postwar boom soon gave way to bust in 1920–21, but as early as the spring of 1919, 500,000 women were out of work. Women fared similarly badly in the depression of the 1930s. In 1933 Herbert Austin, the car manufacturer, claimed to have a cure for the problem of unemployment: he advocated that all women should be sacked. In such a climate, attempts to remove the 'marriage bar' – discrimination against married women – could not succeed. It was quite normal for women clerical workers to be sacked when they married, and, similarly, nurses had to leave the profession if they married. By 1931, 90 per cent of married women did not work, almost exactly the same figure as in 1911, and it was made virtually impossible for a married women to claim unemployment benefit since a married woman's pay was ruled to be a supplement to her husband's. In the same year statistics revealed that 34 per cent of all women were in paid employment, 1 per cent fewer than in 1911. The effects of the First World War thus seemed remarkably short-lived, as Figure 3.2 indicates.

Figure 3.2 *Women in work*

Year	Single	Married	All women	Average female earnings
1911	70%	10%	35%	44% of men's
1931	71%	10%	34%	48% of men's

Nor had the type of work undertaken changed greatly. In 1931, as in pre-war years, more women were employed in domestic service than in any other sphere, and this was the single growth area for women workers during the depression of the 1930s. Similarly, women's wages were still significantly lower than those of men. Only middle-class women made significant gains. By 1935 there were 200 women in the legal profession, while the number of women doctors had grown from under 500 in 1914 to around 2,500.

Girls' education was still not considered as important as boys'. In 1923 the Board of Trade recommended that girls be given less homework than boys because of the household work they were naturally expected to do. The overwhelming majority of girls therefore left school at the age of 14, and only 0.5 per cent continued their education beyond the age of 18. Oxford allocated only 730 places to women, and female undergraduates could only attend classes at the discretion of each lecturer (one of whom was pestered into acceptance, but with an ill grace: 'Oh, all right, but put them where I can't see 'em'). Cambridge had fewer places still, and did not allow women to take degrees until 1947. Clearly a woman's place was not in the lecture theatre in the interwar period; it was still in the home.

There was a cult of domesticity in 1918–39. Governments did their utmost to encourage women to stay at home, emphasising that the breeding of healthy babies was a national duty. State-run Infant Welfare Centres aided the enterprise. Motherhood and employment were depicted as being totally incompatible. This was also the message of women's magazines, whose popularity was at its zenith in the 1920s and 1930s, when about 50 titles were in circulation. *Good Housekeeping* was the most widely read: it held up before its readers an ideal not of meaningful employment but of the home. One escaped not from but into domesticity: everyone's goal was expected to be married bliss and motherhood in an ideal home. Woe betide those who transgressed into motherhood without marriage bonds. Unmarried mothers were often sent to special institutions and forced to give up their babies for adoption. Such 'homes' were virtual prisons, women not being allowed to wander outside the high-walled grounds. As one inmate remembered, 'You were made to know you'd done something wrong in everybody's eyes.'

Signs of change

Yet changes were occurring. There was an increase in the use of birth control, giving some degree of control over the size of families. There was also a greater understanding of women's sexual needs: women no longer lay back and thought of England quite as frequently as they had been supposed to do in Victorian days. In 1918 Dr Marie Stopes published *Married Love*, advocating birth control and insisting that sexual fulfilment was possible for both partners. Such ideas were slow to gain acceptance, however, and printed information was often banned under the obscenity laws. Only after 1930 did doctors agree that it was right to offer contraceptive advice, and then only to married women whose health might suffer from another pregnancy.

Divorce laws were also becoming more equal. From 1923 a wife could divorce her husband on grounds of his adultery, and in 1937 desertion or cruelty became sufficient grounds. But such legal reforms should not disguise the fact that men were still dominant. Most houses were in the husband's name alone, and any income from renting rooms or taking in laundry was regarded as his. Most wives were still as financially dependent as ever upon their husbands.

Conclusion

In 1914 a woman's place was in the home. Should she need to work, then suitable occupations were prescribed by men. Her daughter in 1939 found society's attitudes little altered. Although, at first sight, the 1914–39 period seems to be one of great change – with a breakthrough into the man's world of work during the war and the achievement of the vote in 1918 and 1928 – the day-to-day business of living did not bear witness to these achievements. The Great War was no more than a temporary victory. Women had never been welcome in 'men's' jobs, and the belief that their presence devalued skills was never overcome. Nor did the new-found equality in the eyes of the law, stemming from the vote, pervade society as a whole. Enfranchisement and emancipation are not the same things: the former simply makes possible, but does not guarantee, the latter. Perhaps the feminists became complacent when the vote was granted after the war. Then, when the anti-feminist attack came, it was well orchestrated and well timed. A mixture of threat and incentive ensured that women returned to their 'proper' place and stayed there – until another war demanded their services.

Tasks

1 Study the photograph of women coke-heavers (Figure 3.1). Draw up a list of ways in which this job broke traditional male images of women.

2 The material in this chapter lends itself to debate. This can take place in the mind, as you rehearse the arguments for and against the war being a turning-point for women. But, better still, it can take place in the classroom. Debates are useful because they force you to argue a case, rather than simply repeat facts. They are thus very good preparation for essays, which should also be arguments rather than narratives.

You could set up a debate on votes for women, in 1918 or 1928. Those who find traditional male attitudes quite indefensible should have the role of voicing and defending them: such a task may breed valuable understanding. Be sure to voice views from the interwar period rather than from today. Remember that debates are, essentially, role plays. You are not expected to give a balanced, cautious judgement: instead, you have to marshal the evidence to support a particular viewpoint as best you can. Nevertheless, after the debate you can reach your own final verdict: and, having heard different points of view and been forced to consider a range of evidence, you should be in a good position to do so.

Further reading

Angela Holdsworth, *Out of the Doll's House* (BBC, 1989) – an accessible account.

Elizabeth Roberts, *A Woman's Place* (Macmillan, 1988) – makes good use of oral history.

Martin Pugh, *Women and the Women's Movement in Britain 1914–59* (Macmillan, 1992) – a wide-ranging, up-to-date account.

G. Braybon and P. Summerfield, *Out of the Cage* (Pandora Press, 1987) – relates to both world wars.

Gail Braybon, *Women Workers in the First World War* (Croom Helm, 1981) – a scholarly monograph.

4 Imperial mentalities, 1914–39

The men who governed Britain and the Empire – as politicians, and home and colonial civil servants – were all unique individuals. No two were identical in personality, any more than in physical appearance. Yet they had much in common, in terms of social background, education, conscious beliefs and unconscious assumptions. They are often said to comprise a relatively homogeneous governing class which, around 1914, shared an 'imperial mentality', a common core of values and attitudes derived from the British Empire. This chapter seeks to identify the content, and the origins, of their 'world view' and to establish how far, if at all, it changed under the onslaught of the First World War.

The public schools

The Victorians often boasted that social inequalities were 'removable': everyone of ability, if prepared to work hard enough, could rise in the social scale. Yet the class system, while not rigid, was remarkably resilient, and education was the basic means of perpetuating that system. The so-called 'public' (i.e. fee-paying) schools were the means by which the governing class perpetuated itself. Before 1914, the system was flourishing: there were about 150 public schools, and their Old Boys went on to occupy positions of responsibility at home and abroad. The schools' influence has even been compared in its pervasiveness to the indoctrination of youth in Nazi Germany and Communist Russia.

Formal education was dominated by classics, but emphasis was put not on the intellect but rather on the training of 'character', by means of religious instruction and school games. Many schoolmasters expected almost miraculous results from the playing of cricket and rugby – not only physical health but self-reliance, courage under difficulties, and a love of justice and fair play. Boys would become 'manly' and tough, qualities further developed by the essentially spartan atmosphere of the schools; and by 'playing the game' of cricket, they would learn to 'play the game' of life, never giving way to base temptations, thus ensuring that though they would assuredly have power later in life they would not be corrupted by it.

Supporters of the system believed that it produced Christian, confident and manly gentlemen, whose watchword – because privilege meant responsibility – was 'Duty'. Critics said it produced complacent and narrow-minded 'types', lacking originality or imagination. Certainly public schools must have had a major impact on their pupils. Many historians have judged that, as a result, the public schools did more than any other institution to produce the 'imperial mentality'.

Imperial values

Militarism was one facet of this mentality. School games not only toughened the body but bred competitiveness, and along with games often went drilling, shooting and membership of the Officers' Training Corps. The average public schoolboy toted a gun from an early age. School games were indeed often presented as a preparation for war. Boys would also be subject to propaganda, instilling patriotism, love of the Empire and a disparaging view of foreigners as both vaguely menacing and comically funny. The highest duty to which one could aspire was the defence of the homeland and the Empire. Small wonder, then, that Old Boys readily volunteered to fight for King and Country and treated war, at least at first, as a sort of game.

Another facet was a consciousness of superiority. Public schoolboys were set apart as a superior elite. George Orwell, who went to Eton, dismissed the system as 'a training in class prejudice'. It tended to produce young men whose self-belief made them immune from doubt or self-criticism, but with a certain rigidity of outlook, symbolised by the 'stiff upper lip'. Having been taught to be chivalrous to those less fortunate than themselves (including women, workers and the 'lesser breeds' of the Empire – in fact, virtually everyone else), they therefore found it very hard to meet these others on equal terms. Theirs was an authoritarian, and male-dominated, universe.

The dominant ideology

The public schools undoubtedly contributed to the 'mental set' (the attitudes and habits of mind) of the ruling elite before 1914. But they were not the only source of these ideas. There were many other forms of 'imperial propaganda', and they affected the whole of British society. State schools upheld many of the same values as private ones and thus helped to ensure widespread public support for official policies, transforming elite attitudes into a dominant ideology. At Robert Roberts' school in Salford, described in *The Classic Slum*, teachers 'spelled out patriotism among us with a fervour that with some verged on the religious'. Empire Day was celebrated joyously. 'We drew union jacks, hung classrooms with flags of the Dominions and gazed with pride as they pointed out those massed areas of red on the world map.' The press, literature, music halls, churches, picture postcards and the arts also helped to produce the widespread social penetration of imperialism, establishing the comforting notion that one Englishman was worth a dozen foreigners.

The 'imperial mentality' had several components. Patriotism, enthusiasm for the royal family and the Empire, militarism and an overweening pride in being British were all important ingredients. Most Britons believed implicitly in their right not only to govern the Empire but to establish spheres of influence elsewhere. The ruling Englishman was immensely patriotic, but his interests were not confined to home. Britain was becoming increasingly industrialised: a true sportsman therefore needed the stimulus of an imperial frontier to show his true mettle. The world was his playing field. Nor did he doubt the essentially beneficent impact his involvement was sure to have. This confidence was bolstered by racialist beliefs. Most educated Englishmen believed that just as there was a hierarchy in the animal kingdom, with human beings at the top, so there was a natural hierarchy among the races of mankind. The world's scientists (basing their views on measurements of the skull and of the angle of the jaw) claimed to have proved that the white races were innately superior: the lighter the skin, their simplistic message ran, the higher the race on the evolutionary scale. As the highest race, only palefaces were truly civilised. Perhaps, indeed, God had singled out the British as a new chosen race, to bring the benefits of Christianity, Commerce and Civilisation to the benighted heathens of Asia and Africa.

This world-view partly explains why Britain joined the war in August 1914. This fateful decision was a reflection of the glorious image of war that had been propagated over the preceding decades. Entry also stemmed from the disparaging view of foreigners in the press and from ideas of **Social Darwinism**. To some extent, it was a reflex action: Britain was a great power and unless it took part in the contest, a greater power would emerge on the continent of Europe. It thus reflected Britons' self-image.

The First World War

Many had predicted war; few had imagined the sort of war it would turn out to be. At first perceived as an abstraction (as Glory, Heroism and Valour), it was soon seen in more realistic terms. The turning-point probably came with the slaughter on the Somme in 1916. A poem from

KEY TERM:

Social Darwinism

The term **Social Darwinism** derived from a simplified interpretation of the works of Charles Darwin. Herbert Spencer and others argued that societies were like animals: they would fight, just as animals did, and either win and grow stronger or lose and become weaker. What they could not do was live in peace, at least not for long. War was therefore inevitable. Only the fittest would survive.

early in the war, Rupert Brooke's 'The Soldier', well illustrates the romantic outlook of 1914–15:

> *If I should die, think only this of me:*
> *That there's some corner of a foreign field*
> *That is for ever England. There shall be*
> *In that rich earth a richer dust concealed;*
> *A dust whom England bore, shaped, made aware,*
> *Gave, once, her flowers to love, her ways to roam,*
> *A body of England's, breathing English air,*
> *Washed by the rivers, blest by sons of home . . .*

This is a poem not about war but about the romantic image of war. Full of patriotism and pastoral imagery, it almost makes death appealing! Brooke died in 1915, before he could experience the true reality of trench warfare. Not so **Wilfred Owen**. In 1917 he described a poison gas attack:

> *Gas! Gas! Quick, boys – An ecstasy of fumbling,*
> *Fitting the clumsy helmets just in time,*
> *But someone still was yelling out and stumbling*
> *And floundering like a man in fire or lime. –*
> *Dim through the misty panes and thick green light,*
> *As under a green sea, I saw him drowning.*
> *In all my dreams, before my helpless sight,*
> *He plunges at me, guttering, choking, drowning.*
> *If in some smothering dreams, you too could pace*
> *Behind the waggon that we flung him in,*
> *And watch the white eyes writhing on his face,*
> *His hanging face, like a devil's sick of sin;*
> *If you could hear, at every jolt, the blood*
> *Come gargling from the froth-corrupted lungs,*
> *Obscene as cancer, bitter as the cud*
> *Of vile, incurable sores on innocent tongues, –*
> *My friend, you would not tell with such high zest*
> *To children ardent for some desperate glory,*
> *The old Lie:* Dulce et decorum est
> Pro patria mori.

Dulce et decorum est pro patria mori ('A sweet and fitting thing it is to die for one's country'): the message of governments from time immemorial – and of their innocent dupes, like Rupert Brooke – was in this poem given the lie. In the First World War, men did not die like heroes, they were slaughtered like animals. Owen wrote that his poems were not about 'glory, honour, might, majesty, dominion, or power', nor about poetry, but merely about war and the pity of war.

PROFILE: *Wilfred Owen*

The son of a Shropshire railway-worker, **Wilfred Owen** joined the army in 1915 and was soon commissioned. He suffered in the Battle of the Somme in 1916 and was then invalided to hospital in Edinburgh. He returned to France in 1918, won the Military Cross, but died a week before the armistice. His poems made little immediate mark, but his reputation steadily grew.

By 1917, as casualties continued to mount, there is evidence of considerable war-weariness in Britain. Days lost in strikes more than doubled, and there was talk of a negotiated peace. It seemed that by 1918 the old view of war could no longer be sustained, and that the end therefore came none too soon.

The postwar world

Many have argued that the old 'imperial mentality' came to an end with the close of the First World War. 'That England of the old Victorian men,' wrote H. G. Wells, 'with its empire and its honours and its court and its precedences, it is all a dead body now.' Elgar put aside his jingoistic Pomp and Circumstance marches and in 1919 composed his cello concerto, often interpreted as an elegy not just for the war dead but for prewar England. A new culture developed that rejected the war and the society whose values had spawned it. Artists were now Modernist, putting aside the values that had done so much to destroy the world. This new intellectual elite was sceptical and satirical, debunking previous heroes (as Lytton Strachey did so memorably in *Eminent Victorians* in 1918) and accepting the essential futility of life in 'The Waste Land' (the title of T. S. Eliot's great poem published in 1922). Bloomsbury intellectuals waged war on the values of the past.

The historian Arnold Toynbee described cultural assumptions before the war:

> 'It was taken for granted by almost all Westerners ... that the Western civilisation had come to stay. Pre-1914 Westerners, and pre-1914 British Westerners above all, felt they were not as other men were or ever had been. Westerners were "civilised"; non-Westerners were "natives" in the sense that they had no human rights.'
>
> A. Toynbee, *Experiences* (1969).

The events of August 1914 totally shattered this naive illusion. He, like many others, could not forget the slaughter of 1914–18 because to them this war revealed the essential truth about the world. European cultural pretensions now seemed no more than hollow posturings. It followed logically that Europeans were inadequate to govern other peoples and that empires should be ended. In the past empire-builders had always insisted that they brought peace, the *Pax Britannica*, to warring tribes; but such rationalisations wore thin now that the European tribe had decimated itself. Soon scientists added to the onslaught by deciding that skull measurements revealed evidence about skull size and nothing else. 'Craniology' ceased to be a science and became instead a bizarre hobby of eccentrics. Many intellectuals began to believe that white was not necessarily superior to black. In addition, the theories of Sigmund Freud, which insisted that human beings were subject to unconscious sexual and destructive impulses which they could scarcely begin to comprehend, let alone control, further undermined the imperial world view.

The survival of the old ideas

The very foundations of the imperial world view seemed to be collapsing; and it might be supposed that the old governing elite would realise this more than anyone. After all, a disproportionate number of the officer class had died on the Western Front, including at least 150 heirs to hereditary titles. But in fact old ideas showed a remarkable resilience. This was partly due to people's natural repugnance from unpleasant reality. Rupert Brooke's comforting work sold in far greater quantities than Owen's harrowing offerings. But it was also partly due to government censorship, which had attempted to portray the war in a positive light. Realistic accounts of the war were indeed often censored, just as war paintings or photographs showing dead bodies were expressly forbidden, though exceptions were made if the bodies were indubitably German.

Look at Figures 4.2, 4.3, 4.4 and 4.5. 'Oppy Wood' by John Nash, who became an official war artist in May 1918, conveys the devastation to landscape wrought by war, but not human suffering. Of the two recruiting posters, Figure 4.3 ignores the reality of war altogether, and focuses

Figure 4.2 *'Oppy Wood' by John Nash, 1918, showing the trench system and the desolate, after-battle terrain*

Figure 4.3 *Recruiting poster, appealing to love of the homeland. There is only one answer to the rhetorical question.*

Figure 4.4 *Recruiting poster, appealing to schoolboy dreams of martial glory*

33

Figure 4.5 Neither dulce nor decorum. The reality of war in which around 8 million men died.

on an idyllic green and pleasant homeland, while Figure 4.4 appeals to Britons' love of adventure and martial glory. The image shown in Figure 4.5 was, for many, the all too true reality of war.

The governing class had traditionally been impatient of literary intellectuals, and it remained so. Nor did the public schools encourage too much soul-searching about the war. Those who fell, according to a typical school magazine, 'have died the most glorious death ... a perpetual example of duty nobly done'. *'Dulce et decorum est'* prefaced its growing list of casualties. The impulse to believe that Britain's youth had died in a worthy cause was a powerful one. **John Buchan**, who wrote a 24-volume history of the war, decided that the conflict had

'delivered the world's freedom from a deadly danger, and, though the price was colossal, the cause was worthy ... Most men who fell died for honourable things. They were inspired by the eternal sanctities – love of country and home, comradeship, loyalty to manly virtues, the indomitable questing of youth. Against such a spirit the gates of death cannot prevail. We may dare to hope that the seed sown in sacrifice and pain will yet quicken and bear fruit to the purifying of the world.'

John Buchan and Henry Newbolt, *Days to Remember* (1939).

PROFILE: *John Buchan*

John Buchan (created **Baron Tweedsmuir** in 1935) had a long career spanning politics and literature. He served in South Africa after the Boer War, was an MP from 1927 to 1935 and Governor General of Canada from 1935 until his death in 1940. He also wrote over 50 books, including biographies and best-selling adventure stories. The imperial mentality was very much alive in Buchan and he transmitted imperial values in his novels.

In his Richard Hannay novels, beginning with *The Thirty-Nine Steps* in 1915 and ending with *The Island of Sheep* in 1936, Buchan portrayed a mental world with which the pre-1914 governing class would have been entirely familiar. In simple, action-packed adventure stories, generally set in a variety of foreign locations, he created gentlemen heroes who relished a good fight against 'hellishly clever' but malignant villains. 'Ordinary healthy folk,' insists Hannay, 'don't analyse their feelings': instead they act on intuition, never questioning their racial assumptions (in which 'Dagos' are always 'oily' and a 'nigger band, looking like monkeys in uniform, pounded out some sort of barbarous jingle', and in which Jews are to be found at the back of German aggression or communist conspiracy). In this simplistic moral universe, appearance is a sure guide to character. Anyone with 'gimlet' or 'clear blue' eyes, or with a 'kind mouth', is sure to be reliable; a character whose pupils are not at the centre of his eyeballs, or with 'small pig's eyes', will be unmasked in the end as a villain. A motif of *The Three Hostages* was the 'hideous roundness' of the skull of Hannay's adversary. As for the typical German ('Brother Boche'), he tended to have a head of 'the round bullet type, with no nape to the neck' – perhaps one reason why he was 'as hideous as a hippopotamus' and lacked imagination.

Hannay's world was a man's world, in which true gentlemen were 'bound to play the game'. That meant, if necessary, dying for one's country. There were enterprises in which 'men's lives must be reckoned at less than thistledown': certainly an acre of Britain's precious soil 'was bought cheaply by the blood of the best of us'. It is a rule reiterated throughout Buchan's work. Some things are worth dying for: indeed, war brought out the best in men, pushing them to and even beyond the limits of endurance, enabling the human spirit to 'defy all natural laws'.

The effect of these books, and of those by countless other authors in the interwar period, was to perpetuate the 'imperial mentality'. The First World War therefore did not end prewar habits of mind. Many members of the governing class, and many members of the public, still supported the British Empire, continued to despise foreigners and especially non-whites, and were convinced that Britain was superior to all other countries and so should have an authoritative voice in world affairs. Very many people accepted uncritically such 'outdated' attitudes.

There were probably as many pro- as anti-war books and films in the interwar period. The Modernists might have a large number of intellectuals on their side, but the traditionalists had the majority of popular writers, together with an invaluable ally in the semi-official British Board of Film Censors.

Yet not even the most hardened imperialist could pretend that the world had not changed since 1914. The imperial world view was under siege, and now had a new defensive quality. In 1929 a Buchan character complained that not only was Britain going soft but that in Samarkand one could hear 'the chatter of Bloomsbury intellectuals' and in Lhasa they would be discussing Freud. The old orthodoxy was no longer as dominant: instead there were competing ideologies. Traditional and Modernist ideas formed totally separate camps, and it would be a reckless historian who attempted to quantify the strength of either. Intellectual history from 1914 to 1939 therefore exhibits both stark change and remarkable continuity. Both are reflected in the fact that in 1939 the British people again went willingly to war but in a much more sober mood than in 1914.

Task

Make a list of the factors which, before 1914, made up the establishment's view of Britain's imperial role. Then decide which of these factors were challenged by the war. What was left of the imperial world view by 1939?

Further reading

Samuel Hynes, *A War Remembered* (Bodley Head, 1990) – analysis of literary account of the First World War.

John M. MacKenzie, *Propaganda and Empire* (Manchester University Press, 1984) – a pioneering work, analysing the social effects of the Empire on Britain.

The works of John Buchan – or of other authors, like Edmund Blunden, Robert Graves and Rose Macaulay – may be used by those undertaking personal studies in this area.

5 The Irish settlement of 1922: how was it achieved?

Time chart

1916: Easter Rising in Dublin

1918: Victory for Sinn Fein in 1918 general election: Dail set up

1919: Start of the Anglo-Irish war

1920: 21 November
'Bloody Sunday'

1921: 11 July
Truce signed
6 December
Signing of the Anglo-Irish treaty

1922: March
Irish Free State set up

In the early hours of 6 December 1921 Lloyd George, the British Prime Minister, obtained the signatures of Arthur Griffith, Michael Collins and of three other representatives of Sinn Fein and the Irish Republican Army to one of the most controversial treaties of modern British history. It resulted in the partition of Ireland in 1922, so that the six counties of Ulster with the highest proportion of Protestants remained part of the United Kingdom, while the rest of Ireland became a self-governing Dominion known as the Irish Free State ('Eire' from 1937). Similar ideas had been put forward before, but there was nothing inevitable about this answer – one cannot call it a solution – to the Irish question. The Irish representatives had wanted, above all, a united Ireland and a republic – not partition and the retention of links with Britain – and their acquiescence was in doubt until the very last moment. The treaty was subsequently ratified only with grave misgivings by many Conservative MPs at Westminster, while in Dublin it scraped through the parliament (the Dail) by the narrowest of margins and soon resulted in civil war. It was a treaty preceded, followed and almost written in blood. How did it come about?

Historical background

In 1914 many people believed that Ireland was on the brink of civil war or anarchy. Two communities existed with implacably opposed aims, stemming from contrasting senses of national identity:

■ The Catholics, 90 per cent of the population outside Ulster, believed that Ireland had been exploited for too long by imperialist Britain. Their land had been taken by Protestant settlers, an alien religion established in their midst, and their language and cultural traditions almost destroyed. Admittedly there had been some attempts to make amends – the Protestant Church had been disestablished in Ireland, so that Catholics no longer had to pay tithes to an 'alien' establishment, and legislation had enabled about 60 per cent of Irish tenants to purchase farms from their landlords – but the Home Rule movement was strong nevertheless. Irish Nationalists, led at Westminster by John Redmond, wished to control their own local affairs.

■ However, Protestants, who were a majority in the province of Ulster, believed that they would be discriminated against under a Home Rule regime. Irish Unionists, led at Westminster by Edward Carson, believed that Ulster's manufacturing prosperity would perish if power lay with the rural South and that Home Rule would degenerate into papal 'Rome Rule'.

Gladstone had twice attempted, and twice failed, to bring about Home Rule. On the first occasion, in 1886, he had split his own Liberal Party: the 'Liberal Unionists' joined forces with the Conservatives to maintain the union with Ireland. So deep was the political fissure that Conservatives even endorsed the use of force to combat Home Rule legislation. The phrase first coined in the 1880s, 'Ulster will fight and Ulster will be right', was resurrected by Conservative leader Andrew Bonar Law in 1912. This was an important year for the Irish issue. At Westminster the Liberal government, which was dependent for its survival on the votes of Redmond's Nationalists, introduced a third Home Rule Bill which, under the 1911 Parliament Act, the House of Lords could only suspend for two years. Both sides therefore took up battle order: 100,000 'loyalists' formed the Ulster Volunteer Force and Nationalists responded with the Irish Volunteers. Arms and money were smuggled in from the United States and Germany. In 1914 the Home Rule Act was due to come into operation, setting up a parliament in Dublin, though Westminster was still to control key issues like revenue and defence, and Ulster, or part of it, seemed likely to be allowed to contract out. Civil war seemed a distinct possibility, and the loyalty of Britain's armed forces in any conflict in Ireland was far from certain.

Only the outbreak of the First World War prevented a crisis. The Act was on the statute book (to appease the Catholics) but it was suspended (to calm the Protestants), and it seemed for a time that war patriotism would bind Ireland together. Redmond pledged support for the war effort, and Catholic volunteers outnumbered Protestant ones.

Easter Rising

In 1916 the Easter Rising occurred in Dublin: the Post Office was seized and a republic was proclaimed. But this was the work of small minority groups, like the Sinn Fein ('Ourselves Alone') Party, not of mainstream Nationalists. The British soon re-established control, and they had the support of the majority of the population. Yet a series of executions of rebel leaders produced martyrs and swung public opinion behind the republican cause. Irish playwright Bernard Shaw remarked that the British were 'canonising their prisoners'. Sinn Fein won several by-elections in 1917, and the following year nationalist and republican sentiments were further inflamed by the extension of conscription to Ireland and the arrest of Sinn Fein leaders.

The postwar period

Warfare

By the end of the war, the political position in Ireland had been trans-formed. Redmond's moderate Nationalists won a mere seven seats in the general election; Sinn Fein took 73 (though admittedly with only 40 per cent of all Irish votes). But instead of sitting at Westminster, they declared Ireland to be a republic and formed their own parliament in Dublin, the Dail. The British government passed another Home Rule Act, in 1920: there were to be parliaments in both Dublin, for the 26 southern counties, and in Belfast, for the six Protestant counties of Northern Ireland, though Westminster would have control of key policy areas and retain ultimate sovereignty. Possibly such a measure might have been acceptable before the war but now it was too little and too late. 'We are all Home Rulers today,' proclaimed *The Times* complacently on 26 March 1919 – all, that is, apart from the majority of yesterday's Home Rulers. Sinn Fein fought elections under the Act's provisions – winning 124 of the 128 seats in the South – but only to show their party's dominant level of support; otherwise it ignored the new legislation. Two governments therefore existed side by side: the increasingly nominal rule of the British and Sinn Fein's *de facto* rule, backed up by the Volunteers now reconsti-tuted as the Irish Republican Army (IRA). Lloyd George, Prime Minister of a coalition dominated by Conservatives ('Unionists'), had a full-scale crisis on his hands.

The British government turned first to repression, attempting to re-establish 'law and order'. Certainly law and order did not exist. The shooting of a police constable from the Irish Royal Constabulary in June 1919 in Tipperary is often cited as the first incident. It was certainly not the last, in what the British called an 'insurrection' and the Irish a 'war of liberation'. 'I see no alternative but to fight it out,' declared Lloyd George; 'A republic at our doors is unthinkable.' It was equally unthinkable that he would defy the Conservative backbenchers who formed the mainstay of his government's support. They were adamant that gunmen should be brought to justice and lawful authority reimposed. In their minds, only such a firm policy could dissuade nationalists elsewhere in the Empire from pursuing similar tactics. British soldiers would be fighting for the integrity of the entire British Empire. In the aftermath of the First World War it was relatively easy to find soldiers willing to fight. After April 1920, when the IRA raided Dublin's tax office and destroyed all income tax records, the conflict escalated: the Royal Irish Constabulary was reinforced by the 'Black and Tans' and a division of officers, the 'Auxis'.

Britain went to war without declaring it, soldiers meeting IRA ambushes with equal violence of their own. Atrocities were committed by both sides. For instance:

- on 21 November 1920 ('Bloody Sunday') IRA gunmen killed 14 British soldiers and civilians in Dublin;
- later that day the 'Tans' opened fire on an unarmed crowd at Croke Park in the city, killing 12 and wounding 60;
- that night two leading members of the IRA were shot at Dublin Castle 'while attempting to escape';
- in December much of Cork was burnt, after two lorries of Auxis had been ambushed and killed.

It is impossible to say with accuracy how many died in the troubles, but it is probable that the total of fatalities between January 1919 and July 1921 was not far short of 1,000.

Negotiations

In the midst of the violence it seemed that reconciliation would never be possible. Yet a truce came into force on 11 July 1921. How did this come about? It is not easy to be sure, especially since some of the official British records on such a sensitive period are, predictably, closed to historians. Churchill described it as a reversal of policy seemingly more sudden and complete than any in modern times. It was probably due to several factors:

1 There was a feeling among Sinn Fein leaders that the war was going badly: indeed Michael Collins later contended that the IRA had been at the end of its tether when the truce came, although in fact the evidence on this issue is not conclusive. Certainly it seems likely that the bulk of the Irish population wanted to get back to normal life.

2 On the British side too a war-weariness had set in, not so much among the soldiers (some of whom were glorying in an orgy of violence) as among the public. The British press had, since the end of 1920, been calling for an end to the violence, while some papers had been against it from the beginning.

3 In January 1921 the Labour Party published a highly influential, and detailed, report criticising official policy, and Asquith complained that 'Things are being done in Ireland which would disgrace the blackest annals of the lowest despotism in Europe'. Lloyd George insisted that the critics were a small, self-interested minority, comprising 'Bolsheviks and Sinn Feiners and faddists and cranks of all sorts', but he could not maintain this position for long. In February 1921 General Crozier, a commandant of the Auxis, resigned and urged a truce. Impartial figures like the Archbishop of Canterbury likewise wished to see talks begin, and so did some progressive Conservatives.

4 In addition, international opinion was critical of the government. The United States, the League of Nations and even the Dominions put pressure on the coalition for a change of policy.

5 But alongside moral outrage went a hard-headed concern at the costs of the campaigns at a time when the postwar bubble of prosperity had burst and an 'anti-waste' campaign was under way to reduce expenditure.

Lloyd George had never been as bloodthirsty as his critics believed. His policy of 'reprisals' had been partly a response to Tory backbench opinion and partly a consequence of Sinn Fein's unwillingness to negotiate, while its continuance probably owed much to his absence abroad or absorption in other pressing problems. Now, when George V opened the new parliament at Belfast in June 1921, he issued an invitation to Sinn Fein's president, Eamon de Valera, for talks. A truce was proclaimed on 11 July and de Valera met Lloyd George four times in London later that month. Earlier the Conservative backbenchers would not have countenanced such a meeting with a rebel – indeed even now some complained – and neither would de Valera have been willing to attend. But warfare had made compromise at least possible.

Nevertheless, negotiating a solution was far from easy. Lloyd George hung a large map of the British Empire in the cabinet room to impress de Valera, but the Irish leader merely noted that its projection exaggerated the size of British possessions and that, anyway, colonies represented 'greed and aggrandisement, not power and glory'. Lloyd George, who later said that arguing with de Valera was like trying to pick up mercury with a fork, soon decided that he would have to go further than mere Home Rule and offer instead Dominion status to Southern Ireland. This implied that, while enjoying internal self-government, it would not have full control over its foreign policy or defence and that the British monarch would continue as head of state, to whom local politicians would have to swear an oath of allegiance. He also insisted that Northern Ireland should be able to contract out of a new Irish Dominion. He had, in fact, sketched out the proposals which were to be accepted in December and implemented the following year. But it would be an error to believe that this scheme was the only possible response to the Irish question or that Sinn Fein was bound to accept it. Certainly de Valera was not impressed. In the end, Lloyd George spoke stern words: 'I shall be sorry if this conference fails: terrible as events have been in Ireland, it is nothing to what they will be if we fail to come to an agreement.' But de Valera was undaunted. He took the proposals back to the Dail but would not endorse them. Neither would a majority of Dublin politicians.

The Dail then sent a five-man delegation, dominated by Arthur Griffith and Michael Collins, to a new conference, which opened in London on 11 October 1921. It took two months to strike a deal, a sign that the two sides had fundamental points of difference. Yet the settlement which emerged was very similar to that which Lloyd George had broached to de Valera and on which the Dail could not agree. How did the Prime Minister manage to get his way?

The settlement

Several factors were involved. One was the genuine rapport built up with Griffith and Collins by the British delegates, and especially Conservative leader Austen Chamberlain and fellow Tory Lord Birkenhead. At first relations had been distant, literally so: the two teams were arrayed on either side of a very large table, so that they would not have to shake hands. The Prime Minister had to include leading Conservatives in his team – otherwise he could not possibly hope to secure the acceptance of any resulting settlement by the Conservative backbenchers – but he could not have expected them to hit it off quite so well with the Irish. Another factor is that he himself was a nimble and tireless negotiator – and he needed to be.

The British offered Dominion status, but the Irish pressed the case strongly for a republic. If Britain was worried about its security, they would offer a 'treaty of association' to provide for mutual defence: Ireland would not be in the Empire, but it would be associated with it. They felt strongly on this issue and would compromise only to secure something about which they were even more adamant, the unity of Ireland. But Lloyd George could not compromise on this even if he wanted to: unless the position of Northern Ireland were safeguarded, Parliament would not possibly accept legislation setting up an Irish Dominion. It seemed a classic stalemate.

Lloyd George tried to get his way over the status of a self-governing Ireland by holding out concessions over Ulster. He tried to get the leaders of Northern Ireland to accept an all-Ireland parliament from which they might withdraw after six months – withdraw, that is, unless they preferred to stay in an Irish Dominion where they would have a degree of local autonomy and in which taxation would be lower than in the United Kingdom. He was optimistic that the Ulstermen would accept this proposition on the assumption that Sinn Fein would certainly veto it – whereas Sinn Fein had already accepted! When this Machiavellian scheme fell through, he half promised Griffith and Collins that, if they were prepared to accept a Dominion from which Northern Ireland could contract out immediately, a Boundary Commission would then redraw Ulster's boundaries in such a way that it would be too small to be viable. A partition which looked likely to be merely temporary would, judged the Prime Minister, be much more acceptable to the Irish delegates.

Lloyd George was a brilliant, slippery negotiator. He was also prepared to yield on inessentials, so that, for instance, the oath of allegiance due to the King might be rendered less offensive to republicans. But on the essentials – Dominion rather than republican status and partition – he was adamant. Could he secure agreement? It seemed not. Then, on the afternoon of 5 December 1921, he ceased negotiating and cajoling and presented a stark ultimatum: either they signed the draft treaty of agreement or 'it is war and war within three days ... we must know your answer by 10 p.m. tonight. You can have until then, but no longer, to decide whether you will give peace or war to your country.' With deep solemnity, and superb artistry, he had brought matters to a head – and to a successful conclusion. In the end, a settlement was reached because of Lloyd George's skill and because Collins was not de Valera. Threats had had little effect on the latter, and even now the delegates protested that the terms would first have to be submitted to Dublin. But before the expiry of the deadline, they had agreed to sign. They could have telephoned Dublin, but they did not. Perhaps they realised that the Irish cabinet would veto the deal; now the treaty would at least be debated in the full Dail. Collins insisted – correctly as it turned out – that he was signing his own death warrant, but he signed nevertheless.

Lloyd George had rehearsed his entire repertoire of negotiating skills, culminating in threat – or perhaps bluff? No one can really be sure whether he would have made good his threat to resume the war. At any event, he was jubilant, calling this 'the greatest day in the history of the British Empire'.

Diehards in the Conservative Party were outraged that gunmen were to form the authorised government in Southern Ireland. But the bulk of Conservative MPs accepted the compromise that had been reached: at least Ulster was safeguarded and at least the South was still tied to the Empire and so was not independent. In Ireland itself, however, feelings ran higher. The Irish Free State was proclaimed in March 1922, but the IRA split into the Regulars, supporting the settlement, and the Irregulars, whose opposition was only defeated after a civil war lasting until May 1923. The 'settlement' paved the war for future problems (see chapter 27).

Task: note-taking

All events have causes, and you will already be aware that most events do not come about because of a single reason. Usually a number of factors are involved – some of them very different from one another – and deciding which are the most important is a matter of judgement. Using your judgement to decide the relative importance of the causes of historical events is one of the most important skills a history student can develop. Historians also often find it difficult to distinguish between long-term causes (sometimes called preconditions), medium-term causes (sometimes called precipitants) and short-term causes (sometimes called triggers).

This chapter is the author's attempt to explain, by giving a mixture of narrative and analysis, how the 1922 treaty was achieved. But your notes should attempt to impose a definite framework of causation upon the chapter. Try to divide the chapter into:

- preconditions or long-term causes (for instance, the factors that produced two communities in Ireland)
- precipitants or medium-term causes (such as the British reaction to the 1916 uprising)
- the triggers or short-term factors (including the policies and negotiating skills of Lloyd George).

It is also worthwhile trying to devise a hierarchy of causes, sorting out the absolutely vital issues from the less important. Can you identify a single most important factor? How important were the contributions of individuals (like de Valera and Collins) as against the circumstances? This is an area in which there are no definitely 'right' or 'wrong' viewpoints, though of course not all answers are equally sensible. Whatever your opinion, remember that you must have evidence to back it up.

You must be familiar with a narrative of events, but it should be emphasised strongly that you have to *use* details from a narrative, not merely repeat them. Therefore the more practice you have in formulating arguments, and defending and attacking different interpretations, the more persuasive you will become and the better historian you will be.

Further reading

Robert Pearce, *Britain: Domestic Politics, 1918–39* (Hodder and Stoughton, 1992).

C. L. Mowat, *Britain Between the Wars* (Methuen, 1955) – very useful textbook.

J. J. Lee, *Ireland 1912–85* (Cambridge University Press, 1989) – a lucid, scholarly account.

C. Townshend, *The British Campaign in Ireland 1919–21* (Oxford University Press, 1975) – a monograph covering one aspect of the story.

6 The general strike of 1926

Time chart

1920: Trade union membership reaches peak of 8 million
End of postwar economic boom

1921: Substantial labour unrest, including 'Black Friday'

1925: April
Government returns Britain to the gold standard with the pound
at its prewar value
June
Mine owners propose wage cuts and longer hours; government
responds by giving temporary subsidy to the mines (on 'Red
Friday') and by setting up a royal commission

1926: March
Samuel Report rejected by both sides
4 May
TUC calls a general strike
12 May
End of the general strike
December
Last miners return to work

1927: Trade Disputes Act makes a general strike illegal and requires
trade unionists to 'contract in' if they wish to pay the political
levy to the Labour Party

1933: Trade union membership 4.3 million

The origins of the strike

The 'wave of industrial unrest' which marked the years before 1914 sub-
sided only briefly during the First World War. It resumed after the
armistice and peaked in 1921, when 85 million working days were lost in
strike action. There was then a lull as economic depression, and mount-
ing unemployment, created a new climate in which workers were much
more reluctant to put their jobs at risk by going on strike. Unemployment
levels were particularly high in South Wales, Clydeside in Scotland, and
the north-east and north-west of England, the areas where the 'staple
industries' were located. Britain's capacity to produce coal, steel, ships
and textiles had increased massively under the stimulus of the war, but in
the postwar world these products were not needed in anything like the

KEY TERM:

Gold standard

The **gold standard** was the mechanism which, before the war, had ensured financial stability among the world's leading industrial nations. Each of these countries had tied its currency to the value of a particular amount of gold, and so there were 'fixed', as opposed to variable or 'floating', exchange rates. This regime had provided the stability industrialists always wanted: profits would depend on the amounts sold, instead of varying as the exchange rate rose or fell.

same quantity. The position was probably made worse when, in April 1925, the Conservative government decided to return to the **gold standard**.

Despite the fact that the British economy was weaker in 1925 than before the war, the government returned to the gold standard with the prewar valuation of the pound sterling: as a result, the pound was increased in value, perhaps by 10 per cent. Therefore British exports, at a stroke, were that much more expensive in overseas markets. Many historians believe that the Chancellor of the Exchequer, Winston Churchill, had caused needless problems for British industry – and indeed for industrial relations, since British capitalists responded to increased export prices by trying to cut the costs of production, especially wages.

Just two months after the return to the gold standard, colliery owners insisted that miners' wages would have to be cut and their working day lengthened. Their action reflected not merely the new exchange rate but highly competitive market conditions. Continental mines were highly mechanised and productive, while the British industry was notoriously badly organised and labour-intensive. The miners' response, through their leaders Herbert Smith and A. J. Cook, was an adamant refusal. Hence a strike looked likely.

Another strike would be nothing new. There was in fact a long history of poor industrial relations in the mines, stemming partly from their abysmal safety record. In 1922–4 over 3,500 miners had been killed and almost 600,000 injured in industrial accidents, while many others suffered from respiratory complaints. The miners had hoped that the government's wartime control of the mines would be extended to a full-scale nationalisation, but their hopes had been dashed after the war.

What was new was that the general council of the Trades Union Congress (TUC) promised sympathetic support. Its leaders believed that the miners had a good case and, furthermore, that successful resistance to wage cuts in the mines might prevent reductions for other groups of workers. At this point, the Prime Minister, Stanley Baldwin, stepped in and offered the owners a nine-month subsidy, so that wages and profits could be retained at existing levels. In the meantime a royal commission, headed by Sir Herbert Samuel, would investigate the whole industry.

In March 1926 Samuel reported. He recommended:

- some pits should amalgamate and all should provide better facilities
- the seven-hour working day should not be increased
- there would have to be wage cuts.

But neither side would accept these recommendations, and wearisome last-minute talks failed to produce results. On 3 May the government broke off negotiations, deciding that a refusal by printers at the *Daily Mail* to print an anti-strike editorial meant that the strike had already begun. In fact, the printers had acted unilaterally, so that the TUC, whose leaders wished to avoid a strike if at all possible, felt that it had not been treated fairly by the government.

The scope of the strike

On 4 May 1926 the first – and so far only – general strike in British history took place. Already 1 million miners were not working, locked out by the owners for refusing to accept lower pay and longer hours, and now the TUC called out railwaymen, transport workers, dockers, printers, gas and electricity workers and others – a total of 2.5 million men and women. Engineers and shipbuilders were soon called out in a 'second wave', but not all union members were asked to strike. Health and sanitary workers, for instance, were exempted, and so were those who transported food, though the government refused to make use of them. Even so, it was the most complete stoppage in Britain's history.

As well as being a strike, however, the events of 4–12 May constituted a war of words, a propaganda battle. The players were the British government and the TUC and the prize was the hearts and minds of the people.

The argument

The government side

The Conservative government had many advantages during the strike. It had planned for the conflict well in advance and had no difficulty recruiting volunteers to man essential services. They were also able to issue their own newspaper, the *British Gazette*, which Churchill helped to edit, and to broadcast on the BBC.

From the very beginning the government presented the strike to the public not as an industrial but as a political dispute. Ministers insisted that strikers were challenging the properly elected government of the day (which had won a parliamentary majority of over 200 seats at the last election) and were therefore attempting to subvert the constitution. According to this viewpoint, the strikers were clearly the enemy of the nation, and the general strike was therefore a war which could only be ended by either the unconditional surrender of the TUC or (almost too terrible to contemplate) a revolution and the overthrow of democratic government. In consequence, the government insisted that it had a right to call for the support of all right-thinking men and women.

This was very much the message in the government newspaper, as the following extracts show:

b

Constitutional Government is being attacked ... Stand behind the Government ... The General Strike is a challenge to Parliament and is the road to anarchy and ruin.

(6 May)

a

The General Strike is in operation, expressing in no uncertain terms a direct challenge to ordered government. It would be futile to attempt to minimise the seriousness of such a challenge, constituting as it does an effort to force upon some 42,000,000 British citizens the will of less than 4,000,000 others engaged in the vital services of the country. The strike is intended as a direct hold-up of the nation to ransom.

(6 May)

c

Either the country will break the General Strike, or the General Strike will break the country ... The authority of Parliamentary Government over any sectional combination must be vindicated.

(6 May)

d

All ranks of the Armed Forces of the Crown are hereby notified that any action which they may find it necessary to take in an honest endeavour to aid the Civil Power will receive, both now and afterwards, the full support of His Majesty's Government.

(8 May)

The *British Gazette* gave particular prominence to a statement by the Liberal, Sir John Simon, who insisted in the House of Commons on 6 May that the TUC had no right to call out workers regardless of their contracts and that therefore the general strike was illegal:

e

Take the case of the railwaymen. Most of the railway servants of this country serve under contracts which require that a notice should be given on either side. Every railwayman in that position who is now out in disregard of the contract of his employment is himself personally liable to be sued in the County Court for damages. Let me point out another serious thing. Every trade union leader who has advised and promoted this course of action is liable in damages to the uttermost farthing of his possessions.

Whether this view was accurate or not – and it was not – the publicity given to it was calculated to unnerve the union leaders.

Publicity was also given to Baldwin's broadcast on 8 May, in which he not only justified his government's position but appealed for an end to the dispute:

'What, then, is the issue for which the government is fighting? It is fighting because, while negotiations were still in progress, the Trade Union Council ordered a general strike, presumably to try to force Parliament and the community to bend to its will … Can there be a more direct attack upon the community than that a body, not elected by the voters of the country, without consulting the people, without consulting even the Trade Unionists, and in order to impose conditions never yet definite, should dislocate the life of the nation and try to starve us into submission?

I wish to make it clear that the Government is not trying to lower the standard of living of the miners or of any other sections of the workers …

This is the Government's position – the general strike must be called off absolutely and without reserve. The mining dispute can then be settled … A solution is within the grasp of the nation the instant that the trade union leaders are willing to abandon the general strike.

I am a man of peace. I am longing, and working, and praying for peace. But I will not surrender the safety and security of the British constitution. You placed me in power eighteen months ago by the largest majority accorded to any party for many, many years. Have I done anything to forfeit that confidence? Cannot you trust me to ensure a square deal for the parties, to secure even justice between man and man?'

The Times, 10 May 1926.

The TUC's case

TUC leaders were anxious to disassociate themselves from the notion that the strike was political. They preferred the neutral phrase 'national stop-page' to 'general strike', which had been used in the past by revolutionaries; they refused a donation to the strike fund from the communist trade unions of the Soviet Union; and they insisted that they were merely supporting the miners in their just cause. In the *British Worker*, they contradicted not only the rumours spread in the *British Gazette* that strikers were flocking back to work but the government's basic interpretation of the strike:

a

The threat of revolution exists nowhere save in Mr Churchill's heated and disorderly imagination.

(10 May)

b

We are entering upon the second week of the general stoppage in support of the mine workers against the attack upon their standard of life by the coal owners. Nothing could be more wonderful than the magnificent response of millions of workers to the call of their leaders. From every town and city in the country reports are pouring into the General Council headquarters stating that all ranks are solid ... The General Council ... are especially desirous of commending the workers on their strict obedience to the instruction to avoid all conflict and to conduct themselves in an orderly manner.

(10 May)

c

The position of the General Council may be stated in simple and unequivocal terms. They are ready at a moment to enter into preliminary discussions regarding the withdrawal of the lock-out notices and the ending of the General Stoppages and the resumption of negotiations for an honourable settlement of the Mining Dispute. These preliminary discussions must be free from any condition.

The Government must remember, and the public are asked to remember, that the General Stoppage took place as a result of the action of the Cabinet in breaking off peace discussions ... using as their excuse the unauthorised action of the printing staff of a London newspaper. The responsibility of the present grave situation rests entirely upon the cabinet ... The General Council struggled hard for peace. They are anxious that an honourable peace shall be secured as soon as possible. They are not attacking the Constitution ... They are defending the mine workers against the mine owners.

(10 May)

d

The workers must not be misled by Mr Baldwin's renewed attempt last night [8 May] to represent the present strike as a political issue. The trade unions are fighting for one thing, and for one thing only, to protect the miners' standard of life ...

The Prime Minister pleads for peace, but insists the General Council is challenging the Constitution. This is untrue. The General Council does not challenge one rule, law, or custom of the Constitution; it asks only that the miners be safeguarded ... The Council is engaged in an industrial dispute. In any settlement, the only issue to be decided will be an industrial issue, not political, not constitutional. There is no Constitutional crisis.

(11 May)

e

In many parts of the country excellent amusements and recreation facilities have been provided for the strikers and their families. Special football and cricket matches and a variety of other sports took place yesterday, while there were plenty of indoor attractions, such as concerts, dramatic entertainments, and whist drives. The keen desire of the strikers to keep on good terms with the authorities is exemplified by a novel event at Plymouth, where ... a strikers' team defeated a police team at football by 2 goals to 1.

(11 May)

End of the strike

When Samuel offered to act as an unofficial mediator, the TUC jumped at the chance to end the strike, despite the miners' leaders' refusal to agree. The TUC called off the general strike on 12 May: in effect, they surrendered unconditionally, as the government had insisted they should. The mining dispute had not been settled: the General Council merely hoped that Baldwin could be trusted to secure a 'square deal' for the miners. In fact, his efforts, such as they were, achieved nothing and the mining dispute dragged on till the end of the year, when the men drifted back to work on terms which the owners dictated.

The general strike had not been 'defeated' – since more people were refusing to work on the last day of the dispute than the first – but it had proved a total failure nevertheless. The government won because it was better organised than the TUC, because it had plentiful supplies of volunteers, and because its resources were so much stronger than those of the trade union movement. The unions spent about £4 million during the nine days of the strike – and were uncertain whether they could find more, even if their assets were not seized, as Simon stated they might be; but government expenditure was a lavish £433 million. The General Council could see no prospect of victory, and so decided to end the strike sooner, when their authority was supreme, rather than later, when more radical figures might come to the fore and transform the strike into a political struggle for power.

There can be no doubt that, in the minds of the TUC leaders, the general strike was an industrial dispute. Nevertheless, they were attempting to coerce the government into intervening on behalf of the miners – and to that extent the general strike *was* political. Government statements played on this fact, polarising the issues and obscuring the fundamental industrial aims of the TUC. Many will therefore judge that the government won the war of words with the unions during the strike.

Task: evaluation of evidence

Interpreting source material

All examination syllabuses now require that A and AS students become familiar with a variety of source materials. This book is itself a 'source' – of information about the past. It also provides you with a wide variety of sources (or 'documents' or 'texts') for the period 1914–79. These include both written and visual material. You will need to know how historians recreate the past on the basis of such material, and you will be encouraged to use these materials yourself.

What kinds of questions should you ask as you work through sources of different kinds? The following is a brief checklist:

1 Do I understand what I am reading or looking at? Comprehension is a crucial skill, and unless you understand what message is conveyed, you won't be able to move on to ask more sophisticated questions of the source. If you do not understand, don't just settle for ignorance. Ask questions and discuss what the source is about with fellow students. May your difficulty be because words have changed their meanings? Remember that a decent dictionary is a wonderful research tool: get into the habit of using one regularly and effectively.

2 What is the context of the source? No source can be understood on its own. You must be aware of its context. Examine its date and try to relate it to what is happening around that time. In other words, bring your existing knowledge to bear.

3 What is the 'witting' and 'unwitting' testimony of the source? Distinguish between these two, i.e. between the message the author is consciously trying to convey and the information he or she reveals without intending to (for instance about his or her own character or about the things he or she takes for granted).

4 How reliable is the source? Is it telling me the truth? Remember that sources are always partial, since there is no such thing as an all-wise and all-seeing observer able to give the whole truth about anything. On the other hand, only rarely is a source a pack of lies, and when it is your wider knowledge will usually make this obvious. Much more commonly, you are given part of 'the truth', and therefore your skill lies in knowing what to rely on and for what purpose. Also, remember that the reliability of a source is relative not absolute: sources can be more, or less, reliable.

A clue to a text's reliability often lies in its 'provenance' (i.e. its background, the reasons why it was produced). You must always try to identify the authors or originators of texts: find out as much as you can about them and ask whether they were in a position to provide reliable information. In addition, ask why a source was produced: after all, its function may radically affect the weight we give it as evidence. Don't take the easy route by noting that a document is biased because its author is biased, and leave it at that. After all, every observer, describing an event, is writing from a particular point of view, even if he or she is trying to tell the truth. Note the bias, by all means, but then go on to try to understand it and, by this means, make allowances for it. In some instances, the bias of a source may itself be its major historical significance.

5 What is the mood of a text? Once you are certain of the literal meaning of a document, you then have to try to 'breathe life' into the source. Try to recreate in your mind the scene which the text represents. One way of doing this is to try to imagine the mood of the author. Read the text to yourself in various tones of voice. You'll be surprised how the 'meaning' of the document can change! You then have to use your judgement to decide which mood is most likely to be the correct one.

6 Is the evidence I have sufficient for my purpose? If your purpose is to recreate an aspect of the past, then the answer will almost certainly be 'No'. Good historians want to know more and more and are rarely, if ever, satisfied. Therefore look for other sources to corroborate ('back up') what your evidence tells you and to place it in as full a context as possible. You therefore need to learn to relate one source to another – not least because many examination questions ask you to explain what you can work out by comparing two or more presented sources. This may seem an artificial exercise, but it is a valid way of testing a wider skill – the ability to gather information from different sources and then to select what you need for your particular purpose.

7 What uses can I put this source to? Everything that survives from the past is evidence, in some way, about the past, and therefore all sources are useful for *something* – and most are useful for a range of purposes. You should never conclude, because of some obvious deficiency (gaps in the evidence, clear bias of the author, an incorrect date in a text, etc.) that it is 'useless'. Historians should be like Autolycus, Shakespeare's 'snapper-up of unconsidered trifles', in *The Winter's Tale*. Leave nothing unconsidered: the choice of one word, rather than another, may be a clue revealing its author's state of mind to us. Be critical of your sources, by all means, but be critically positive rather than negative.

8 Why do sources disagree? This is an important question to ask, but often the answer is not so very difficult to fathom, if you think about it. The originators of historical sources are subjective, with biases, prejudices and 'blind spots' – in other words, they are real human beings, like you, not objective robots. Even if the evidence is a seemingly objective photograph, don't forget that a photographer had to point and focus the camera, and that the exact angle of vision, and the focal length of the lens selected, can change a scene dramatically. Most often sources differ in a complementary way, presenting different aspects of the same reality. Sometimes they flatly contradict each other, perhaps because of unconscious error or deliberate deceit. Consider all such disagreements as a challenge to further enquiry or investigation. A historian is very much in the position of a judge at a trial: the evidence from witnesses is often contradictory, so contradictory that the complete truth may never be established. But it is often possible to establish what happened 'beyond reasonable doubt'. The historian always has to reach a definite verdict, even though the nature of the evidence may be such that the verdict should be a cautious and qualified one.

This chapter includes several sources from the two sides in the general strike. Read them again and then answer the following questions:

1 *The government case*
   i Examine the figures in statement **a**. Given that Britain's total population was almost 46 million, was it correct to say that 4 million were trying to coerce 42 million? Explain your answer.
   ii Give examples of the use of 'military' language or imagery in these extracts. Why do you think that such language was used by those who opposed the strike?
   iii Sir John Simon, in statement **e**, insisted that he was a neutral in the strike, merely clarifying a point of law. Does the evidence of his statement suggest that this was so? Give examples of particular words and phrases used by Simon to support your answer.
   iv Establish the ways in which Baldwin's broadcast of 8 May was shrewd and skilful. Was it also accurate and honest? Do you think that, on balance, he was addressing the general public or the General Council of the TUC? How might TUC leaders have replied to each of his paragraphs?

2 *The TUC case*
   i Examine extract **c** carefully. Did the TUC state its case in 'simple and unequivocal terms'? In particular, what do you think it meant by an 'honourable settlement' and an 'honourable peace'? Why did it not explain how the strike was 'defending' the miners against the colliery owners?
   ii Explain whether, in your opinion, the General Council was correct in insisting that there was no constitutional crisis and no threat of revolution.
   iii Why do you think extract **e** was included in the *British Worker*? What is its significance? Is it merely a 'space-filler' or is it highly revealing of TUC tactics and attitudes?
   iv Is there any sign from these extracts, from 10 and 11 May, that the TUC would call off the strike on 12 May?

BUSINESS AS USUAL.

Figure 6.1 Cartoon by Strube on the aftermath of the general strike: the British Lion is back at work. The Lion: 'Now where were we, Miss, when that fellow interrupted us?'

3 Finally, study the cartoon in Figure 6.1, published in the wake of the general strike. Remember that a cartoon is not simply an amusing illustration: it is also a historical text, which should be scrutinised slowly and carefully. Cartoons always contain more information than is apparent at first sight.

The cartoonist, Strube, is summing up Britain after the experience of the strike. The victorious British Lion is back at work again. Write a brief account, 40–50 words, of the 'message' of the cartoon. In particular, (i) try to identify the general mood conveyed by the drawing, (ii) point to particular details in the cartoon which are used to represent the effects of the strike, and (iii) try to establish the political stance of the cartoonist.

Further reading

Robert Pearce, *Britain: Industrial Relations and the Economy 1900–39* (Hodder and Stoughton, 1993) – chapter 5 looks at the causes and consequences of the strike, and at why it lasted only nine days.

C. L. Mowat, *Britain Between the Wars* (Methuen, 1955) – a good, solid account.

For greater depth, consult the volumes, all called *The General Strike*, by M. Morris (Penguin, 1976), P. Renshaw (Eyre Methuen, 1975), G. A. Phillips (Weidenfeld and Nicolson, 1976) and R. A. Florey (Calder, 1980).

7 Interwar politics: the reasons for Conservative dominance

The dimensions of Conservative success

Looking back on the 1918–39 period, almost all historians have been struck by the degree to which a single party – the Conservative (or Tory) Party – dominated British politics. This chapter questions why the Conservatives were in office for so long and won such a consistently high number of parliamentary seats. But before attempting to find the reasons for this dominance, we have to be certain exactly what it is we are trying to explain. How dominant were the Conservatives? This is illustrated by the following chart.

Interwar politics: general elections and governments

General election, December 1918:   Coalition – 478 seats (47.6% of votes), including 335
                Conservatives (32.6% of votes)
        Labour – 63 seats (22.2% of votes)
        Asquith Liberals – 28 seats (12.1% of votes)

        1918–22: Coalition government

General election, November 1922:   Conservatives – 330 seats (37%)
        Labour – 142 seats (29.4%)
        Asquith Liberals – 41 seats (14.6%)
        Lloyd George Liberals – 47 seats (9.2%)

        1922–3: Conservative government

General election, December 1923:   Conservatives – 258 seats (38.1%)
        Labour – 191 seats (30.5%)
        Liberals – 159 seats (29.6%)

        1923–4: Labour government

General election, October 1924:   Conservatives – 419 seats (48.3%)
        Labour – 151 seats (33%)
        Liberals – 40 seats (17.6%)

        1924–9: Conservative government

General election, May 1929:	Conservatives – 260 seats (38.2%)
	Labour – 288 seats (37.1%)
	Liberals – 29 seats (23.4%)
	1929–31: Labour government
General election, October 1931:	Coalition – 554 seats (67%), including 473 Conservatives (55.2 %)
	Labour – 52 seats (30.6%)
	1931–5: National government
General election, November 1935:	Coalition – 429 seats (53.3%), including 387 Conservatives (47.8%)
	Labour – 154 seats (38%)
	Liberals – 21 seats (6.7%)

We can see from the chart that the Conservatives were not merely the most successful political party in the period but that they were over-whelmingly dominant. They were in office for the whole of the interwar period apart from the two periods of Labour administration, in 1924 and 1929–31, and on neither occasion did Labour have a parliamentary majority. In 1924 Labour was a much smaller parliamentary group than the Tories, who also won more votes, though fewer seats, than Labour at the 1929 election. Indeed the Conservatives won more votes than any other party at every general election in the whole of the interwar period. They were in office alone on two occasions and dominated the coalitions of the period, the Lloyd George Coalition that followed the First World War and the two National governments. Some commentators even began to fear that Britain had succumbed to one-party rule.

Reasons for dominance

1 The electoral system

The information in the chart above itself provides a partial explanation for Tory success. It will be immediately apparent that the number of votes given to each party, expressed here as a percentage of the total popular vote, bears little correlation with the number of seats won. Look, for instance, at the figures for the 1922 election: the Conservatives won a substantial overall majority in terms of seats and yet polled only 37 per cent of all votes. Only once did the party win a majority of votes, in the special circumstances of 1931 (see chapter 8), and yet they regularly achieved political power. Under another electoral system, the Conservatives would not have been nearly so successful.

The party was the beneficiary of the British 'first-past-the-post' system, whereby whoever polls the highest number of votes in a constituency becomes its Member of Parliament. He – or she from 1918 – does not need to win a majority of the votes cast. Under this system a party can, theoretically, win every single seat in the House of Commons while polling far fewer than 50 per cent of popular votes. In practice, the system regularly distorts voting patterns, magnifying often small victories in terms of votes into major victories in terms of parliamentary seats and thus in terms of political power.

The Conservatives benefited not merely from the general but from the precise form of democracy in Britain. The 1918 Representation of the People Act was to their advantage. It preserved 'plural voting', so that owners of business premises outside their constituency of residence could vote twice, and graduates could also vote for University seats. Both of these categories of voters were likely to be Tories. In addition, the legislation effected a significant redistribution of seats to Conservative advantage. Several safe seats in the Home Counties were subdivided to form a larger number of equally safe Conservative seats. Finally, the Act gave the vote to many women, initially at the age of 30, and it seems likely that the Conservatives secured the largest share of the female vote between the wars.

Conservatives also gained from events in Ireland. After the 1922 Anglo-Irish treaty (see chapter 5) Irish Nationalist MPs, who had traditionally supported the Liberals, now sat in their own parliament in Dublin, leaving at Westminster, as staunch Conservative supporters, only MPs from Ulster.

2 The Conservative Party machine

Britain's electoral system certainly made possible the dominance of the Conservatives, but it did not make it certain. It was the Conservative Party machine which had the job of capturing the votes needed for success, and it was well suited to the task, winning the support of traditional, upper-class Britons (from whom it drew its candidates and much of its funding), the lower middle class (who provided most of the active constituency workers) and a proportion, perhaps around a third, of the working class (without whom an election could not be won). The wealth of its supporters meant that the party could afford more publicity material, posters and leaflets, mobile cinema vans and organised speakers than any other party. In fact, it employed more paid agents than the other parties combined. In 1939, when Labour had 133 full-time agents in the constituencies, the Conservatives had over 450. They were also able to contest every single constituency in the country at election time. Female volunteers and fund-raisers were especially prominent, and by 1930 women's branches of local Conservative associations had probably in excess of 1 million members. An added advantage was that the press, often owned by prominent Tories, gave consistent support, especially at election time.

3 Weakness of the opposition parties

Conservative dominance may well be seen, at least to some extent, as a consequence of the weakness of the opposition groups.

a The Liberal Party had been dominant before the First World War, but the split between Asquith and Lloyd George in 1916 (see page 14) was a fatal blow from which the party never really recovered. Perhaps the Liberals were doomed anyway: it has been claimed that their ideology of *laissez-faire* and free trade was increasingly irrelevant to modern needs; but no one around 1914 could have predicted such a rapid decline as occurred after the war. Even when the Conservatives jettisoned Lloyd George as the Coalition Prime Minister in 1922, the Liberals fought as two separate and opposed groups in the election of that year. Lloyd George then agreed to serve under Asquith, and after the election of 1923 the Liberals held the balance of power in the Commons, but the 1924 election – marked by a fear of communism – saw them reduced to a mere 40 seats. It seemed a death-blow to the party, which could not afford to contest many more than half of the country's constituencies. Lloyd George then resumed leadership, after the retirement of Asquith, and replenished party coffers from his own political fund (amassed partly from the sale of honours when he had been Prime Minister).

In 1929 the Liberals put themselves forward as the party of economic radicalism, offering to cure unemployment. But the results of this, in many ways very impressive, effort were disappointing: while the Liberal popular vote blossomed from under 3 million to over 5 million, their seats grew to a disappointing total of only 59. Even so, Lloyd George temporarily held the balance in the Commons, and it is clear that a revival of Liberal fortunes was harming the Conservatives. But in 1931 the Liberals were irrevocably split in the crisis that led to the formation of the National government and thereafter they ceased to be a real force in Parliament.

b There were many reasons why Labour was unlikely to overthrow Conservative dominance. First, it was a new force in politics: it had only been formed in the first years of the century, and its organisation was not as efficient, or well funded, as the Tories. Second, the party

Figure 7.1 Punch's comment,
1919, on the short-sightedness of
strikes. The Goose: 'Have you
realised, my good sir, that if you
proceed to extremes with that
weapon my auriferous [gold-
bearing] activities must inevitably
cease?'

THE GOOSE THAT LAYS THE GOLDEN EGGS.

suffered from being identified with one class only, the industrial workers, and also with revolutionary communism.

It was all too easy for the right-wing press to present the Labour Party,
and its allies the trade unions, as being revolutionary, communist-
inspired and opposed to the real interests of the nation. This is the
essential message of the two *Punch* cartoons in Figures 7.1 and 7.2.

Yet in every election in the 1920s Labour increased its share of the popular vote, so that by 1929 it was the largest single party in the
Commons. The party was becoming respectable. The political crisis of
1931 (see chapter 8) was then its undoing. Labour's leaders and best-

Figure 7.2 *In this cartoon of 29 October 1924* **Punch** *endorsed the Zinoviev letter and branded the Labour Party as crypto-communist and blatantly unpatriotic. Footnote to the cartoon: [In a document just disclosed by the British Foreign Office (apparently after considerable delay), M. Zinoviev, a member of the Bolshevist Dictatorship, urges the British Communist Party to use 'the greatest possible energy' in securing the ratification of Mr. MacDonald's Anglo-Russian Treaty, in order to facilitate a scheme for 'an armed insurrection' of the British proletariat.]*

ON THE LOAN TRAIL.

known political personalities, like Ramsay MacDonald and Philip Snowden, resigned from the Labour cabinet to form a coalition, and it was widely felt that the party was not sufficiently responsible to take unpopular decisions in the national interest. All the old fears of Labour's unfitness to govern were revived at the general election, so that its tally of seats in the Commons fell catastrophically, from 288 to 52. Its popular vote held up reasonably well, and by 1935 it secured almost as many votes as in 1929, but it was still in no position to challenge the Tories.

4 Conservative unity

Both the Liberal and Labour Parties were split for part of the interwar period. In contrast, the Conservatives were much more united. At the Carlton Club meeting in August 1922 the Conservatives suffered their own fissure: Tory leader Austen Chamberlain and several colleagues maintained their support for Coalition leader Lloyd George and so refused to serve in the government set up by Bonar Law. But this was only a relatively minor and short-lived split. Stanley Baldwin, Law's successor as Conservative Prime Minister, used his time in opposition in 1924 to bring his erstwhile colleagues back into the Tory fold.

Coalitions can often be divisive of party unity, but this was not so for the Conservatives between the wars. The Lloyd George Coalition was immensely to their advantage, allowing them to gain valuable ministerial experience. It also enabled them to cash in on Lloyd George's popularity, as 'the man who won the war', in the election of 1918. In addition, they survived – unlike the Liberals – with their unity substantially intact. The Coalition formed in 1931 was even more in their interests. The atmosphere of national crisis enabled them to win the election of that year by a tremendous majority. The Tory Party alone – fighting on the patriotic, 'national' banner – won a small majority of the popular vote and a large majority of seats. Indeed so comfortable for the Conservatives was the National government that they made no effort to leave it: they simply devoured those groups of non-Tories who remained with them, and they even thought of changing the name 'Conservative' to 'National'.

5 Good luck

The Conservatives also had their fair share of luck in the interwar period. The disunity between Asquith and Lloyd George was fortunate for them, and so was the 'red scare' – the Zinoviev letter – during the 1924 general election. Had trade union leadership during the general strike been more determined – and especially if union leaders had had the foresight to make proper preparations before the strike – the Conservatives might not have earned such praise from the public for their handling of the dispute. Also, it was certainly to their advantage to lose the election of 1929, leaving Labour to grapple with the economic blizzard that soon engulfed Britain, as it did most of the world. The willingness of MacDonald and other Labour ministers to serve in the National government was also lucky.

6 Conservative successes

There are, however, more positive reasons for the Conservatives' dominance in the interwar period. Their record in office convinced many people that they were competent administrators who, while taking no unnecessary risks, would foster progressive reforms. Contributory old age pensions were begun in 1925 for all workers and their wives; in 1926 the Central Electricity Board modernised the production and distribution of electricity; and in 1929 local government was reformed. In foreign affairs, too, things seemed to be going well, at least in the period up to 1935. There was substantial harmony in Europe, so that many could believe that 1914–18 had indeed been a war to end all wars. The standard of living also improved considerably for the great majority of people in the country. High unemployment was the great failure of the period, but most people believed that there was simply no solution to this blight, and the Conservatives could be reassured that the unemployed tended to be concentrated in a relatively small number of 'depressed areas', comprising constituencies which were likely to return Labour MPs anyway. (See chapters 9–12 for a more thorough evaluation of the performance of interwar politicians.)

Leading Conservatives between the wars were widely respected and trusted. This was especially true of Stanley Baldwin (leader 1923–37): he was not dynamic, and indeed many people found him rather dull. His policies were summed up in the phrase he suggested as the Tory slogan for the 1929 general election, 'safety first'. Perhaps he, and other Conservatives, realised that, in view of their own advantages and the weakness of the other parties, they did not have so much to win elections as to avoid losing them. But Baldwin offered what many people wanted – stability – in contrast to both the upheavals of the First World War and the dislocation and revolutions occurring on the continent of Europe in the 1920s and 1930s. He was thus a profoundly reassuring figure. He was not heroic, but perhaps this was not a heroic age in Britain. Even so, he was a progressive in Conservative terms, and he did his best to combat the 'diehard' right wing of his party, which believed that doles and pensions would harm the moral fibre of the nation.

The Conservatives under Baldwin were pragmatic. They stood for national unity, for patriotism, peace and progress. This was a wise programme, for who would oppose such desirable ends? (Which of us is not, at least in theory, against sin?) By pitching their appeal at this broad level the Conservatives were sure to alienate as few potential Tory voters as possible. Baldwin declared that he stood for 'even justice' between man and man, 'a square deal', and insisted that he understood the average working man far better than the Labour Party. Such rhetoric undoubtedly made him an asset. Some people voted Conservative because they were Tories, but others did so because Baldwin was Baldwin, a man considered in some ways above party politics. One working man said of him in 1935, 'What I likes about Baldwin, 'e don't sling no mud'.

Conclusion

Looking back, we can identify the reasons which explain Conservative dominance in the interwar period. Indeed it is not difficult to establish a substantial and convincing set of explanations, ranging from the structure of politics to the role of key individuals and the part played by important events. Hence it is tempting to ask more refined questions; to ask, for instance, whether Tory dominance was due more to positive factors (such as their own strengths and policies) or to negative and fortuitous ones (the weakness of the opposition and lucky breaks). This is an issue well worth considering – and students are also urged to formulate factors other than those identified in this, necessarily brief, chapter.

It is also worth remembering that, to contemporaries, Tory dominance seemed by no means assured from 1918 to 1939. Indeed what in retrospect seems a period of relative political stability, sandwiched between the violent upheavals of the two world wars, appeared at the time to be one of uncertainty – and not surprisingly so, in view of the aftermath of the Great War, the general strike, the depression and mass unemployment, the political crisis of 1931 and the turmoil caused by Hitler's foreign policy. Hence the Conservatives never considered themselves the inevitable party of government, and this lack of complacency must be considered another reason for their dominance.

Task: note-taking

This is a very broad chapter: you are therefore urged to read this chapter without taking detailed notes straightaway, although you will need to be familiar with the framework of the governments. Come back to the reasons for Conservative dominance after you have read the subsequent chapters (8–14) in Part One. These will put flesh on some relatively bare bones. Then you should be able to cross-reference your notes, and so avoid too much repetition. Also, remember to use the index. But do return to the main issue in this chapter. Decide for yourself which factor, or combination of factors, best explains Conservative success. Do you give most weight to the circumstances of the time (including the economy), the weaknesses of the opposition (including the British fascists) or to Conservative strengths (in terms of policies and personnel)?

Further reading

Robert Blake, *The Conservative Party from Peel to Churchill* (Fontana, 1970) – readable account.
John Ramsden, *The Age of Balfour and Baldwin, 1902–40* (Addison Wesley Longman, 1978) – a more academic approach.
A. Seldon and S. Ball (eds), *The Conservative Century* (OUP, 1994) – collection of stimulating essays.

8 The crisis of 1931

Time chart

1900: Founding of the Labour Representation Committee

1918: New constitution for Labour

1923: Formation of first Labour government

1924: Zinoviev letter helps Conservatives to win election

1929: May
Formation of second Labour government
October
Wall Street Crash heralds depression

1930: Mosley Memorandum rejected by Labour

1931: July
Publication of the May Report, leading to a run on the pound
24 August
Labour's cabinet cannot agree on expenditure cuts: MacDonald forms a National government
September
MacDonald expelled from the Labour Party; Britain forced off the gold standard
October
General election: Labour reduced to 52 seats

The most dramatic and controversial political crisis in twentieth-century British politics occurred in 1931, when MacDonald's minority Labour government was replaced by a National government. What caused this political realignment? How important were the financial and economic circumstances of the time? Might there even have been a conspiracy of bankers and other capitalists to bring down the Labour government? And what was the role of **Ramsay MacDonald**, the Labour leader who stayed on as Prime Minister in an administration dominated by his former political enemies? Was he, as many admirers thought, the saviour of the nation; or was he, on the contrary, a traitor to the working class, as many of his former colleagues insisted?

PROFILE: *James Ramsay MacDonald*

B orn in 1866, the illegitimate son of a Scottish seamstress, **Ramsay MacDonald** was the first Secretary of the Labour Party. He entered the House of Commons first in 1906 and was Labour leader from 1922. A hard worker and an inspiring speaker, he was also a moderate, anxious to show that the party was respectable. He believed that socialism would only come by slow, gradual stages. Colleagues found him secretive and aloof. He was Britain's first prime minister to have no previous ministerial experience. After 1931 his health deteriorated rapidly, and in his final period as Prime Minister, up to 1935, he was in some ways a figure of fun, known in the Commons as 'Ramshackle Mac'. Churchill once dubbed him the 'Boneless Wonder'. MacDonald died in November 1937.

Historical background

Labour had come a long way since its formation in 1900 as the Labour Representation Committee. (The name 'Labour Party' was not used until 1906.) A breakthrough came in 1918 with the adoption of a new constitution which not only made the party structure more efficient but gave Labour a distinctive 'socialist' position: it promised to work towards a society based not on conflict and inequality but on planned production, stemming from the common ownership of the means of production. Labour MPs had also done much to calm the exaggerated fears of many members of the middle classes that the party favoured violent revolution and would overturn all the country's most sacred traditions – in short, that it was secretly communist.

The first Labour government, in 1924, had been a minority administration which had lasted only nine months, but it had certainly done much – by doing very little – to dispel some of these wilder myths. There was a Labour government in office, to the acute dismay of some, and yet very little changed: the Empire was not disbanded, plans were made to expand the Royal Navy, the family unit survived intact, and people's Post Office savings were not confiscated by the state. Labour, dominated by the civil servants, seemed respectable and fit to govern. During the subsequent election campaign, in October 1924, the *Daily Mail* published a letter, supposedly written by the leading Bolshevik Zinoviev, calling for revolution in Britain, and this encouraged Liberals to vote Tory; but Labour still increased its vote by 1 million.

Perhaps the real danger was not that Labour might be revolutionary but that it might be absorbed into the 'establishment' and lose its reforming zeal. Many on the left of the party certainly feared this, and they were further dismayed when MacDonald – always anxious to seem respectable – refused to give any support to the general strike in 1926. But most Labour supporters had few such qualms. They believed that the tide of history was running in their favour, and that in due course their party would achieve an overall majority and could then introduce 'socialism'. There seemed good reason for their confidence. In the 1920s Labour's popular vote grew from 22 to 37 per cent, and the party seemed on the brink of a breakthrough to real power.

Labour did remarkably well in the general election of 1929, the first election in British history which saw universal adult suffrage. The party won over 37 per cent of the popular vote and a total of 288 seats. Admittedly they were somewhat lucky, since the Conservatives, with 38 per cent of votes, won only 260 seats. But MacDonald had no hesitation in forming a government, despite the fact that the Liberals held the balance in a 'hung Parliament'. He was optimistic that his administration could succeed. A further period of competent Labour rule would, he believed, result in still more votes and seats at the next election.

The second Labour government

The government's record was good in foreign affairs, where Labour promoted harmony between France and Germany. But foreign policy took second place to domestic. Labour had the misfortune to be in office when the Great Depression began, triggered by the collapse of the stock market on Wall Street in the United States. Between 1929 and 1931 the value of British exports fell by half, while unemployment rose month after month, from 1.1 million to 2.8 million. Government revenue plummeted, as fewer people were paying taxation; but government expenditure, especially on unemployment benefit, rose steeply. What could Labour do?

There was no lack of advice from economists. Most traditional thinkers believed that the country could not go on living beyond its means and that the only viable option was to cut expenditure and balance the budget, even though this would mean reducing unemployment benefit. This was the course of action favoured by Labour's Chancellor, Philip Snowden. Others advised introducing protection (tariffs on imported goods). This was favoured by the Conservatives, though Snowden as a convinced free-trader did not agree. Public works seemed a possible way of reducing unemployment: Lloyd George had endorsed these at the previous election, but they would prove expensive at a time when public expenditure already seemed too high. Cambridge economist John Maynard Keynes and trade union leader Ernest Bevin advised coming off the gold standard (which, since 1925, had fixed – and probably overvalued – the pound at 4.86 dollars). Abandoning the gold standard would allow sterling to float downwards and thus make British exports cheaper and so more competitive abroad; but the consensus among economists was that abandoning gold would generate runaway inflation. Indeed the gold standard was such a fixed point in the firmament of most economists that they did not even consider abandoning it.

Labour's attitude was negative. At first, it was optimistic, hoping that the depression would cure itself. Hence when a junior minister, Sir Oswald Mosley, put forward a wide-ranging package of proposals, in 1930, he was turned down flat. There seemed to be a certain satisfaction – even smugness – among leading Labour figures that the capitalist economy was failing. Hadn't socialists always said that capitalism meant poverty and unemployment, ills which would not exist in a properly socialist economy and society? The only problem with this reasoning was that it did not help matters. Labour's socialism was therefore, as Robert Skidelsky has argued, utopian: it explained the past and promised the future but had nothing constructive to offer the present.

Soon Labour prevaricated because the options seemed too terrible to contemplate. If it pursued a deflationary policy, slashing government expenditure, it would be harming the unemployed, one of the most vulnerable groups of the working class, the very people Labour had been formed to represent. On the other hand, if it adopted untried and expensive policies like setting up major public works, and thus reflated the economy, it might well make matters worse. In this situation, the government set up committees and commissions to make recommendations; but this was merely a way of buying time, in the hope that, in the meantime, the world economy might somehow improve. The government thus drifted. But things got worse, not better.

The crisis of August 1931

Labour's problems came to a head at the end of July 1931. Banking failures abroad (and the loss of British investments) coincided with a severe balance of payments deficit. On top of this, on 31 July, the May Report was published. A committee on national expenditure had been set up in February under the businessman Sir George May: it now issued an alarmist report predicting a massive budget deficit of £120 million and recommending increased taxation of £24 million and expenditure cuts of £96 million, including a 20 per cent cut in unemployment benefit ('the dole').

MacDonald's cabinet set up a committee to consider May's recommendations and then dispersed for the summer holidays. But they could not maintain such a leisurely approach. The report led to a further crisis of confidence in sterling, fuelling a run on the pound, and ministers had to be recalled for urgent meetings.

Snowden was adamant that now drift must end: expenditure cuts had to be made and the budget balanced. He drew up a package totalling £78 million, to include a 10 per cent cut in unemployment benefit. If tough action were not taken, he insisted, the standard of living of all working people would plummet. MacDonald backed him up, and the proposals were put to the cabinet on 19 August, in a session lasting almost 12 hours. But the whole cabinet would only agree to cuts totalling £56 million, leaving benefits intact. The cabinet seemed divided down the middle. Further debate followed. Snowden insisted that the delay made necessary the negotiation of an international loan and that American bankers would only supply the necessary funds providing the 10 per cent cut in unemployment benefit were guaranteed. On the other side, the Trades Union Congress threw its weight against cuts. Snowden was opposed by an equally implacable Arthur Henderson, the Foreign Secretary and a much respected figure in Labour ranks. He believed that it was immoral to impose cuts on those least able to bear them. On 23 August a final vote was taken: 11 members voted for cuts of £78 million and nine (including eight trade unionists) voted against. MacDonald, who as Prime Minister did not vote, had little choice but to tender the resignation of his government. He immediately left for the Palace.

Formation of the National government

The following day MacDonald informed his cabinet colleagues that the Labour government was indeed at an end but that he himself, together with Snowden and J. H. Thomas, would take his place in an emergency National government. He would thus continue as Prime Minister. There had been calls in the press for such an administration, and the King, George V, had pressed MacDonald to do his patriotic duty by heading it. The opposition leaders had also urged him on. MacDonald had held regular talks with them, mainly because, lacking an overall majority, he needed their support to get measures through Parliament. He also needed to keep them informed when it looked as though they might have to take over from his own divided cabinet. As for the Conservatives, they reasoned that, if unpopular public expenditure cuts had to be made, it was better that they be imposed by a National government rather than a solely Tory administration. There is also good evidence that Neville Chamberlain, Conservative number two, believed that a National government, by detaching Labour's leaders, would wreak havoc with the future of the Labour Party.

MacDonald did not get permission from Labour to join a coalition (as, for instance, Arthur Henderson had done during the First World War). Indeed he did not even trouble to tell the Parliamentary Labour Party, most of whom had no inkling of what was afoot. Small wonder, then, that the party felt aggrieved or that, electing Henderson as its new leader, it proceeded to expel MacDonald, Snowden, Thomas and the few other defectors.

The National government

The new government made cuts in public expenditure (including a 10 per cent cut in the dole and in the salaries of government employees) and increased taxation. The budget was balanced, but a renewed run on the pound, fuelled partly by a refusal of the fleet at Invergordon to obey orders, convinced the Governor of the Bank of England, Montagu Norman, that there was no choice but to abandon the gold standard. To make matters worse, MacDonald, despite assurances that the National government was a temporary alliance rather than an electoral force, called a general election. This was catastrophic for Labour. All the old scare stories were revived and the party seemed discredited. The election was fought in an atmosphere described by one contemporary as 'jingoistic panic', and most electors voted National out of patriotism. Perhaps the surprising thing, in this atmosphere, is that the Labour popular vote held up so well.

Conclusion

What was MacDonald's role in these events? Was he really the traitor to his party and his class that critics averred? These broad questions can be narrowed down to four more specific ones, for which reasonably clear-cut answers can be found.

1 *Why did MacDonald support his Chancellor in calling for cuts in the dole?* Throughout his career MacDonald had wished to make Labour into a party of government. To his mind, that meant overcoming two major problems, the dual stigma that Labour was a one-class party interested only in industrial and economic issues and, more generally, that it was irresponsible and 'unfit to govern'. He himself had therefore always concentrated on foreign and imperial affairs and was vastly ignorant of economic policy, and so he was the last man to ignore the consensus of expert advice on budget issues. He knew that Labour's critics would rejoice at nothing so much as the failure of the party through adopting radical, untried policies. Far better, in his view, to take unpopular decisions in the national interest – and he was profoundly dismayed that so many of his colleagues would not agree with him.

2 *Why did MacDonald agree to head a predominantly Conservative administration in October 1931?* Convinced that Labour would not do what was necessary to tackle the financial crisis, MacDonald had certainly been willing to resign. But he was convinced by George V and by the opposition spokesmen that his presence in a new National government would be popular in the country and internationally. No doubt such notions flattered his vanity, but he does seem to have believed that such an alignment was in the national interest and, at first, that it would be merely temporary.

3 *Why did MacDonald not communicate his intentions more clearly and openly to his Labour colleagues?* MacDonald hoped to return to Labour ranks after the financial crisis had been settled, but his failure to secure Labour approval for his actions was almost guaranteed to anger colleagues and make this impossible. The fact is that he had long been isolated in the party, disliking his colleagues as much, if not more, than they disliked him. He was most at home in London's high society, a fact which fuelled later speculation that he had been corrupted by what the *New Statesman* termed the 'aristocratic embrace'. A man of very humble origins, he had certainly sprung from the people – a long way from them! He had been Labour's official leader since 1922, but in fact he had never been more (in the words of Beatrice Webb) than 'a magnificent substitute for a leader'. He had never led people in the sense of taking them with him; he had simply been Labour's star performer, a fine platform orator, brilliant at rolling his Rs. He was a lonely man who found it very difficult to communicate his real feelings. Most Labour figures found him an enigma. Hence the secrecy over his actions in August 1931 was typical of him.

4 *Why did MacDonald break his word and call an election under the National banner?* Labour expelled MacDonald at the end of September 1931, leaving him no party to which to return. Hence he was in a very difficult political position. Perhaps he should have resigned rather than accept Conservative calls for a general election the following month, but the far easier course was to acquiesce in a further period as Prime Minister. It should perhaps also be said in defence that his health was poor. He had always worked tirelessly, staying up late into the night to work through his boxes of official papers. As a result, he suffered badly from a variety of stress-related ailments, especially insomnia, as his diary poignantly

reveals. It therefore seems all the more likely that he was swept along under the pressure of events in August and September 1931, rather than making a series of considered judgements.

No one can reasonably argue any longer that MacDonald masterminded the political crisis of 1931. He had not planned events days, let alone years, ahead. In fact there was probably never a prime minister less in control of events. He must therefore be acquitted of the charge of traitor. He was not the 'Lucifer of the Left'. He did what he thought was best. On the other hand, neither was he the saviour of the nation, as supporters insisted. The cartoon in Figure 8.2 is therefore remarkably inaccurate. He was no boffin, experimenting to find exactly the right political mix capable of solving Britain's problems. (Nor was the 66-year-old Mac-Donald so sprightly a figure as portrayed here.) He had no real understanding of economic theory; he simply hoped that the orthodox economists were right in their views. He let others convince him that he was indispensable to the nation's recovery, but by no positive action of his own did he help to bring about recovery.

What of the supposed conspiracy of the bankers? Does this carry more conviction? At first sight a case can be made out. International bankers did insist on a 10 per cent cut in benefits as a precondition for a loan. May this not have been a ploy to engineer the downfall of a Labour – a *socialist* – government and install a safer capitalist one? Furthermore, having sacrificed Labour on an altar of gold, the banking community then performed a very skilful U-turn and demanded that, after all, the gold standard should be abandoned. What had seemed almost sacrosanct under Labour became eminently disposable once Labour was out of office.

Yet such reasoning does not stand up to scrutiny. The bankers had been asked for their advice and gave it, much as the TUC had done. Their call for a balanced budget, involving unemployment benefit cuts, was standard business practice: after so many banking failures, they wanted some assurance that their loans would eventually be repaid. And why should they have wanted to unseat a government which had scarcely shown itself particularly 'socialist' over the previous years? As for the abandoning of the gold standard, this was caused by the pressure of investors switching out of sterling. Financiers did not want it to happen. One has only to read the papers of Montagu Norman, Governor of the Bank of England, to see the patent reluctance with which he recommended action to the government.

'Conspiracy theories' are unnecessary to explain the crisis of 1931. Events can be readily understood by straightforward historical means. So can the

THE MASTER CHEMIST.

Figure 8.2 *MacDonald as hero: the dispassionate scientist and the country's saviour. 'Professor' MacDonald is saying 'Now if only these rather antagonistic elements will blend as I hope, we'll have a real national elixir.' The reality was very different from this image.*

theories themselves. They were surely a product of the unwillingness of left-wing thinkers, mesmerised by their own propaganda on the lengths to which evil capitalists would sink to preserve their power, to face the shortcomings of the second Labour Government. MacDonald and the bankers were convenient scapegoats.

Task: answering essay questions

Essay questions on the 1931 crisis are common. The following is typical:

'Was the Second Labour Government betrayed by Ramsay MacDonald in 1931?'

Helpful hints: How is this question best approached? First, you must analyse the question. What are the key words? The most important is obviously 'betrayed', and this must be defined. What was the nature of the alleged betrayal? It cannot be that MacDonald *blundered* into a position where he was aligned against his former Labour colleagues, since 'betrayal' presupposes a large measure of conscious design. It must be that he deliberately sacrificed his party, and his principles, in order to remain as Prime Minister. Nor is 'betrayed' a neutral or value-free term: it is highly critical. Therefore, if you think that what MacDonald did was sensible, then you would argue that he did not betray his party. Another key word is 'Was': you are not asked 'to what extent?' but a much more clear-cut – indeed stark – question, one which tends to invite 'Yes' or 'No' as the main plank in your answer. It is also worth thinking about the date: 1931 is specified, but clearly more precise dates are implied – 24 August, when the National government was formed, and 27 October, when the election was held. The whole of the year is relevant only if you think MacDonald was intending and planning the downfall of the government for the whole of this period.

Establishing the exact meaning of a question is absolutely vital: without this you cannot write a good answer. Never write generally on this issue or topic, always answer the precise question set.

Next you must begin to plan your answer. Always avoid narrative (starting, say, with the formation of the government and gradually working your way up to its demise). One way of avoiding this is to do the opposite: start with the end of the government and look back, isolating the issues and themes which helped to cause it. Remember the vital importance of backing up all your arguments with carefully selected facts and evidence: unsubstantiated generalisations – i.e. mere assertions – will not get good marks. In your final paragraph, come back to the wording of the question and hammer home your argument as clearly as possible.

Further reading

Robert Pearce, *Britain: Domestic Politics* (Hodder and Stoughton, 1992).

D. Marquand, *Ramsay MacDonald* (Cape, 1977) – the best biography of MacDonald.

S. Ball, *Baldwin and the Conservative Party: The Crisis of 1929–1931* (Yale University Press, 1988).

Andrew Thorpe, *The British General Election of 1931* (Oxford University Press, 1991).

9 Stanley Baldwin: reasons for his political survival

Stanley Baldwin (1867–1947) dominated interwar politics to a greater extent than any other individual. He seems to bestride the period like a colossus, and indeed interwar Britain is sometimes called 'the age of Baldwin'. His political career, remarkable for the length of time he spent in high political office, can be summarised as shown in the chart.

1908–37:	Conservative MP for Bewdley
1917–21:	Financial Secretary to the Treasury
1921–2:	President of the Board of Trade
1922–3:	Chancellor of the Exchequer
1923–37:	Leader of the Conservative Party
1923–4:	Prime Minister
1924–9:	Prime Minister
1931–5:	Lord President of the Council (with greater authority than the Prime Minister Ramsay MacDonald)
1935–7:	Prime Minister

He was out of office between 1918 and his retirement in 1937 for only the two brief periods of minority Labour administration; he was leader of the Conservative Party for 15 years; and he was Prime Minister on three separate occasions. This is a remarkable record.

How do we account for this political longevity? How was Baldwin able to survive at the top of the greasy pole of politics for so long? There are two basic explanations. The first is that he was a man of supreme political skill who earned and kept his position by merit. Winston Churchill, for instance, once referred to him as 'the most formidable politician I have ever known'. But the second view is that he was, quite simply, very lucky: he was a mediocre man, without great talent or even industry, who survived for so long due to a remarkable series of lucky breaks.

Elements of luck

The elements of sheer good fortune throughout Baldwin's career are glaringly obvious. They may be summarised as follows:

▓ Defeated at Kidderminster in the 1906 general election, he was returned unopposed two years later for Bewdley after the death of the incumbent MP, his own father. He inherited not only a sizeable fortune, based on his family's ironworks, but that invaluable political asset, a safe seat.

▓ It was also fortunate that he was born into a family which staunchly supported the Conservatives, a party which was to dominate politics between the wars (see chapter 7).

▓ In the next six years, he spoke on only five occasions in the Commons and seemed destined to remain a silent but loyal backbencher, one of a group often dismissed as 'lobby fodder'. But the Great War intervened. At the age of 50 Baldwin became Financial Secretary to the Treasury in 1917. He served under two Chancellors, Bonar Law and Austen Chamberlain, neither of whom was impressed with his work; but in 1921 he entered Lloyd George's cabinet when the resignation of Bonar Law through ill health necessitated a reshuffle.

▓ The major breakthrough in his career then came with the ending of the coalition between Conservatives and those Liberals loyal to Lloyd George in October 1922: not only was Lloyd George consigned to the political wilderness but he took with him most of the leading Tory figures (including Austen Chamberlain, Birkenhead and Balfour), leaving Bonar Law to form a 'government of the second eleven' in which Baldwin could claim a place. He was made Chancellor of the Exchequer, but only after another man had turned down the post.

▓ Baldwin was not particularly successful in this role, and indeed the Prime Minister wrote anonymously to *The Times* criticising his settlement of war debts with the United States; but it formed the springboard from which he became premier after the resignation of the terminally ill Bonar Law. Bonar Law would not recommend a successor – so little confidence had he in the available candidates – and Baldwin was only chosen because, with the Conservatives still split, there was no real alternative apart from Lord Curzon, who had the double disadvantage of being a peer and a man of overweening arrogance. At least Baldwin sat in the Commons, had some experience of high office, and – perhaps his most attractive quality – seemed a refreshing change after the dynamic Lloyd George, whose excessive promise of creating a 'land fit for heroes' had not been fulfilled. A memorandum extolling Baldwin's virtues from Bonar Law's secretary, which the King mistook for Law's own, may have been the final stroke of luck which swung the decision his way.

Having become Prime Minister largely by a bizarre combination of lucky chances, which he himself preferred to see as divine providence, Baldwin survived by a generous helping of good fortune. Again, there are many examples of this:

■ He was certainly lucky to remain as party leader after calling an unnecessary general election in November 1923, on the issue of protection, which led to the first Labour government. No one challenged his leadership because it was clear that Labour would not last very long, and it was thought politically unwise to change leaders just before another election.

■ It was also lucky when, on Labour's resignation the following year, the Conservatives were able to exploit the 'Red Scare', arising from the (probably forged) Zinoviev letter, to achieve a massive majority.

■ Baldwin was fortunate to be in office in 1924–9, a period of détente in Europe and of growing economic prosperity.

■ He was fortunate also to lose the general election of 1929, when the Great Depression was about to wreak political as well as economic havoc.

■ Nevertheless defeat on this occasion, after a campaign centred on Baldwin as the embodiment of trustworthy 'safety first', seemed likely to end his career. Even supporters admitted that he was a poor leader of the opposition, and he would probably have been replaced if rivals of sufficient stature had come forward to challenge him. He survived only by the narrowest of margins, and probably only the formation of the National government in 1931 (see chapter 8) safeguarded his position as party leader.

Perhaps Baldwin was the sort of man who needed luck as a substitute for hard work. He had a reputation for being lazy. Certainly he lacked the stamina of most other prime ministers and did not work particularly hard while in office, even when doubling up as Prime Minister and Chancellor of the Exchequer for three months in 1923. As a result, he is not associated with any particular act of Parliament or treaty. He simply chose ministers – not always very wisely, as with Churchill's appointment to the Exchequer in 1924, and seldom promoting younger men – and let them do their work with minimum interference, which usually meant none. 'Whatever you do,' he wrote to his Foreign Secretary in 1927, 'I will support you.' But neither Austen nor Neville Chamberlain, who were primarily responsible for the major reforms of his periods as premier, noticed particularly active support from their leader. He was particularly fortunate in that the younger half-brother, Neville, remained loyal despite harbouring a certain contempt for him.

Some of Baldwin's greatest so-called triumphs were due as much to his opponents as to himself. The general strike of May 1926 (see chapter 6) lasted only nine days, and Baldwin took the credit for its defeat, but the mass of strikers was solid: it was the general council of the TUC, whose members had authorised the strike only with patent reluctance, who got cold feet and decided to call it off. A more skilful negotiator than Baldwin might possibly have prevented a strike in the first place. Similarly, his handling of the abdication crisis in 1936 was fortunate. He was determined that the new King, Edward VIII, should not be allowed to marry an American divorcee and remain on the throne. The abdication was therefore a consummation he devoutly desired; but his success was due as much to Edward VIII's willingness to give up the throne as to anything he himself did. As Beaverbrook said to fellow royalist Churchill: 'Our cock won't fight.' Baldwin was therefore able to retire, in May 1937, amid considerable popularity. His timing was immensely fortunate: it was his ill-fated successor, Neville Chamberlain, who had to grapple with Hitler's aggression.

Elements of skill

Chance took Baldwin to Downing Street, and chance kept him there, but not without his stir. Baldwin did not rely entirely on luck. He was also a skilful politician. This took several forms:

■ He showed courage, as revealed at the fateful Carlton Club meeting in October 1922, when he was the only cabinet minister to speak out against Lloyd George. No time-server, and secure in the family fortune, he was prepared to leave politics rather than continue to work with someone he regarded as immoral. He made a fine speech at the club attacking Lloyd George as a 'dynamic force ... a very terrible thing' who had split the Liberal Party and was in the process of splitting the Conservatives.

■ Though generally lacking the eloquence of Lloyd George or Ramsay MacDonald, Baldwin could sometimes rise to unaccustomed oratorical heights, as with his attack in March 1931 on press barons Beaverbrook and Rothermere: their selfish aim, he insisted, was 'power without responsibility – the prerogative of the harlot throughout the ages'. An effective use of words must therefore be considered another element of his skill as a politician. He always sounded reasonable and sincere and was particularly effective on radio and on newsreels, which both became politically important in the interwar years. Baldwin was probably heard and seen, through the media, more than any previous politician in British history. In his first election broadcast, in 1924, he spoke over the radio in authentic and effective conversational tones, as if he were addressing each individual. He even broke off in mid-sentence to light his pipe, the sound of the striking match being clearly audible. In contrast, the other two party leaders were inept: they had the microphone taken to the public meetings which they were addressing and so sounded far less intimate and convincing in people's homes. Over the years Baldwin retained his common touch on the radio: in the 1935 general election, for instance, it was said that he 'has his feet on our fenders'. Many people could have written Baldwin's speeches – in fact, many people did! – but only Baldwin could have delivered them with such conviction.

- Baldwin was also a good 'House of Commons man', with an uncanny ability to sense the mood of MPs. Indeed Tory backbencher at the time Harold Macmillan described him as a 'sensitive artist' in politics, while left-winger Aneurin Bevan considered him the most consistently adroit of parliamentary performers. Baldwin made a particular effort to get on well with Labour MPs. Left-winger Manny Shinwell found him 'friendly and approachable'; and when another Clydesider, David Kirkwood, referred to him as 'Uriah Heep' (parading a false humility), Baldwin 'very gently asked him afterwards if that was how he really appeared'. The result was that Kirkwood 'felt very ashamed of himself' and was quickly won over. It is doubtful if any prime minister ever made fewer political enemies.

- Baldwin was highly respected not only within Parliament but in the country as a whole. In the course of his political career, he gained a reputation for being a fair-minded statesman, a man of complete integrity who could always be trusted – not brilliant, certainly, but fair-minded and honest. Baldwin, with a candour unequalled in any other modern politician, admitted that he was 'not a clever man' and that, indeed, he sometimes made mistakes. He seemed to have the genuine virtue of humility. The civil servant Tom Jones, who knew Baldwin well, judged that he was 'one-half contemplative and non-political', more preacher than politician. Certainly he believed in the Christian virtues. The salvation of England, he once said, lay not with the five-syllable French derivative 'proletariat' but in four words of one syllable each: 'faith, hope, love and work'. Above all, he believed in peace. His earnest prayer, he told the House of Commons, was 'Give us peace in our time, O Lord.'

Such homely philosophising often enabled him to take the heat out of a tense parliamentary situation. It was also vague enough not to rule out, or to prescribe, any particular policies: and as a result, he was a pragmatic Conservative. While insisting in 1934 that Conservatives could not go wrong if they stuck to the principles Disraeli had laid down at the Crystal Palace in 1872 – namely, 'the maintenance of our institutions and of our religion; the preservation of our Empire, and the improvement in the condition of our people' – he nevertheless insisted that no precise formula spelled political salvation and that therefore 'the sheet was quite clean' – no policies were self-evidently necessary or forbidden. The pragmatic Baldwin was therefore able, despite professing belief in free-market forces, to accommodate his party to a degree of collectivism and social reform which angered his right wing.

A shrewd political operator

The image

Baldwin was unlike any other contemporary politician. As Arthur Bryant wrote in 1937: 'Here was a politician who was scarcely a politician at all.' Whoever thought of Baldwin thought of 'Honest Stan', a pipe-smoking, pig-keeping countryman, unimaginative but as solid as a rock. He was not dashing or elegant – and his clothing was deplored by *The Tailor and Cutter* – but this made him all the more human. In short, he was the sort of man you could identify with and trust. As such, he was elevated in the popular consciousness above the ruck of party politics, as in the cartoon from *Punch* (Figure 9.1) published in the aftermath of the general strike. This was not a man bothered about the applause of the public (or about sartorial elegance!): instead he was, resolutely and determinedly, concerned with the safety of the ship of state. He stuck 'quietly to his job'. Baldwin's evident sincerity seemed to rule out any attempt to use satire against him.

On his retirement in 1937 *Punch* published a similar illustration (see Figure 9.2). There seems nothing distinguished about the short and stocky figure, while his glance upwards at John Bull has an unmistakably modest air. Similarly, his work of ploughing seems humdrum and even menial, though certainly suitable for this country-lover. But he had earned the plaudits of the nation for an essential job slowly but surely done.

But do these illustrations represent the real Baldwin? It seems very unlikely. (After all, he suffered a virtual nervous collapse at the end of the general strike and made very few efforts to solve the continuing coal dispute.) Baldwin employed no firm of public relations experts to advise on his 'image', but it is arguable that he nevertheless was careful to foster an image that rebounded to his political advantage. Austen Chamberlain remarked in 1935 that he would head a chapter on Baldwin 'Sly, Sir, devilishly Sly!' because, despite the common image, he was really 'one of the shrewdest politicians', as well as one of the most egotistical of men.

Figure 9.1 *Stanley Baldwin as he wished to be seen, as the man who could be trusted. He is steering the good ship GENERAL STRIKE past rocks labelled COAL CRISIS! Caption read:*
John Bull (to the pilot) *'You've got us through that fog splendidly.'*
Mr Baldwin (sticking quietly to his job) *'Tell me all about that when we're past these rocks.'*

THE MAN IN CONTROL.

The real Baldwin was totally unlike his image. He was an industrialist not a countryman, nervous (with a facial tic and a habit of sniffing audibly at papers and books) rather than unimaginative. He was complex and clever, not simple and slow. Most people believed him to be modest, yet he often voiced the astounding claim that he understood the British people and spoke for them. He also had a shrewd eye for the main political chance:

■ It was generous of him, as Financial Secretary to the Treasury, to donate £120,000 to the nation, 20 per cent of his wealth; but he announced the gift in a letter to *The Times* signed 'FST', and so it was hardly the anonymous, selfless gesture he claimed.

Figure 9.2 Baldwin's retirement in May 1937: the image – but not the reality – of the humble, unsophisticated countryman. Farmer Bull says 'Well done Stanley: a long day and a rare straight furrow.'

THE WORCESTERSHIRE LAD

- He resigned immediately after losing the 1929 election, despite the fact that Labour did not have an overall majority, because anything else would 'look unsporting', not because it would be wrong.

- In 1935 he cashed in on the resignation of Labour's leader, George Lansbury, by calling an election earlier than originally intended.

- Had Baldwin been as principled as he made out, he would surely have resigned with his Foreign Secretary, Sir Samuel Hoare, over the Hoare–Laval plan (wherein Britain and France indulged in secret diplomacy despite assurances that they supported the League of Nations) at the end of 1935.

■ His moderate political position also owed a good deal to shrewd calculation. He told a junior colleague that to be leader of the Conservative Party, one should adopt a middle position between the extremes of the party, 'between Harold Macmillan and Henry Page Croft. I do so and that is why I am still here.'

■ Some may judge that he played cynically on his image as the plain, blunt man – ordinary but trustworthy – for political advantage. When, during the 1935 election campaign, he insisted 'I think you can trust me by now', this was the culmination of a whole series of similar claims which, repeated often enough, were accepted as truth. Tom Jones did not get it quite right: Baldwin was not one-half non-political: rather he forged a seemingly non-political image as a most effective political weapon.

Conclusion

Baldwin's career was a long one. It would therefore be unreasonable to suppose that a single factor – even one as multifaceted as 'luck' or 'skill' – could account for his political survival. As we have seen, both these factors played their part: indeed both were crucial. Although, at first sight, they seem to be alternatives, in reality they complemented each other. Baldwin was indeed immensely lucky to survive for so long, and without good fortune would not have remained in high office or indeed have achieved it at all; but it is equally true to say that without determination and skill he would surely have fallen. But this is not to say that each factor was equally important at all stages of his career: indeed, a full understanding of Baldwin's survival will emerge only from a thorough study of his career and, almost, of the whole interwar period.

This chapter has focused solely on the reasons for Baldwin's political survival. The issue of whether he – and other interwar politicians – used their power constructively is taken up in the next chapter.

Task: evaluating cartoon evidence

Cartoons are often valuable forms of evidence for the historian, but they need some care in interpretation. Political cartoons are rarely intended to be 'funny' as such. The cartoonist hopes to bring a smile of recognition to the reader's face by showing a familiar figure in an unreal – but symbolically important – role: Baldwin as pilot or ploughman, for example. For the historian, such cartoons reveal how people at the time thought of their subjects.

Study the *Punch* cartoon from 1926 (Figure 9.1):

a In what ways does the cartoonist suggest that the general strike was a crisis?

b Who do you think 'John Bull' was, and why is he shown having a conversation with 'Mr Baldwin'?

c What message is the cartoonist trying to give about Baldwin's abilities?

Now look also at the cartoon from 1937 (Figure 9.2):

d What points of similarity, and what points of difference, can you note about these two cartoons?

e Use the evidence of these cartoons, and other evidence from this chapter, to explain the dominant impression of Baldwin that was given to the British people. Suggest possible reasons why this impression was so often conveyed.

Further reading

K. Younger, *Baldwin* (Weidenfeld and Nicolson, 1976) – a short, entertaining account.

K. Middlemas and J. Barnes, *Baldwin* (Weidenfeld and Nicolson, 1969) – an important, but very long, biography.

10 Interwar politicians: 'rule by pygmies'?

Interwar Britain has, generally, been portrayed by historians as a depressing period. It began hopefully enough: Britain had won the war and there were hopes of building a 'land fit for heroes'. But such hopes soon proved delusory. The foul stench of the trenches gave way to the bitter odour of despair. Postwar economic boom was replaced by bust, as prices tumbled and unemployment mounted. The Roaring Twenties failed to roar in Britain, while industrial troubles escalated to produce the costly general strike in 1926. In the 1930s – the 'devil's decade' – things were even worse. Unemployment rose to 3 million in the early years of the decade, and at its end Britain entered another world war, one even more destructive than the first. The whole period seems one of catastrophic decline for what had once been a great country.

Most historians have blamed the politicians for what happened. One of the most knowledgeable historians of the period, Charles Loch Mowat, in *Britain Between the Wars* (1955), wrote that between 1922 and 1940 occurred 'the rule of the pygmies'. One might object to the terminology as having racist – or at least 'sizist' – overtones; but the implication is clear enough. Politicians like Baldwin, MacDonald and Chamberlain, and the lesser fry who swam meekly in their wake, were simply unequal to the challenges they faced as the country's leaders, and, instead of making matters better, they made them worse. For a long time this view was generally accepted. Certainly A. J. P. Taylor, in *English History 1914–45* (1965), delighted in exposing the inadequacies of all and sundry. But more recently historians have defended interwar politicians and have claimed that they had substantial successes to their credit. This chapter examines the historiographical controversy that has occurred, and in so doing considers how historical judgements are made.

The case against the politicians

The arguments of those who agree with Mowat are based on the failure of the politicians to solve Britain's major problems.

Economy and unemployment

A fundamental problem was high unemployment. Throughout the 1920s there were at least 10 per cent of the insured population (about 1 million people) out of work. Figures were much higher for most of the 1930s, reaching 22 per cent in 1933 (almost 3 million people). In fact, these official totals were underestimates of the real problem, since not all the unemployed were on the official registers. The situation was particularly bad in certain regions of the country, the 'depressed areas'. Over 60 per cent of the insured population were unemployed in Merthyr Tydfil in South Wales, for instance, and over 70 per cent in Jarrow in the North-East in the mid-1930s. (For more details of the interwar economy, see chapter 12.)

Government response was incompetent. The return to the gold standard at the prewar parity in 1925 (see page 47) hastened decline, while also aggravating industrial relations, and most of the measures taken to alleviate the situation, like protection in 1932, had little impact. Ministers devoted far more attention to reorganising the system of unemployment benefit than to creating new jobs. Yet they could have done much more. Maynard Keynes, the most brilliant economist of the period, was devising a system of 'demand-management' whereby government could actively create employment by increasing its spending and so boosting the demand for goods and services. Certainly the political parties accepted in 1944 that they could ensure a high level of employment, and in the 1950s and 1960s – when Mowat and Taylor were writing – mass unemployment was no longer a problem.

Poverty

Many government measures actually harmed the welfare of the people. Cutting the dole by 10 per cent in 1931, for instance, simply reduced spending power and so harmed employment prospects. The cuts also led to a deterioration in the health standards of the poorest in the community, including an increased incidence of rickets in the schoolchildren of the depressed areas. Governments in fact did very little to combat poverty between the wars. Seebohm Rowntree found that in York in 1936 about one-third of the working-class population lived in poverty. There was a great health divide between the classes. Public schoolboys, for instance, who enjoyed a better diet, were on average 4 inches (10.16 cm) taller than those attending state schools. In 1938 a survey revealed that malnutrition was a direct cause of the death of as many as 3,200 women each year in childbirth. Further evidence came in 1940. The state of evacuated working-class children created a scandal: over 12 per cent of those evacuated from Newcastle, for instance, did not have proper shoes, and 50 per cent were infested with lice. Clearly politicians were not responsive to the real needs of the mass of the electorate.

Foreign policy

Foreign policy must be reckoned a third area of failure. Britain had been on the winning side in 1918, and for much of the interwar period Germany suffered far more hardship and destitution than Britain. Why was Britain therefore unable to prevent a second war? The answer seems obvious: appeasement. Instead of rearming and opposing Hitler's demands with superior force and an effective coalition of allies, politicians meekly gave way to his demands and by so doing increased both his appetite for territory and his contempt for a decadent Britain. Hence the Second World War was 'the unnecessary war'. It would not have occurred had British politicians shown more moral fibre. But they would not tackle Hitler any more than they would unemployment (see chapter 11, on appeasement, for further details).

Reasons for failure

How can these failures be explained? Critics would say that a lot of the blame must go to politicians, who saw political power as an end in itself not as a means towards fostering a better life for the British people. Inevitably the prime ministers must be singled out. Baldwin was a lazy man who preferred to shut his eyes to problems in the hope that they would go away. Likewise MacDonald, especially in the National government, retreated into incoherence. Both were old men in the 1930s, and so was the Prime Minister at the end of the period, Neville Chamberlain, and the health of none of them was good. In 1935 the 69-year-old MacDonald, who was incapable of making an intelligible speech in the House of Commons, gave way as premier to Baldwin, who was only a year younger and was becoming increasingly deaf. Waiting in the wings to take over was Neville Chamberlain, the 66-year-old gout-ridden Chancellor of the Exchequer. Why were there so few new men thrusting into positions of prominence? Perhaps the answer lay in the Flanders mud where so many had perished – and where positive thinking and optimism had also been casualties. The shadow of the First World War cast its gloomy light over the next decades.

Another vital factor was the political structure of Britain. A party could achieve a sizeable majority in the Commons without winning a majority of the people's votes. What mattered most, therefore, was party unity, and this tended to keep out of office talented men and creative men – like Lloyd George, Oswald Mosley and, to some extent, Winston Churchill – who did not always toe the party line.

The defence of the politicians

Many historians have defended the interwar politicians, arguing that the detractors have judged unfairly. The major biographers of the Prime Ministers – Middlemas and Barnes for Baldwin, Marquand for MacDonald, and Dilks for Chamberlain – have all treated their subjects sympathetically, attempting to empathise with them in very difficult situations. The more we know about these men, they argue, the more we understand that they did their best and that, moreover, they have substantial achievements to their credit. The opening of government papers after only 30, rather than the traditional 50 years, from 1967 has facilitated this quest for true understanding.

The economy

In the 1960s H. W. Richardson introduced the revisionist view that the 1930s were a period of substantial economic growth and modernisation. He concentrated not on the depressed staple industries but on the so-called 'new industries', including chemicals, motor vehicles and synthetic textiles. Looked at from this perspective, the British economy seems far more impressive. There was also a 'retailing revolution'. There were indeed high levels of growth and productivity between the wars. If some areas of the country saw continuous high unemployment, others saw high levels of employment as well as population growth, as British workers moved to where the jobs were.

In the 1970s and 1980s, and now in the 1990s, most economists no longer believe that Keynes had the answer to unemployment. Consequently, critical judgements about the interwar politicians for ignoring his advice are no longer so severe. (Indeed Keynes's theories were not fully worked out until 1936, with the publication of his *General Theory*, and therefore it is not surprising that governments failed to follow his advice.) Perhaps there was no choice for politicians but to allow market forces to operate, so that gradually the old staple industries would cut back to a size warranted by the market for their goods. John Ramsden has argued that the politicians were quite right to turn a deaf ear to Keynes during the crisis of 1931: had they taken his advice there would have been a collapse of business confidence and the economic depression would have been much more severe. Certainly right-wing historians are these days more likely to praise the National government's economic record than to criticise it.

Poverty

Undoubtedly poverty existed in interwar Britain. But the issue needs to be seen in perspective. Poverty was exacerbated everywhere in the world by the depression of 1929–33, on the banks of the Benue in northern Nigeria as in the shipyards of the Clyde. The key issue, surely, is whether, on the whole, things were getting better or worse in the interwar period. Many contemporaries judged that things were deteriorating: the novelist J. B. Priestley, for instance, insisted in 1939 that 'the England of 1914 was superior, in every important department of national life, to the England of today'. But there is hard statistical evidence that they were quite wrong.

Average life expectancy certainly rose: it was 52 years for men in 1910 but 61 years in 1938. For women it increased over the same period from 55 to 66 years. Maternal mortality did not fall, at least until the late 1930s, but infant mortality certainly did, from 76 deaths of babies under the age of one year per 1,000 live births in 1929 to 55 per 1,000 in 1938. In his famous book *Food, Health and Income* (1936), John Boyd Orr criticised nutritional standards, but he acknowledged that the diet of the whole population had improved on pre-1914 days. Poverty undoubtedly existed, but on a smaller scale than earlier. This is clearly apparent if we compare Rowntree's 1936 survey of York with the one that he had undertaken in 1899. Using the same criteria, he established that at the latter date poverty had declined by over 55 per cent. In the Second World War, only one-third were found to be unfit for military service, compared with two-thirds in 1914–18.

Governments' social policies may have been cautious and low-key, but they were undoubtedly beneficial nevertheless. They promoted a shorter working week, typically 48 hours in 1939 compared with 54 hours in 1918, and the 1938 Holidays with Pay Act established a week's paid holiday as the norm. Expenditure on social welfare grew from 5.5 per cent of Britain's gross national product just before the First World War to 13 per cent in 1938. Admittedly Britain's social services were far from adequate to meet the needs of the people, but even so they were among the most advanced in the world.

Foreign policy

Over the last two decades there has been a remarkable shift in historical views on appeasement. No longer do the issues seem quite as simple as they used to do, when the Second World War was the 'unnecessary war' which could have been avoided but for the short-sighted feebleness of the 'guilty men'. Appeasement now seems based upon a realistic appraisal of Britain's economic weakness. The country already had to defend its vast and sprawling empire. How could it do this and be expected to ward off the challenges of Germany, Italy and Japan, especially when there were so few reliable allies at hand? To David Dilks and others, appeasement was a 'natural' policy for Britain to follow.

Democratic success

In addition, the defenders of the interwar politicians would point to an important, but often unsung, success for which they were responsible. Detractors may criticise the electoral system, but the fact is that democracy flourished in Britain while elsewhere it was collapsing. Democracy came about through legislation in 1918 and 1928, and it worked. Voters regularly turned out at elections and they did not become cynical about the politicians. The undemocratic Communist Party and the British Union of Fascists were never able to mount a real challenge.

Democratic success was admittedly a complex phenomenon, but the interwar politicians deserve a share of the credit. Perhaps Baldwin should be singled out. He saw the need to convince electors, by honest administration and by avoiding unrealistic election promises, that they could trust the politicians. He also wished to prevent powerful industrial conglomerates, on the one hand, and mass trade unions, on the other, from producing class confrontation on a truly Marxist scale. Hence he attempted to evoke a sense of common patriotism that would bind all citizens together. The speeches to which he gave real attention were not those on specifically political topics but addresses entitled 'Christian Ideals', 'Democracy and the Spirit of Service' and, above all, 'England', in which he evoked a pre-industrial idyll:

> 'To me, England is the country, and the country is England ... The sounds of England, the tinkle of the hammer on the anvil in the country smithy, the corncrake on a dewy morning, the sound of the scythe against the whetstone, and the sight of a plough team coming over the brow of a hill, the sight that has been seen in England since England was a land...'
>
> Stanley Baldwin, *On England* (1926).

No other prime minister has ever waxed lyrical over the smell of wood smoke or scutch fires! But these were not deranged ramblings. Baldwin's non-political musings had the very definite political purpose of making Britons forget what divided them in the light of their common heritage. Only with a sense of common citizenship, he believed, could democracy flourish.

Conclusion

We have seen in this chapter – and there is further evidence in chapters 9, 11 and 12 – that historians have differed widely in their assessment of the work and the calibre of interwar politicians. It should be easy for you to understand why they have disagreed. Partly it is due to the sources that are available. The release of government papers, after the 1960s, has allowed us to see politics 'from the inside' and thus more sympathetically. It is also due to our own 'angle of vision'. We see the past from the perspective of the present day, conditioned by the political experiences through which we have lived and by our own particular interests, political viewpoints and temperaments. The past is so diverse that we can never hope to see all its many aspects, and hence each historian tends to pick out different ones as important.

The 'rule by pygmies' debate has highlighted different aspects of the interwar period. To take one example, the economy: historians have established that the period was both 'the best of times' and 'the worst of times'. Many millions of people suffered acutely during the depression of the 1930s, while millions of others saw rising standards of living. Some historians (the 'pessimists') have picked out the negative aspects, while the 'optimists' have done the opposite. Of course all self-respecting historians try to give a balanced view, but what exactly is the correct balance and how do we compare, say, poor maternal mortality rates with the setting up of the Central Electricity Board? No two historians are likely to agree on this.

Evaluations of the politicians are thus partly dependent on our view of the interwar years, an uncomfortably full period – certainly in terms of surviving records. There is the added difficulty that it is never easy to evaluate particular personalities. Lloyd George and Winston Churchill, the premiers during the First and Second World Wars respectively, have often been excessively praised by biographers, creating the impression that in the interwar years political leaders were, in contrast, all tame mediocrities. But perhaps it was the situation between the wars, when there was no heroic battle to be fought against foreign foes, which gives this impression.

Did interwar politicians pursue the best policies available to them? We must grapple with this question if we are seriously to evaluate their political stature. But what a hard question it is! So much depends on the theoretical issue of 'what would have happened if ...?' What if the government in 1931 had introduced Keynesian techniques to combat depression? What if, in 1936, the government had taken firm action to eject Hitler's troops from the Rhineland? Controlled experiments are, alas, not available to historians, and therefore such questions will never be answered definitively.

In short, everyone is bound to make different evaluations of the stature of interwar politicians. The view of the present writer is that there is much to be said for, and much against, Baldwin, MacDonald, Chamberlain and all the others, but that they erred too much on the side of caution. On the whole, therefore, we should criticise rather than praise. But this is not to dismiss the politicians as 'pygmies'. Nor is it to say that you should agree. At the end of this chapter it is hoped that you will be well on the way to formulating your own views, that you will be able to argue your case with those of different opinions, and that you will be aware of the criteria by which your judgements are made. Hopefully, too, you will be searching for more information – and will be willing to modify your views in the light of that information.

Task

One way of appreciating why there is so much disagreement about the stature of the interwar politicians is to rehearse a range of viewpoints, selecting the best evidence to support each of them:

a Compose an attack on the interwar politicians from the point of view of a postwar Keynesian.
b Compose an attack on the interwar politicians from the point of view of a sympathetic biographer of Winston Churchill.
c Give a defence of the politicians from a biographer of Stanley Baldwin.

You should be able to make out a good case for each of these standpoints. But are they equally valid? A classroom debate should help you to explore this issue; and once each group within the class has reported, you should be able to judge which argument is the strongest.

Further reading

See the volumes recommended for the other chapters in this section of the book. Also valuable are:

Andrew Thorpe, *Britain in the 1930s* (Blackwell, 1992) – this provides an excellent, short introduction.

H. W. Richardson, *Economic Recovery in Britain 1932–9* (Weidenfeld and Nicolson, 1967).

11 British foreign policy and appeasement: Chamberlain in the dock

Time chart

1919: The Treaty of Versailles

1924: The Dawes Plan, scaling down reparations

1925: The Locarno Treaty: Germany accepts its western borders

1929: The Young Plan, further scaling down reparations

1930: Rhineland evacuated, five years ahead of schedule

1933: Hitler comes to power in Germany

1935: The Stresa Front (Britain, France, Italy), disrupted when Mussolini invades Abyssinia

1936: 7 March
Hitler remilitarises the Rhineland

1937: May
Chamberlain replaces Baldwin as Prime Minister

1938: March
Hitler annexes Austria
September
The Munich Conference: Sudetenland ceded to Germany

1939: March
Hitler invades Czechoslovakia; Britain guarantees Poland
23 August
Hitler and Stalin sign the Nazi–Soviet Pact
1 September
Hitler invades Poland
3 September
Britain declares war on Germany

No issue in foreign policy this century has been more controversial than **appeasement**, and no prime minister has been more praised and more vilified than Neville Chamberlain. Not surprisingly, Chamberlain's appeasement has spawned an extensive historiographical debate. This chapter investigates these issues and asks whether Chamberlain should be praised or censured for his foreign policy in 1937–9.

Foreign policy before Chamberlain

The Versailles Settlement

Britain, along with France and the United States, was on the winning side in the First World War. Its representatives, and especially its Prime Minister, Lloyd George, therefore had the very difficult job of helping to produce a settlement with the defeated powers, including Germany. Most historians have been critical of the settlement, not least because another world war started only 20 years afterwards.

The treaty with Germany has been criticised on two counts. First, Germany was given a sense of grievance. In particular, the Germans complained about the following points:

- The 'war guilt' clause blamed Germany and its allies for starting the war, whereas most Germans felt that they had been acting defensively.

- Germany lost 13 per cent of its land in Europe, and 7 million inhabitants.

- While other groups were given **national self-determination**, the Germans were denied the right to join together: not only were millions of Germans forced to live as minorities in other countries, but the *Anschluss* (the union of Germany and Austria) was forbidden.

- Germany also lost all its colonies.

- There was to be an army of occupation stationed in the Rhineland – that part of Germany which bordered France and through which the Germans had invaded in 1870 and 1914 (see Figure 11.4 on page 101) – for 15 years. Thereafter it was to be kept permanently demilitarised.

- Germany could maintain an army of no more than 100,000 men.

- Germany was to pay reparations (calculated at £6,600 million in 1921) for some of the damage inflicted on its enemies.

On the other hand, some critics, especially in France, believed that the settlement was too moderate. Germany, they believed, should have been so weakened that it would have been unable to start another war at any time in the future. As it was, Germany was still a potentially strong state. Its population, for instance, was greater than France's or Britain's. Nor were there any practical means of enforcing the terms of the Treaty of Versailles, so that the German army, though reduced in size, was never scaled down to 100,000 men.

In effect, Versailles was both too harsh and too weak: it gave Germany a sense of grievance and left it with the potential for becoming strong

Détente

The term **détente** denotes a lessening of tension in international affairs and the growth of reconciliation between former enemies. Historians have debated whether the years 1924–9 in Europe saw real or only delusory détente.

enough to redress those grievances in the future. Germany seemed weak around 1919–23; but eventually the problem would be German strength.

Détente

Neither the French nor the Germans found Versailles acceptable. The French wanted security against German revival, while the Germans wanted equality of status. In 1923 there was confrontation: the French occupied the Ruhr, the industrial heartland of Germany, when the Germans fell behind with reparation payments. Yet neither side gained by this confrontation, and both soon learned to compromise. In 1924 reparations were scaled down with the Dawes Plan, as they were also in 1929 with the Young Plan, and the Germans agreed to pay them. Furthermore, by the Locarno Treaty of 1925 both France and Germany agreed to accept their common border, with Britain and Italy acting as guarantors. By this freely negotiated treaty, the Germans accepted that the Rhineland would be permanently demilitarised. It seemed, finally, that Franco-German enmity had ended. Contemporaries believed that the problems of the past were over and that peace was assured. Further promising signs were soon apparent: in 1928, in a peace pact, most of the world's leading nations renounced war; the League of Nations (the international body set up by Versailles to solve international problems peacefully) seemed to be doing well, and Germany was admitted as a member for the first time in 1926; and in 1929 the French agreed to evacuate troops from the Rhineland ahead of schedule. All seemed set fair.

The impact of Hitler

A blow to international affairs was delivered by the economic slump which hit the world in 1929. It was not so easy for powers to cooperate in this new climate, especially since several powers turned to aggression in their search for new markets and, perhaps, to provide diversions for their citizens from austerity at home. For instance, in 1931 Japan invaded Manchuria. Another blow came when Hitler achieved power in Germany in 1933. He immediately left the world disarmament conference and the League of Nations. He also rearmed much more openly than his predecessors in Germany and insisted that what remained of the Treaty of Versailles should be scrapped.

The response of the international community was muted, even when, in March 1936, Hitler broke not only Versailles but also the Locarno Treaty by sending German troops into the Rhineland. There were several reasons for the lack of retaliatory action:

◼ Hitler's demands seemed to be just. Historians had decided that the First World War had been an accident: Versailles, which was based upon false notions of German war guilt, was therefore immoral and ought to be revised.

■ Most countries were grappling with their own economic problems and did not want to be diverted by international issues.

■ Certainly no other country wanted to face a possible war, especially since conflict was likely to be even more destructive than in 1914–18.

■ Britain, France and Italy had formed the Stresa Front in 1934 to deter Hitler, but the Italians had invaded Abyssinia in 1935, so ending this alignment. This invasion also destroyed the credibility of the League of Nations, which did no more than impose feeble and unsuccessful economic sanctions.

■ Hitler was still, in many ways, an unknown, enigmatic figure. Perhaps he would settle down once his immediate grievances had been solved. Certainly many admired the way in which he was solving Germany's economic problems and restoring the Germans' self-respect.

■ Hitler was thought to be a potentially valuable ally against Stalin's Russia. At all events, a strong Germany would be a valuable buffer against Soviet expansion westward.

Britain's attitude to Germany was conciliatory. Its politicians wished to see German grievances satisfied without recourse to war. In short, its policy was appeasement.

The National government in Britain recognised that Germany was a potential aggressor – but that seemed all the more reason to appease Hitler, especially since the Italians and Japanese were also potential aggressors, who might threaten Britain's Empire. In addition, a moderate programme of rearmament was begun. The Prime Minister from 1935 to 1937, Stanley Baldwin, was unlikely to pursue a dynamic foreign policy: he was suffering from poor health and, anyway, had no real interest in foreign affairs. (Revealingly, he once changed the seating arrangements at an official dinner so that he would not have to talk to the foreign guests.) Under Baldwin, appeasement was largely passive. Not so under his successor, **Neville Chamberlain**.

Chamberlain's foreign policy

Chamberlain had a good record in domestic politics, and most observers decided that he was an extremely capable politician. As Prime Minister from May 1937 he recognised that foreign policy was paramount and, in business-like fashion, set about trying to solve the problems.

PROFILE: *Neville Chamberlain*

The son of Joseph Chamberlain, and half-brother to Austen (Foreign Secretary 1924–9), **Neville Chamberlain** served as Lord Mayor of Birmingham in 1915–16 before entering the House of Commons in 1918 at the age of 50. He was twice Minister of Health in the 1920s and served as Chancellor of the Exchequer in 1923–4 and 1931–7. He was a dynamic and constructive minister, showing a capacity for administrative efficiency and reform. He once said that he was unable to contemplate any problem without trying to find a solution to it. No one doubted that he had earned the position of premier. His weakness was a reputation – well-deserved – for being cold emotionally. He also found it hard to disguise feelings of contempt for the Labour opposition and even for some of his own colleagues. Many found him arrogant, though others believed this was a façade covering up deep-seated insecurity. Mussolini predicted that his 'uniform of a bourgeois pacifist' would act on Hitler like the taste of blood to a wild beast. Chamberlain died in 1940, aged 71.

Under Chamberlain, appeasement continued to be British policy. For instance, Britain scarcely complained when, in March 1938, Hitler sent his troops into Austria, bringing about the *Anschluss* (see Figure 11.4). But Chamberlain's appeasement was much more active than Baldwin's. When Hitler demanded the Sudetenland (containing 3 million Germans) from Czechoslovakia in the summer of 1938, even at the cost of war with the Czechs and their French allies – a war which might involve Britain – Chamberlain flew to meet Hitler three times. The third occasion was at Munich in September, a meeting which is generally thought to symbolise appeasement. The Czechs were abandoned by the West and were forced to give Hitler what he wanted without a fight. Chamberlain also sought a personal meeting with Hitler, and together the two men signed a declaration that Germany and Britain had no intentions of going to war again. This was the piece of paper which Chamberlain waved to the cheering crowds at Heston airport: it meant, he said, not only 'peace with honour' but 'peace in our time' (see Figure 11.2). Public opinion was massively relieved that war had been avoided. Chamberlain was compared with Christ, he was called the greatest statesman of any age, streets were named after him and statues of him were erected. In the *Punch* cartoon shown in Figure 11.3, he was praised by John Bull, the traditional symbol of the British people. The cartoonist has even 'improved' Chamberlain's appearance: in reality, he was a tall, angular man with a 'pin head'. (Lloyd George once said he had the smallest head of any man he had ever known, and therefore was not to be trusted.)

Figure 11.2 *Chamberlain on his return from Munich. He was, for a time, the most popular man in Britain.*

Yet six months later, in March 1939, Hitler invaded the remainder of Czechoslovakia, despite having insisted that the Sudetenland was his last territorial demand. Chamberlain then, under pressure to do something, guaranteed Poland, which might be Hitler's next target. But even this did not deter the German leader. On 23 August 1939 he signed a pact with Stalin, to stop Britain doing so and to ensure that the Soviets would not intervene against him, and on 1 September he invaded Poland. Two days later Britain declared war on Germany. Chamberlain had been praised excessively; but now he began to be criticised. His dove-like innocence, said one critic, made him fit only for a stained-glass window; another added that he had 'eaten dirt in vain'. When the war began to go badly for Britain, in the early summer of 1940, Chamberlain was called one of the 'Guilty Men' who had betrayed their country.

Figure 11.3 Chamberlain, considered (briefly) the saviour of world peace, receiving the praise of John Bull, who says: 'I've known many Prime Ministers in my time, sir, but never one who worked so hard for security in the face of such terrible odds'. In reality, Chamberlain did not 'mediate' at Munich at all.

A GREAT MEDIATOR

The case for the prosecution

Chamberlain has been heavily criticised for his role in appeasing Hitler. The points generally made against him include the following:

◼ His background in municipal politics and domestic affairs unfitted him for diplomacy (so that he saw foreign affairs through the wrong end of a municipal drainpipe); in addition he was simply too old in 1937 (at 68) to adapt to new issues.

◼ He never understood Hitler. His appeasement was based on the

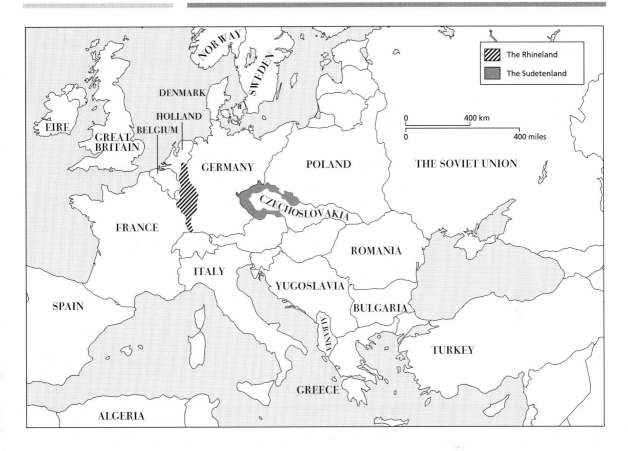

Figure 11.4 *Europe in the 1930s*

assumption that Hitler was a reasonable man, whose demands stemmed from legitimate grievances, whereas in reality Hitler was a power-hungry tyrant whose appetite for conquest grew by what it fed on. He did not want merely to revise Versailles: that was just a first step towards European, and perhaps world, domination. Chamberlain's 'piece of paper', and the words he addressed to the cheering crowds, showed his naivety and wishful thinking. It was hardly honourable to sacrifice the Czechs: the Sudetenland was not only the industrial heartland of Czechoslovakia, it also contained Czech defensive fortifications.

■ Appeasement was a counter-productive policy. It did not deter Hitler; it positively encouraged him. After meeting Chamberlain, he thought he could get away with anything: 'Our opponents,' he said, 'are little worms. I saw them at Munich.' Furthermore, Hitler was strengthened by every peaceful conquest. Had Britain fought in 1938 it would have had the Czechs and their armies as allies; but by 1939 Czech forces had been taken over by Hitler.

■ He did not rearm fast enough, and therefore Britain was extremely vulnerable at the start of the Second World War.

He did not make enough effort to win allies for an anti-Hitler coalition. He seemed to treat the French with as much contempt as he showed for the Labour Party, and when President Roosevelt suggested, in January 1938, a world conference to discuss key issues he damned the idea – which might possibly have seen the emergence of the United States from isolation – as 'drivel'. In particular, he was highly suspicious of the Soviet leader, and made no real attempt to form a pact or alliance with the Soviet Union. The First World War alignment – Britain, France and Russia – could not therefore be resurrected.

Critics believed that Chamberlain was totally misguided in his approach to Hitler, if not indeed wilfully blind. Several contemporaries thought this. One was the cartoonist David Low. According to the cartoon in Figure 11.5, Czechoslovakia was not 'a far-away country of which we know nothing', as Chamberlain insisted, but the keystone of Western defence.

Yet the greatest of the anti-appeasers was Winston Churchill, who campaigned tirelessly against Chamberlain's foreign policy in the 1930s. For instance, after the Munich settlement, Churchill told Chamberlain that he had chosen dishonour rather than war, but that war would come

Figure 11.5 *David Low on the fatal, short-sighted complacency of the appeasers.*

WHAT'S CZECHOSLOVAKIA TO ME, ANYWAY ?

nonetheless. Churchill was also a very influential historian, with his six-volume history of the war. In the first of these he described 'how easily the tragedy of the Second World War could have been prevented', if only Britain had stood up to Hitler instead of appeasing him. The Second World War was therefore the 'unnecessary war'.

Later writers have taken up these themes. Richard Lamb has resurrected the charge that Chamberlain was a 'guilty man', and Mrs Thatcher has recently apologised to the Czech President for the Munich agreement. Anthony Adamthwaite and Richard Cockett have drawn attention to the ways in which Chamberlain's government attempted to censor the British media to create a more favourable impression of the Nazi regime. It has also been pointed out that appeasement did not stop in March 1939, when Britain guaranteed Poland, for Chamberlain did his best to persuade the Polish leader, General Beck, to make concessions to Hitler. He also hoped, as Parker has argued, that the guarantee would force Hitler to reopen negotiations with Britain. Furthermore, when Poland was invaded, on 1 September, Chamberlain did not immediately make good his guarantee to Poland. Instead he only declared war on Germany when a potential revolt of backbenchers in the Commons forced his hand. Even then he made no attempt to wage war, and in the spring of 1940, when Hitler began to move westwards, Chamberlain was one of those in favour of a negotiated, compromise peace.

Chamberlain always insisted that he was not a pacifist and that he would fight when there was no alternative; but perhaps he was an unconscious pacifist. Certainly many breathed a sigh of relief when, in May 1940, he made way for Winston Churchill as wartime Prime Minister. He had done his best, critics averred, but that best had not been good enough: his control of foreign policy had brought Britain to the very verge of disaster.

The case for the defence

With today's general public, Chamberlain is still largely regarded as a figure of fun, symbolised by his return from Munich with the infamous 'piece of paper'. But a good case can be made for Chamberlain. Certainly he waved the paper, according to his Parliamentary Private Secretary Alec Douglas-Home, not because he thought Hitler could be trusted but because he feared that he could not. By ensuring maximum publicity for Hitler's promises, he would stand exposed as a liar if he subsequently broke his word. There was thus far greater shrewdness to Chamberlain's appeasement than critics allow. For instance, he was not taken in by Hitler: he once called him 'the commonest little dog' and a man who was 'half mad'.

The case for Chamberlain rests on many points, among which the following are some of the most important:

■ Chamberlain was aware of British defence and economic weaknesses. He knew that it was not possible to pursue 'forward' policies. At the time of Munich, the Chief of the British General Staff, General Ironside, wrote that 'Chamberlain is of course right. We have not the means of defending ourselves and he knows it ... We cannot expose ourselves now to a German attack. We simply commit suicide if we do.'

■ It was impossible to help the Austrians, Czechs or the Poles. Britain could make gestures on their behalf, but they would not be aided thereby. The Poles were slaughtered in September 1939, even though Britain declared war.

■ He was also aware that Britain had too few allies. He rebuffed Roosevelt's idea of a world conference, but this was realism. Chamberlain believed that it was best to count on nothing from the Americans but words – and, after all, the USA was deep in isolation (emerging only when they were attacked by Japan in December 1941). As for the French, with their political instability and general weakness, they were not, in his opinion, particularly valuable allies – and, what is more, they were as much in favour of appeasement as Britain. The Soviets were an unknown quantity; but Chamberlain reckoned that Stalin was no more attractive than Hitler. This too, many say, was a realistic assessment.

■ On the other hand, Britain had too many potential enemies. There was not only Germany but also Italy and Japan. Britain was so vulnerable partly because its empire was so large and scattered: indeed it was called, by the military expert Liddell Hart, the greatest example of over-extension in history. If Britain became involved in a war with one power, the others were very likely to cash in by making their own attacks. This is precisely what happened in 1940–41. It was this contingency which Chamberlain was determined to prevent if he could.

■ Chamberlain hoped to avoid war: only in this way could Britain remain a relatively wealthy and important power. But while hoping for the best, he insisted that he was preparing for the worst. In short, he rearmed, increasing defence expenditure significantly when he was Chancellor and then Prime Minister. Defence spending rose from 3.3 per cent of gross national product in 1935 to 5.6 per cent in 1937 and reached 21.4 per cent in 1939. Chamberlain decided that in view of economic weaknesses, Britain would have to adopt a defensive strategy in any war: he thus put the emphasis on the Royal Air Force – and on radar and on fighter planes – rather than the army, a strategy which paid off in 1940 when the RAF won the Battle of Britain.

- In 1939 Britain was better able to cope with war than it would have been in 1938. In particular, British people were now more united. Furthermore, they now, unlike in 1938, had the full support of the Dominions as well as the sympathy of neutral nations.

- Churchill's analysis of German policy in the 1930s was faulty. He said at the time of the *Anschluss* that Hitler had a precise timetable of aggression, which was unfolding stage by stage. In fact this was not the case: Hitler had broad aims, no more, and these did not include war with Britain. Churchill also exaggerated the degree to which Germany was economically and militarily prepared for major war.

Since the release of official government papers, many – though certainly not all – historians have become sympathetic to Chamberlain, now seeing his problems 'from the inside'. They argue that, in view of Britain's weaknesses and problems, the attempt to avoid war was sensible. Perhaps a policy of greater firmness would have deterred Hitler; perhaps indeed bluff would have done the trick. But Britain had no margin of strength and therefore Chamberlain pursued the only realistic option open to him. Chamberlain's biographer David Dilks, and other historians, therefore call confidently for a verdict of 'not guilty'.

Assessment

No simple summary can do justice to the debate on Chamberlain and appeasement. But several points are worth making. First, the debate has perhaps been polarised too much between those 'for' and those 'against' Chamberlain. Surely Chamberlain was neither 'guilty' nor 'innocent'; and similarly appeasement cannot be seen as either a totally sensible or a completely foolish policy. Perhaps, however, there came a point – March 1939 possibly – after which appeasement passed from a largely coherent response to Hitler's revisionism to one based more on wishful thinking. William Rock has argued this position. Second, the debate on appeasement hinges not only on facts but on assumptions of how other, alternative policies would have worked. For instance, what would have happened if Britain, perhaps backed up by France, had applied sanctions after Hitler entered the Rhineland? Would subsequent events have worked out better, from Britain's point of view? This is a question on which all can speculate, but which no one can answer definitively.

In a recent book John Charmley has argued that Churchill had a romantic, and totally unrealistic, vision of Great Britain and its capacities. Chamberlain was therefore quite right to seek to avoid war and to try to appease Hitler. There was simply nothing Britain could do to help Hitler's victims in eastern Europe. So far Charmley's case is familiar ground, but instead of praising Chamberlain he in fact criticises him – for ending appeasement and declaring war against Germany. Had Britain stayed out of the war, so the argument runs, British wealth would not have been drained in 1940–45 and this country would not have become dependent economically on the United States. This is a stimulating argument, but it presupposes that Chamberlain had the political power to avoid a declaration of war in September 1939, which is a moot point, and that a victorious Hitler would not sooner or later have attacked Britain, another highly contentious assumption. We may be certain that the historiographical debate will long continue.

Tasks

1 Carry out the following tasks:

   a Define appeasement.

   b Explain why the appeasers were so frequently vilified during and after the Second World War, and why historians' views tended to be so hostile.

   c What revisions to the traditional interpretations have the 'defenders' of Chamberlain made? What kinds of evidence have they used in their reassessment?

   d Summarise the strengths and weaknesses of the traditional and the revisionist interpretations.

   e Now you should formulate your own verdict on Chamberlain's foreign policy.

2 This chapter, on 'Chamberlain in the dock', lends itself to a mock trial, in which prosecuting and defending counsel call a series of witnesses (including experts on British defences and economic strength in the 1930s, and perhaps Hitler, Churchill etc.). Observe orderly court procedure, and do not neglect jury deliberations.

Even if you do not actually role play a trial, it would be a stimulating intellectual exercise to compose a five-minute speech either attacking or defending Chamberlain. Even if – or especially if – you find that neither an attack nor a defence does justice to Chamberlain, and the complex problems he had to face, the exercise will have served a useful function.

Further reading

Alan Farmer, *Britain: Foreign and Imperial Affairs, 1919–39* (Hodder and Stoughton, 1992) – an accessible account.

Paul Kennedy, *The Realities Behind Diplomacy* (Fontana, 1981) – very valuable for the economic and military background.

J. Charmley, *Chamberlain and the Lost Peace* (Hodder and Stoughton, 1989).

R. A. C. Parker, *Chamberlain and Appeasement* (Macmillan, 1993).

12 British economic performance, 1918–39

> ## *Chronological survey*
>
> *1918–20*: There was a postwar boom. Investment and the demand for goods were both high, and industrial production rose 20 per cent within two years of the end of the war. Unemployment was consequently low.
>
> *1920–22*: In December 1920 the bubble burst and a brief but acute depression began. The prices of goods fell, industrial production slumped, and unemployment reached 2 million (18 per cent of the insured workforce) in June 1921.
>
> *1923–9*: Years of gradual recovery. There was no boom, as in the United States and elsewhere, and throughout the period there were 1 million people (10 per cent) out of work. Britain suffered 'current account' deficits (i.e. the value of goods imported exceeded the value of those exported), and the country's share of world exports fell. But 'invisible exports' (the profits from banking and investments overseas) prevented an overall balance of payments deficit. Furthermore, industrial production grew by an average of almost 3 per cent a year (higher than in the prewar years), while productivity (output per worker) also increased substantially. New industries (chemicals, motor vehicles and electrical engineering) did well.
>
> *1929–32*: The Great Depression. Britain had not performed as well as many of its rivals in the 1920s, but now it did not do as badly. There was no banking collapse. Even so, the prices of goods fell; the value of British exports was almost halved, causing a balance of payments deficit; and unemployment mounted. In 1931–2 almost 3 million people were out of work (22 per cent). Many thought that the whole capitalist system was breaking down.
>
> *1932–9*: Economic recovery. Unemployment dipped in the final months of 1932, and thereafter recovery was slow but unmistakable, apart from in 1937–8 when there was a short-lived recession. But by 1939 there were still 1.5 million unemployed. However, by this date production totals significantly exceeded those of 1929, as a result of an annual growth rate in the 1930s of at least 2 per cent and possibly 3 per cent. Exports did not reach their prewar levels, but

there had been a significant expansion in the domestic market: new consumer goods industries flourished, including electrical equipment and cars, and there had been a housing boom. Over half a million cars were manufactured in 1937, and in the whole of the decade 2.7 million houses were built. New 'service' industries – such as retailing, insurance, advertising and entertainment – also grew rapidly. At the end of the decade government rearmament programmes also boosted the economy.

Features of the economy

Unemployment

Unemployment scarred the economy, detracting from British economic performance between the wars. Unemployment was a personal blight for the men and women, and their families, who were directly affected, as may be judged from the fact that an average of two unemployed men committed suicide every day in the early 1930s. But unemployment also harmed the whole economy. Those out of work were not paying taxes and were unable to buy more than a minimum of goods, thus reducing demand, and moreover they had to be supported by state benefits, in other words by those in work, who in consequence had less money to spend on goods. No economy can be working at optimum levels with so many people out of work.

KEY TERMS:

Cyclical unemployment

Cyclical unemployment refers to unemployment caused when the trade cycle dips, often due to world trends. It is likely to be only short term, as the rise in the cycle will produce new jobs.

Structural unemployment

Structural unemployment refers to unemployment caused by the nature, or structure, of the economy; as such it cannot be expected to solve itself, as the trade cycle picks up. The root cause of structural unemployment at this time was that Britain was too dependent on its labour-intensive staple industries (textiles, coal, iron and steel, and shipbuilding).

Why were there so many unemployed? There are essentially two answers to this question:

1 The 'trade cycle' (the sum total of all economic activity, formed by world as well as domestic trends) has peaks and troughs (the latter occurring in 1921–2, 1929–33 and 1938). Boom tends to give way to bust, and high employment levels tend to be followed by low ones. This is the nature of capitalist economic activity, and hence one would expect employment levels to vary. There was bound to be **cyclical unemployment,** and the interwar period saw its fair share of this.

2 But Britain also saw long-term **structural unemployment**. This stemmed from the decline of the staple industries, which had served Britain well in the nineteenth century, but whose products were no longer required in such vast quantities. This was because other countries were tending to satisfy their own needs or to import from elsewhere, or because substitutes had been found (like oil for coal and synthetic fibre for cotton). The First World War had seen an insatiable demand for the products of the staple industries, but the end of the conflict saw massive overcapacity in Britain or, to be more exact, in certain regions like the Clyde, South Wales, the North-East and Northern Ireland – soon to be known as the 'depressed areas'. For instance, unemployment rates were over 3.5 times higher in South Wales than in London in 1937.

The result was that while some areas saw recovery from 1933 and the growth of consumer affluence, others continued to suffer depression. While the new industries, which tended to be capital-intensive and so not to employ so many workers, saw relatively high wages, the staple industries – which accounted for a larger, though declining, proportion of industrial output – tended to remain technologically backward and to pay lower wages. This structural unemployment was only really ended by mobilisation for the Second World War.

The standard of living

1 Positive aspects

Everywhere in the country those in work experienced rising standards in the interwar period. Wage rates tended to fall, but prices fell even more sharply. This was a period of deflation not inflation: the prices of goods and services became cheaper (something Britons have had no experience of since the Second World War). During the 1930s 'real wages' (that is, wages in relation to prices) probably rose by over 15 per cent, giving people far more disposable income to spend on luxuries. The government judged that in 1938 the average British family, which was now smaller than before the war, had twice the real income of a family in 1913–14. Hence consumer goods industries were boosted and so was the entertainments industry. New 'picture palaces' (see Figure 12.1) became a feature of most towns. Britain could boast no less than 5,000 cinemas in the 1930s, with 20 million tickets being sold each week. By the end of the 1930s over 11 million people took a holiday at the seaside each year, and Billy Butlin's holiday camps became firmly established.

It has even been calculated that those living on unemployment benefits were better off than they would have been, before the First World War, if in full-time unskilled employment.

2 Negative aspects

The above represents the positive side of the interwar experience. But there are negative aspects as well. Those on unemployment benefits were certainly better off than their counterparts in the nineteenth century, but most social scientists calculated that they were still suffering from acute poverty. Adding to their burdens was the household means test, intro-

Figure 12.1 *One of Britain's 5,000 cinemas in the 1930s, a symbol of growing affluence.*

duced in 1931: the dole of anyone out of work for over six months was reduced if any member of the family were earning money, or if the family possessed savings or valuable possessions. And if many people were better off than ever before, they still had poor diets. The expert John Boyd Orr calculated in 1936 that 4.5 million people had diets that were inadequate in all respects, and that only one-third of Britons had healthy diets.

Health standards were much lower in the depressed areas than elsewhere. To use one of the most basic measuring sticks, consider infant mortality – see Figure 12.2.

Figure 12.2 *Infant mortality in 1935*

	No. of deaths per 1,000 live births
Home Counties	42
Glamorgan	63
Jarrow	114

Assessing economic performance

Reaching a verdict on the interwar economy is far from easy, for reasons which should now be apparent:

■ The interwar economy changed vastly over time, and, because of the trade cycle, that change was not in a single direction.

■ The 'economy' is not a single entity but a vast collection of diverse activities, varying greatly from one area of the country to another. Indeed even within the same region there were exceptions to general trends.

■ Economic history is not separable from social history. Judgements about the economy inevitably involve judgements about human beings, and it is never easy to balance the hardships of one against the benefits of another.

In short, judging economic performance is not the objective, factual task it might at first sight appear. Like all historical endeavours, it involves 'interpretation' as well as 'fact'. This is true even when we come to consider statistics, those invaluable, compressed sources which sometimes seem to convey the impression that history (or at least economic history) is a science. But let us consider how two sets of statistics for the interwar period may be used.

Figure 12.3 indicates the falls and rises in economic activity, both in terms of industrial output and unemployment.

Students should always remember Disraeli's scathing comment that there exist 'lies, damned lies and statistics', and should treat statistics cautiously:

■ First, always be very careful about what statistics really tell us. The 'index of industrial production' for instance, is certainly not a foolproof guide to the whole British economy between 1918 and 1938. Indicating levels of *industrial* output, it says nothing whatsoever about agricultural production or the service sector, which was becoming more important in the economy. Are the figures an index of the *value* of goods produced, in which case have prices been adjusted to take account of deflation? Or are they indicative of amounts produced? In Figure 12.3, since no indication is given, the safest bet is that the index relates to amounts. Nor are the unemployment figures foolproof indicators of how many people were out of work: they reflect only the registered unemployed, and there were, in the early 1930s, probably another 0.75 million who were unemployed but, for one reason or another, not on the registers.

Figure 12.3

Year	Index of industrial production (1924 = 100)	Average unemployment totals (millions)
1918	73.8	not available
1919	81.3	n.a.
1920	90.3	n.a.
1921	73.5	n.a.
1922	85.0	1.7
1923	90.0	1.4
1924	100.0	1.2
1925	103.9	1.3
1926	98.4	1.2
1927	113.4	1.2
1928	110.2	1.2
1929	115.2	1.3
1930	110.8	2.0
1931	103.7	2.7
1932	103.2	2.7
1933	110.1	2.3
1934	121.1	2.2
1935	130.3	2.1
1936	142.0	1.9
1937	150.5	1.5
1938	146.4	1.9

■ Also, remember that the index's figures are merely annual averages, which may disguise what was really happening in the economy. The figure for 1920 gives no indication of the onset of a depression at the end of the year; only monthly totals would do this. Similarly, the 5 per cent increase from 1928 to 1929 should not lead us to suppose that all sectors of British industry experienced this rate of growth. On the contrary, there may have been contraction in some sectors, and much higher rates of growth in others. Hence no sector may have grown by exactly 5 per cent! This point is equally relevant to the unemployment totals. Figures varied from month to month, and traditionally unemployment was (and still is) higher in the winter than the summer. The average annual totals can therefore be misleading.

■ Analysing these figures poses many difficulties. How, for instance, should we measure recovery from the Great Depression? We could say that by 1937 production was almost 46 per cent higher than in 1932. This figure – obtained by deducting the 1932 figure from that of 1937 and then comparing the result as a proportion of the 1932 index

– i.e. $(150.5 - 103.2)/103.2$ – is undoubtedly correct, and it makes the recovery seem remarkably good. But it is equally valid to compare the 1937 figure with that of 1929, the point at which the depression began, and by this method the rise in production was a far less impressive 27 per cent. Hence statistics, by being presented in one way or another, can create very different impressions. Much also depends, for indices, on which year is assigned the base figure of 100: all subsequent calculations are skewed by the starting-point. If 1929, rather than 1924, were rated at 100, the changes in the 1930s would appear as relatively greater on the index.

■ Finally, one always needs to ask how statistics are compiled and whether they are likely to be reliable. The more one delves into this, the more one generally becomes suspicious about accuracy. Often the original compilers of statistics indicate that they should be treated with caution, advice often omitted by those who subsequently quote them.

The conclusion must be that statistics are useful, in their place and when treated with the utmost care, but that they are not the short cut to historical understanding which most of us, in lazy moments, would like to believe exists. Generally they show trends in the economy, but no more, and they are not to be treated as Holy Writ.

Conclusion

The dole queue is a traditional symbol of the interwar British economy. This is realistic, given the persistently high levels of men and women out of work; but it cannot be *the* symbol of the period. Alongside it needs to be placed a symbol of growing affluence, such as the production line at Cowley, one of the new Marks & Spencer stores or one of the glittering new 'picture palaces'. The 'hungry thirties' and the 'affluent thirties' are only half-truths: we need to combine them to arrive at the real truth.

The First World War had posed great challenges to the British economy. On the debit side, it enabled rivals to replace British exports in overseas markets; it fouled up the complex international system of banking and finance, forcing the government to sell overseas assets and hastening the decline of the City of London as the world's financial capital; and it also produced vast over-investment in the staple industries. On the positive side, it stimulated increased mechanisation and the creation of several new industries, like aircraft production, which were to be important for the future.

The interwar economy reflected both these positive and negative stimuli. The economy continued to undergo modernisation, while the growth of new industries added an important fillip of diversification to the economy. Increased mechanisation led to substantial rises in productivity as well as to the fall in the price of mechanical and electrical goods which boosted consumer demand. But the ailing staple giants continued to bulk large in the economy, and a fall in demand for their products abroad led to massive lay-offs. Britain therefore emerged from the interwar period with stark regional variations.

Economic judgements cannot be more objective or absolute than those in political or social history. Historical truth is always relative, and therefore we need comparisons. One comparison is between the different regions in Britain. Another is between Britain's overall economic performance in 1918–39 with that, say, before the First World War. The annual rate of growth of British industrial production was around 2 per cent in 1913–37, compared with 2.3 per cent in 1900–13, no great statistical difference. Rates of economic growth and of productivity between the wars were relatively good. Another useful comparison is between Britain's economy and those of its rivals between the wars. Here too British figures hold up well. There was no real boom in the 1920s, but then the depression starting in 1929 was all the shallower. 'Structural unemployment' was worse, but 'cyclical' unemployment was not as bad as elsewhere. In 1913–37 the USA achieved a higher growth rate (2.9 per cent), but France and Germany lower ones (0.8 and 1.2 per cent respectively); and in the 1930s Britain's growth rate outstripped even that of the United States. In 1939 Britain was fourth in the world table of economic producers, behind the United States and Germany (which had been ahead in 1914) and the Soviet Union. Only the latter had overtaken Britain between the wars, by means of the tyrannical five-year plans of Stalin. Britain's decline in the world's economic league table only became precipitous after 1939.

Britain's overall economic performance was in many ways impressive, forming a contrast to the preconceived images of the interwar period, and especially of the 1930s, that most people hold. Increased production, together with cheaper imports of raw materials, made possible a higher standard of living for most Britons. But a substantial number of people were unable to take a full share in this growing prosperity. We therefore need a dual vision on a period which, paradoxically, was both 'the best of times' and 'the worst of times'. As Seebohm Rowntree, who had surveyed York in 1899 and again in 1936, wrote:

> 'The economic condition of the workers is better by 30 per cent than in 1899, though working hours are shorter. Housing is immeasurably better, health is better, education is better ... Great though the progress made during the last forty years has been, there is no cause for satisfaction in the fact that in a country so rich as England, over 30 per cent of the workers in a typical provincial city should have incomes so small that it is beyond their means to live even at the stringently economical level adopted as the minimum in this survey, nor in the fact that almost half the children of working-class parents should spend the first five years of their lives in poverty and that almost a third of them live below the poverty line for ten years or more.'

Quoted in J. Stevenson and C. Cook, *The Slump* (1977).

One can only wonder what the British economy might have achieved in the interwar years had it not been for the problem of unemployment.

Task: note-taking

Although some students may find this chapter to be child's play, others will find it daunting. Economic history undoubtedly has its difficulties. It is therefore advisable to read the chapter slowly and carefully. Make your notes during a second reading. Once the contents have been grasped, you will realise that it is, in reality, a straightforward account.

1 Use the evidence in this chapter to draw up two columns, one of which gives the advantages for a historian of interwar Britain of using statistics and the other of which gives the disadvantages.

2 Does the evidence support the view that most British people were better off in 1939 than they had been in 1918? Quote examples to support your view.

3 Why do you think that historians have found it difficult to come to a clear conclusion about British economic performance between the wars?

Further reading

Robert Pearce, *Britain: Industrial Relations and the Economy, 1900–39* (Hodder and Stoughton, 1993) – chapter 4 provides a fuller account than the present chapter.

Stephen Constantine, *Social Conditions in Britain 1918–39* (Routledge, 1983) – brief but stimulating.

J. Stevenson and C. Cook, *The Slump* (Cape, 1977) – an excellent survey.

B. W. E. Alford, *Depression and Recovery? British Economic Growth 1918–39* (Macmillan, 1972).

13 Unemployment and social conditions in the 1930s: Orwell's *Wigan Pier*

The depression of the 1930s led to a number of minutely researched studies, establishing such facts as how many people were unemployed, average life expectancy in particular parts of the country, income levels, family size, etc. Such surveys are very valuable, yet also impersonal and somewhat arid. Small wonder, then, that historians sometimes turn to the lively personal impressions of writers. Probably the most widely consulted literary source on life, work and unemployment in the north of England is George Orwell's *The Road to Wigan Pier*, published in 1937.

This chapter seeks to assess the value of this piece of evidence. What reliable information does it give us, and what are its advantages as a historical source? Everything that survives from the past can yield useful knowledge, and therefore we should always adopt a positive approach as historians. On the other hand, we must also be critical, for sources are written by ordinary human beings – people with biases and prejudices and who, sometimes, even tell lies. In order to interpret *The Road to Wigan Pier*, therefore, we need to know not only about the book but about its author. We should also compare this source with others, in order to check reliability.

PROFILE: *George Orwell*

George Orwell (who was born Eric Blair in 1903) holds a unique place in English literature as the man who made political writing into an art. He was born into a middle-class family, was educated at Eton and worked for a time in the imperial civil service; but he soon took up writing full time and gained a reputation as a fearless opponent of totalitarianism. He generally wrote out of first-hand experience, and so his writings are of immense importance to the historian. He attained fame after the Second World War with *Animal Farm* (1945) and *Nineteen Eighty-Four* (1949). He died in 1950.

The contents of *Wigan Pier*

Housing

Whoever reads the book will immediately be aware of one of its major advantages – readability. This is no dry-as-dust study but an immensely entertaining account of personal experiences. Having lived in the south of England and abroad, Orwell was experiencing industrial conditions for the first time, and rather than stay in a comfortable hotel, he took a room in a cheap lodging-house, above a tripe-shop, run by the Brookers.

Anyone beginning the first chapter is unlikely to stop before reaching its end, as one revolting – but fascinating – detail succeeds another. We learn that Orwell's bedroom, which he shared with three other lodgers, 'stank like a ferret's cage' in the morning; Mr Brooker had a 'peculiarly intimate, lingering manner of handling things', so that the slices of bread and butter he prepared always bore black thumbprints; and Mrs Brooker had a habit of wiping her mouth with bits of newspaper, which would litter the floor for hours, and an even more nauseating habit of repeating the same self-pitying phrases over and over again. One can well believe the rumour that blackbeetles swarmed over the tripe in the cellar. Certainly the kitchen table was rarely cleaned: Orwell used to 'get to know individual crumbs by sight and watch their progress up and down the table from day to day'. Small wonder, one may think, that he decided to leave when a full chamber pot appeared under the breakfast table. And yet, in Orwell's view, the tripe-shop was 'fairly normal as lodging-houses in the industrial areas go'.

Later portions of the book contain full and frank details of other houses in Wigan and Barnsley, often transcribed directly from Orwell's notebooks. He related room sizes, measured by himself, details of rent and rates, sleeping arrangements, whether there was infestation by bugs, and the distance to the nearest lavatory. Such descriptions constitute very valuable historical evidence, though, as Orwell knew, imagination is needed to breathe life into them. Words themselves, he wrote, were feeble things. 'What is the use of a brief phrase like "roof leaks" or "four beds for eight people"? It is the kind of thing your eye slides over, registering nothing. And yet what a wealth of misery it can cover!'

People

Orwell's aim was to penetrate into the psychology of people living in such conditions. This can be seen in his description of a woman, one of about 1,000 people living in some 200 caravans in Wigan:

'One woman's face stays by me, a worn skull-like face on which was a look of intolerable misery and degradation. I gathered that in that dreadful pigsty, struggling to keep her large brood of children clean, she felt as I should feel if I were coated all over with dung.'

She and others were not living that way from choice, as many foolish middle-class people imagined, but from necessity born of the housing shortage. The rent for a caravan was the same as for a house.

Orwell went on to describe the diet of local people, and he transcribed a weekly budget made out for him by an unemployed miner and his wife. Their entire allowance of 32 shillings (£1.60) a week was spent on rent, food and other necessities, leaving nothing for the replacement of utensils, bedding and furniture. Perhaps the food they bought was not the most nutritious possible, since more might have been spent on vegetables and fruit and less on sugar, but to Orwell this was understandable enough. A millionaire might enjoy living off orange juice and Ryvita biscuits, he noted, but not an unemployed man. 'When you are unemployed, which is to say when you are underfed, harassed, bored, and miserable, you don't *want* to eat dull wholesome food. You want something a little bit "tasty".'

Mining

Another section of the book covers mining, one of the staple industries of the period; a declining industry but one still vital for Britain's livelihood. Orwell not only gave statistics on accident rates, but helped to bring home their significance to his readers. Every year one miner in six was injured in accidents down the pits and one in 900 was killed (figures ignoring those harmed by respiratory diseases). Orwell compared such casualties with those sustained in a minor war, and yet they were so much taken for granted that each mining company used a rubber stamp (bearing the words 'death stoppage') to note deductions from pay as compensation for the bereaved. Orwell also examined miners' pay slips to show that they were not paid at all generously, despite hazardous and heavy work.

The coalminer's work was described in a chapter containing some of Orwell's finest prose. Not content with second-hand information, he himself went down several pits. Getting to the coalface, by crawling along low tunnels, was an ordeal in itself.

> *'You have not only to bend double, you have also got to keep your head up all the while so as to see the beams and girders and dodge them when they come. You have, therefore, a constant crick in the neck, but this is nothing to the pain in your knees and thighs. After half a mile it becomes (I am not exaggerating) an unbearable agony ... When finally you get back to the surface you have been perhaps three hours underground and travelled two miles, and you are more exhausted than you would be by a twenty-five-mile walk above ground.'*

Yet this journey to and from the coalface ('which to any normal person is a hard day's work in itself') was unpaid – 'like the City man's daily ride in the Tube' – an extra, sandwiched between seven and a half hours' hard labour. The men at the coalface (often a thin seam between gigantic layers of rock) would operate noisy cutting machinery, after which 'fillers' would shovel something like two tons of coal an hour on to conveyor belts, all in an atmosphere thick with black dust. A coalmine, Orwell summed up, fitted his mental image of hell: 'heat, noise, confusion, darkness, foul air, and, above all, unbearably cramped space'.

Miscellaneous

The book covers these issues and much else besides. Orwell described the sheer ugliness of the industrial landscape, Sheffield being the ugliest town in the Old World, and its sulphurous stench. He also drew attention to the physical degeneracy of the people: even children's teeth had a bluish hue, due to calcium deficiency, and most adults had lost all of their own teeth. 'Teeth is just a misery,' one woman told him. He also gave a graphic account of 'scrambling for coal', whereby local people boarded moving trains to gather the small nuggets of coal which had no commercial value but which could provide some warmth in winter. They did this despite liability to prosecution, and the even greater hazard of accidents. One might suppose that, in view of the hardships of life in this area, the local people might either have become revolutionary or have despaired altogether. But neither was the case, in Orwell's view. A whole population settled down to life on the dole without going spiritually to pieces:

> *'Families are impoverished, but the family-system has not broken up. The people are in effect living a reduced version of their former lives. Instead of raging against their destiny they have made things tolerable by lowering their standards ... they have kept their tempers and settled down to make the best of things on a fish-and-chip standard.'*

He mused that perhaps cheap luxuries (like gambling, chocolate, mass-produced smart clothes, the movies and strong tea) had averted revolution in Britain.

Most readers find *The Road to Wigan Pier* an interesting and moving book. We are all of us, at first sight, convinced that Orwell is a reliable historical witness. His opinions were on the surface and undisguised, and he had the humility, at times, to admit ignorance. But how reliable is the book? A jolt is delivered when, after the documentary Part I, Orwell, in Part II, gave some autobiographical information. This is extremely useful, since in order to evaluate a source we first need to know about its author. The shock comes in that he delivered a series of prejudiced judgements, condemning those who believed in pacifism or feminism or birth control, or who wore sandals, and mocking little fat men with 'obscenely bald' heads. In fact, the more we read Part II, and learn about Orwell, the more we question whether the documentary part of the book is really as reliable as we assumed.

Orwell's diary

It is always wise, whenever possible, to compare one historical source with others covering the same area. *The Road to Wigan Pier* should be compared with writings like J. B. Priestley's *English Journey* (1933), as well as with the social surveys that were held. But there is an even more relevant source, the diary Orwell kept when he was in the north of England. Comparison between the two shows that the finished book contained less straightforward factual reportage than at first seems to be the case. Also very valuable are Orwell's personal papers, now available at University College, London.

Housing

In comparison with the diary's more sober account, the depiction of the tripe-shop in *The Road to Wigan Pier* appears fanciful and even misleading. 'At supper you still see the crumbs from breakfast': this was the rather prosaic origin of his phrase about getting to know individual crumbs by sight. One of the lodgers in the house was an unemployed man who liked the portentous phrase 'Matrimonial chains is a big item'. Yet the diary reveals that he lodged not with the Brookers but at a much better place, where Orwell had first stayed in Wigan. In the book Orwell left the tripe-shop on the spur of the moment, as the full chamber pot appeared; but in the diary the unemptied pot appeared on 21 February and he continued to lodge there for another week, before leaving for a prearranged port of call.

Orwell judged that the tripe-shop was typical of lodging-houses. But such a view is totally unacceptable. Research has established that it had a reputation for being probably the worst lodging-house in Wigan. The diary concedes that it was 'appreciably dirtier and very smelly' compared with his first lodgings in the town, but the published book ignored the more respectable establishment.

In his first chapter, Orwell came up with an exaggerated version of the worst conditions in Wigan and then, perversely, described them as typical. The fact is that it was very difficult for him to judge what was typical or exceptional during his stay. Nowhere in *The Road to Wigan Pier* did he say exactly how long he had been in the North, but he did write that 'For some months I lived entirely in coalminers' houses'. In fact, his diary reveals that he stayed in the north of England from around 5 February to 26 March, and he was not staying in miners' houses all that time.

A study of Orwell's personal notebooks also reveals that he did not always transcribe details of housing conditions in the North accurately.

The mines

Orwell's account of travelling underground to the coalface is not fiction. He went down three pits, and there is evidence to corroborate the statement that he suffered physically as a result of travelling underground bent almost double. But even so, there are inaccuracies in this section of the book.

'I have before me five pay-checks belonging to a Yorkshire miner, for five weeks (not consecutive) at the beginning of 1936,' wrote Orwell; and he then proceeded to average out their gross weekly wages. These slips survive in the Orwell papers, and we can now see that Orwell was not accurate in the calculations he made, miscalculating the gross averages. Nor was he correct about the period they covered. One bore no date at all, and only one of the others was for early 1936: the rest were for March and April 1935.

Other inaccuracies

Orwell's papers reveal that he tampered with the weekly budget supplied to him by an unemployed miner and his wife. The original list totalled slightly more than the allowance of £1.60. A comparison between the 'scrambling for coal' episodes in the original (diary) and later (published) versions also reveals discrepancies. In the diary account, fewer people were involved: instead of a 'couple of hundred men', there were 'not less than a hundred men' involved.

Perhaps the best indication of the way Orwell revised his diary comes with his account of a woman glimpsed from a train at the start of spring:

> *'I had time to see everything about her – her sacking apron, her clumsy clogs, her arms reddened by the cold. She looked up as the train passed, and I was almost near enough to catch her eye. She had a round pale face, the usual exhausted face of the slum girl who is twenty-five and looks forty, thanks to miscarriages and drudgery; and it wore, for the second in which I saw it, the most desolate, hopeless expression I have ever seen. It struck me then that we are mistaken when we say "It isn't the same for them as it would be for us," and that people bred in the slums can imagine nothing but the slums. For what I saw in her face was not the ignorant suffering of an animal. She knew well enough what was happening to her – understood as well as I did how dreadful a destiny it was to be kneeling there in the bitter cold, on the slimy stones of a slum backyard, poking a stick up a foul drainpipe.'*
>
> George Orwell, *The Road to Wigan Pier* (1937).

This is a stunning, and moving, piece of writing; but the diary version, for 15 February, is significantly different.

> *'Passing up a horrible squalid side-alley, saw a woman, youngish but very pale and with the usual draggled exhausted look, kneeling by the gutter outside a house and poking a stick up the leaden waste-pipe, which was blocked. I thought how dreadful a destiny it was to be kneeling in the gutter in a back-alley in Wigan, in the bitter cold, prodding a stick up a blocked drain. At that moment she looked up and caught my eye, and her expression was as desolate as I have ever seen; it struck me that she was thinking just the same thing as I was.'*
>
> George Orwell, *The Collected Essays, Journalism and Letters of George Orwell*, vol. 1 (1970).

Conclusion

The Road to Wigan Pier contains factual inaccuracies and fabrications. As an accomplished novelist, Orwell could not resist embellishing what he saw. Despite its seductively direct tone, it is a more subjective book than it appears at first sight. Orwell intended to secure a certain response from his readers, perhaps because, as a left-winger, he wanted to shock people and create a climate suitable for widespread reform.

It also contains many omissions. He could not cover all aspects of the life he saw. Was it prejudice or simply a 'blind spot' in his mentality that he ignored the role of women workers, in the textile mills and at the pit heads? In addition, he only considered male workers as physical beings, ignoring their political and trade union activities. And why did he ignore sport and pubs and all scenes of enjoyment or jollity? Perhaps he was simply too gloomy a man to bother with such things.

Certainly he was a pessimistic type, and his temperament may have cast more of a pall over Wigan than really existed. But in the diary he said quite a bit about working-men's clubs and their comic turns; hence the finished *Wigan Pier* seems to have undergone a certain self-censorship.

Nor should we accept Orwell's views that, in the 1930s, things were getting worse and worse. Admittedly they were bad, but Orwell insisted that, on average, English people were declining physically. This was simply not true. He lacked proper historical perspective, drawing instead on his own unreliable childhood memories of prewar days.

We know a tremendous amount about George Orwell, about his background and the way he came to construct *The Road to Wigan Pier*. As a result, we can see that the book is by no means a foolproof historical source. But that does not mean that it is of no value: indeed knowledge of the book's inaccuracies and its author's biases positively enhance its historical worth. All books and authors – and all historical sources – have their drawbacks, and if we can identify them we can make allowances for them. We should therefore treat every source as, in this chapter, we have treated Orwell's book. How many texts would survive scrutiny as well as *The Road to Wigan Pier*?

Task: evaluation of evidence

It is worthwhile comparing the two accounts, from the finished book and the diary, on page 122:

1 Make a list of their differences. You should be able to spot half a dozen.

2 Which of the two is the more likely to be accurate? Explain the reasons for your choice.

3 Could Orwell be certain of the woman's age? (It is noteworthy that elsewhere in the book, Orwell estimated a lodger's age at 28, only to find later that he was 43!)

4 Do you trust Orwell's ability to read her mind? (You might also look back at the passage describing the woman living in a caravan

(page 118). How convincing do you find the comparison between her feelings and those of Orwell if coated with dung? Full marks if this struck a false note with you when you first read it!)

5 Do you think it really matters to a historian of the 1930s if the longer, more elaborate version is a fictionalised account of what happened? May it not be 'poetically' true – or, as Orwell was fond of saying, 'essentially' true? This is a difficult issue. It seems to the present author that it does matter. Orwell may have intended the woman as a symbol of Wigan life, as a representative figure, but we should beware of accepting his view. He could not judge objectively, and indeed was not trying to get at the truth: instead he wanted to give the lie to those unsympathetic people who thought that nothing need be done about slum poverty because people got used to it and so were not really so badly off. Hence he projected his own feelings on to the woman, despite the fact that, elsewhere in the book, he gave reliable evidence that people did get used to it, at least some of the people some of the time. Asking a man when the housing shortage began, he received the reply 'when we were told about it'.

6 How much reliance should a historian place upon Orwell's work as evidence of social conditions in interwar Britain? Use both Orwell's writing and your own knowledge of the period, and be certain to explain the reasoning behind your verdict.

Further reading

George Orwell, *The Road to Wigan Pier* (Penguin, 1937).

The Collected Essays, Journalism and Letters of George Orwell, vol.1 (Penguin, 1968). This contains Orwell's diary.

J. B. Priestley, *English Journey* (Heinemann, 1934). This should be read as carefully and as sceptically as *The Road to Wigan Pier*.

14 Why did fascism achieve so little support in Britain?

In the late 1930s the German novelist Thomas Mann described **fascism** as 'a disease of the times, which is at home everywhere, and from which no country is free'. Fascism did indeed seem to be spreading rapidly: beginning in Italy, its adherents took control in Germany, Austria, Spain, Poland and elsewhere. Yet fascists in Britain came nowhere near to winning power. So why did fascism fail in Britain? This chapter attempts to answer this question. But of course to explain why something did *not* happen is even more difficult than to explain why something did! Answers therefore must be speculative to some extent.

Outline of events

First of all, we must look at the landmarks of fascist history in Britain, centring on the major fascist party, the British Union of Fascists (BUF), founded by **Sir Oswald Mosley**.

PROFILE: *Sir Oswald Mosley*

The son of a wealthy landed family, **Oswald Mosley** served as a Conservative MP (1918–22) before becoming an Independent in 1922 and joining the Labour Party in 1924. He served in MacDonald's second Labour government from 1929 to 1930, before resigning when his Memorandum on Unemployment was rejected. He had urged the government to take positive action to remedy unemployment, but was defeated by party loyalty and conservatism. He then founded the New Party, all of whose candidates were defeated at the 1931 election. Despairing of democracy, whose machinery he decided was a hundred years out of date, Mosley visited Italy, was impressed by the dictator Benito Mussolini, and founded the British Union of Fascists. Mosley's supporters, like Mussolini's, were called the Blackshirts. He died in 1980, at the age of 84.

Time chart

1932: **1 October**
The BUF officially launched. Considerable support from the press, especially from Rothermere's *Daily Mail*

Mid-1934: The movement has approximately 50,000 members: the fascist bandwagon seems to be rolling

1934: **7 June**
Mosley's meeting at Olympia, with a crowd of 12,000, disrupted by hecklers, who are ejected with considerable violence. Rothermere withdraws his support

Late 1935: Membership has fallen to about 5,000 members. Internal feuds and financial problems

1936: **4 October**
The 'Battle of Cable Street': fascists ty to march from the Royal Mint into the East End of London, but are opposed by anti-fascists. Over 100 people injured and about 100 arrested

1936: **December**
The Public Order Act passed, banning the wearing of political uniforms (even armbands) and giving the police extra powers to ban marches and meetings. The BUF has about 15,000 members

1936–9: Mosley runs one-issue campaigns, such as 'Stand by the King' (during the abdication crisis) and 'Stop the War' (urging that Hitler should be given a free hand in eastern Europe). He intends to fight the next general election, due in 1940

1939: **September**
The BUF has approximately 22,500 members when the Second World War starts

1940: **23 May**
Mosley arrested, together with over 700 other leading British fascists, under Defence Regulations. He is released in 1943, when his health is poor and Britain no longer in danger of a German invasion.

The chronological information given in the time chart – on Mosley himself, on fascist violence, on anti-fascism and on government legislation – goes a long way towards explaining why fascism in Britain failed to mobilise mass support.

Mosley and BUF members: lack of ability?

Fascism as an ideology is based upon the importance of the leader, who was supposed to be virtually infallible. In Italian fascism Mussolini was popularly believed to be always right, and in Germany so was Hitler. But this puts a tremendous onus on the leader; and it has often been thought that, in Britain, the would-be fascist dictator, Oswald Mosley, was simply inadequate for this role. A. J. P. Taylor, for instance, once called him no more than a 'highly gifted playboy' who lacked staying power and was often away enjoying himself with his rich friends in Venice instead of working determinedly for the cause. According to this interpretation, he was an inauthentic figure, merely playing at being a dictator: he was like a ham actor. Corroborative evidence for this interpretation comes from Mosley's previous political instability. He had jumped from the Conservatives to the Labour Party, and then shifted ground again, forming the New Party. For some anti-fascists, it was (and is) almost a self-evident truth that no fascist could have real ability. Orwell said that it would be hard to find a man more barren of ideas than Mosley: he was 'as hollow as a jug'.

Yet these criticisms are probably overstated. Certainly Mosley had made a name for himself as a Labour minister in 1929–30. His main fault seemed to be not lack of ability – indeed some commentators marked him out as a successor to Ramsay MacDonald as Labour leader – but lack of patience. He was not prepared to bide his time and accumulate seniority within Labour ranks; instead, he rocked the boat, calling for positive actions to combat the depression. It should also be noted that, once he had made a commitment to fascism in 1932, he never thereafter wavered in his political allegiance. In other words, he *did* have staying power. He also worked very hard. In his first five years as a fascist leader, he wrote three books and 100 articles. He also made an average of over 100 speeches a year and was an effective orator. Certainly he managed to secure fanatical adherence from some of his followers. His 1932 publication, *The Greater Britain*, contained a more coherent political analysis than that provided by any European fascist leader.

This is not to say that, in reality, Mosley lived up to the image of the heroic, all-powerful and all-wise leader. Of course he did not, but then no one could – not even Hitler or Mussolini. Such supermen were the products, to a large extent, of propaganda. But it is to assert that, probably, Mosley was of such stuff that an effective propaganda machine could have made him seem superhuman. Study the two photographs of Mosley (Figures 14.1 and 14.2). In Figure 14.1 Mosley is unconvincing and smug:

trying to cast a hypnotic gaze towards the camera, he merely succeeded in looking goggle-eyed. But Figure 14.2 is much more effective. Surrounded by his admiring supporters and by fascist paraphernalia, he seemed entirely at home. And note how his gesture has religious overtones.

Yet lack of ability may nevertheless have been a factor in the BUF's failure. Mosley was a poor administrator, party funds suffered because of petty pilfering in the mid-1930s, and he never seemed to attract lieutenants of real calibre, without which no party can succeed. His two best-known assistants, A. K. Chesterton and William Joyce, were both rabid anti-semites and indeed both quarrelled with Mosley and left the Union before 1939.

It has also often been pointed out that the bulk of the BUF's membership consisted of 'marginal' men and women. Indeed some have seen them as cranks. A female member in Lancashire in 1935 described her own branch as:

> 'a mixed crowd ... For every good, normal member we got several who were cranks – and worse ... with waste paper basket ideas. We seemed to attract them somehow ... How could we possibly get on with the Cause when Mormon clashed with Pacifist, Catholic with ex-Communist, Methodist with C. of E. and anti-vivisectionist with Christadelphian? It was almost like a comic opera.'
>
> K. Lunn and R. Thurlow (eds), *British Fascism* (1980).

Yet to seek to explain the failure of the BUF by the nature of its membership is not to provide a satisfactory explanation. Why were the fascists unable to recruit more able and committed followers?

Fascist violence: a cause of alienation?

There can be no doubt that the violence which erupted at the Olympia meeting in June 1934 proved a turning-point in Mosley's fortunes. Until then he seemed to be doing very well, and membership stood at a healthy 50,000. Some supporters, like Lord Rothermere, who actually printed BUF enrolment forms in his *Daily Mail*, looked upon Mosley as a dynamic Conservative and a great improvement on the weaker figures in the National government: he seemed to be someone who would reimpose national discipline and restore people's pride in being British. But Olympia changed all that. The publicity given to the meeting, and to the

Figure 14.1 *Sir Oswald Mosley, the would-be dictator. Decisively dynamic or decidedly daft?*

Figure 14.2 *Mosley on the march: the devoted leader surrounded by his admiring supporters.*

strongarm tactics of the Blackshirt stewards in ejecting hecklers, tore the veil of respectability from Mosley's Union. No longer would Rothermere – or other respectable figures from the right of British politics – provide support. Further harm was done when, at the end of June, Hitler murdered his rivals in Germany in the so-called Night of the Long Knives. The BUF was damned by association. Henceforth Mosley found it very difficult to hire halls for his meetings. He took to organising marches instead, but these too – especially the 'Battle of Cable Street' – resulted in bloody clashes with anti-fascist demonstrators.

In fact, as Robert Skidelsky and other historians have shown, this violence generally originated not with Mosley but with communists, Jews and others who were willing to fight for the anti-fascist cause. A rousing speaker, Mosley had wanted to be heard, and to enthuse his audience, not to be continually interrupted. But as the 1930s wore on, the BUF became more extreme, using violence as a political weapon and voicing openly anti-semitic remarks. In 1936 Mosley changed the name of his party to the British Union of Fascists and National Socialists; above his desk he hung photographs of George V, Mussolini and Hitler; and he married, in Berlin, a woman who idolised Hitler, Diana Mitford.

Mosley failed partly because he used violent tactics but also because of the activities of the opposition. In particular, the Communist Party of Great Britain (CPGB), founded in 1920, mustered effective anti-fascist support. It should also be remembered that in Italy and Germany the fascists came to power when there was perceived to be a real chance of a communist coup. Fascism thus spread partly in reaction to communism, but in Britain there was no real communist threat. The Communist Party had 16,000 members in 1938, almost as many as Mosley, and in effect the CPGB and the BUF cancelled each other out.

The character of the British people: reality or delusion?

It has often been said that the national character of the British people not only explains the failure of British fascism but doomed the movement from the start. The British were a gentle, freedom-loving people who would have no truck with a violent – and moreover intellectual and foreign – ideology like fascism, especially since it was anti-semitic. Perhaps, therefore, this is the fundamental cause of its failure.

Yet many doubt the existence of 'national character', or at least insist that substantial variations exist between the millions of people who compose a nation. Furthermore, it should be noted that there was a substantial history of anti-semitism in Britain. Many contrived to interpret the Russian Revolution of 1917 as a Jewish conspiracy, and legislation had been passed in 1905, 1914 and 1919 to restrict the number of Jews entering Britain from eastern Europe. In addition, many of the ideas which helped to form fascism as an ideology derived from the works of British thinkers – Charles Darwin and Herbert Spencer, who insisted that life was a struggle in which only the fittest survived; Houston Stewart Chamberlain, who believed in the supremacy of the Teuton race and the inferiority of Jews; and Thomas Malthus, who insisted that population growth would exceed food supply, thus necessitating a search for living space (*lebensraum*). It is perhaps not surprising, therefore, that Mosley's BUF was not the first – nor the last – fascist group in Britain. Indeed some would say that the British Empire, based as it was on the supposed superiority of white Britons, provided a breeding ground for fascist ideas. Certainly several political commentators in the 1930s believed that Britain was relatively free of the fascist virus not because Britons were immune to the disease but because those most susceptible were in the Empire, helping to govern those whom Kipling called 'lesser breeds'. In addition, Britain had undergone the First World War, which is often held to have contributed to the emergence of fascism later. Several prominent British fascists, including Mosley, Chesterton and the novelist Henry Williamson had served with distinction in the Great War. Many veterans believed that democratic politicians, in their failure to produce a 'land fit for heroes', had let them down badly. Furthermore, many people who had not fought in the war were nevertheless conscious – and dissatisfied – that their once great nation was in a state of decline.

In the present state of knowledge it would be unwise to assume that fascism was alien to British culture or that it was doomed to failure from the start. Many highly cultured and civilised countries fell prey to fascism in the interwar period, and it is surely arrogant to assume that, in certain conditions, the British would not have succumbed. Fascism only seemed 'unBritish' when, in the Second World War, Britain took up arms against Germany and Italy.

Government actions and the parliamentary system: key factors?

In 1934 the government gave the police extra powers to search for seditious literature; but the main political effort to deal with the BUF came with the 1936 Public Order Act. Henceforth members of the Union could not wear their black uniforms, and it was also much more difficult for

Mosley to arrange marches. This was a real blow to the BUF; but it was hardly a knockout punch, as many historians used to assume. After all, membership increased after 1936, particularly in the East End of London and in the north of England. The government therefore contributed to the containment of fascism, but no more. On the other hand, perhaps the government was right not to make martyrs of the fascists. Draconian measures might have bred sympathy for their victims. They might even have transformed the politicians at Westminster into fascists. The German philosopher Nietzsche once remarked that those who fight against dragons become dragons themselves. In other words, a virulent anti-fascist campaign from the government might have led to the curtailment of civil liberties, thus producing fascism 'by the backdoor'. But in Britain democracy was preserved.

Nor was Mosley correct in saying that the British democratic system was 100 years out of date. British parliamentary government had changed considerably since 1832, when the Great Reform Act was passed. In particular, the franchise had been extended, so that by 1928 all men and women aged 21 or over could vote. British people realised the benefits of being able to turn out a government at the polls, and at general elections at least 70 per cent of the electorate voted. Mosley undoubtedly underestimated the resilience of democracy, which had become deep-seated. Institutions were stronger than the charismatic appeal of individuals.

On the other hand, the undemocratic nature of the British system also enhanced its strength. The 'first-past-the-post' system made it extremely difficult for new parties to secure representation at Westminster – and unless they could gain a foothold, it was almost impossible to grow stronger and become dominant. British elections in the interwar period regularly secured a majority of seats for a party without a majority of votes. This may not have been democratic, but at least it made for strong government, without the constant necessity to cobble together coalitions. Proportional representation – though undoubtedly democratic – made it much easier for fascist parties on the continent to grow and flourish.

The timing of the BUF: Mosley's bad luck

The time chart also points to another reason for fascism's failure in Britain. The BUF was founded in October 1932, too late for it to secure maximum impact. Fascists (and communists) argued that the traditional capitalist system, based upon free-market competition, was breaking down, resulting in escalating unemployment and economic crisis. Hence a thorough political change was needed to give new life to the economy and prevent mass suffering. There were grounds for supposing that, in Britain, this was true. At the start of 1932 there were, officially, almost 3 million people out of work (22 per cent of the insured workforce), and these figures underestimated the real problem. Had matters got worse and worse, then perhaps the BUF might have become increasingly popular: certainly many people might well have decided that the old political parties were as bankrupt as Mosley insisted. But instead the situation substantially improved. Between 1932 and 1937 industrial production grew by 46 per cent, with unemployment sinking to 1.5 million by the latter date. Many people began to experience real affluence for the first time, while the unemployed tended to pin their political hopes on the left rather than the right. In other circumstances, Mosley lamented, it could all have been very different.

The start of the Second World War: the final blow

As a fascist, Mosley had often played the patriotic card, or tried to. He wished to whip up nationalistic fervour, though this was not so easy in a country like Britain, which had no territorial grievances. There were no pockets of British people living under what they regarded as foreign rule; there was no land whose ownership Britain disputed with another country. Indeed some suspected, because of his connections with fascists abroad, that Mosley might fail to defend Britain against its enemies.

Mosley always responded indignantly to this suggestion, arguing that he was a great patriot who would defend his native soil with his dying breath. On the other hand, he insisted that there was no reason to pick a quarrel with Germany or Italy. His policy was to defend and develop the Empire, leaving Europe to the Europeans. Only this policy, he repeated, would bring prosperity to these shores and reverse national decline; and only this would prevent Britain being dragged into another world war.

However, most Britons realised that the Prime Minister, Neville Chamberlain, was doing his best to avoid another war. It was also becoming apparent that Hitler was a violent aggressor from whom Britain had much to fear. When, therefore, Britain declared war on Germany on 3 September 1939, most Britons accepted that it was necessary. But the fight against fascism abroad meant that British fascists were a potential fifth column whose activities could not be tolerated. There was no public criticism when Mosley was imprisoned in 1940, only when he was released, because of ill health, in 1943.

Conclusion

The British Union of Fascists did not attract more than about 50,000 supporters (not much more than 0.1 per cent of the population). Mosley's movement achieved political prominence but never seemed likely to achieve political power. The reasons for this are many. Several of them have been outlined above, and perhaps these, taken together, do explain why fascism achieved such low levels of support in Britain. But it is important to realise that they do not provide a full explanation. Many more factors could be put forward. For instance, how important was the system of unemployment relief? Just after the First World War, Lloyd George introduced 'uncovenanted benefit': those whose insurance cover had expired could nevertheless claim the 'dole'; in addition there would be extra benefits for dependents. Perhaps these measures prevented a revolution. It has also been said that the existence of the monarchy was vital for Mosley's failure. The British (so the argument runs) were as susceptible to hero worship, flag-waving and feelings of patriotic fervour as any other people; but in Britain these potentially dangerous emotions were directed, quite harmlessly, towards the royal family, instead of towards politically powerful individuals. Thus the monarchy, the undemocratic element in the British constitution, helped to preserve democratic machinery.

The BUF can be written off as an immense failure, as something alien to British culture and irrelevant to mainstream history. But this is an arrogant and sterile perspective from which to view the fascist phenomenon. It is more fruitful to see fascism as part and parcel of the British experience between the wars. A study of the BUF tells us not only why fascism failed but sheds light on diverse aspects of British politics, economy and society.

Task: writing essays

'The main reason for the failure of fascism in Britain was that economic improvements in the 1930s gave most people little reason to support an extremist political organisation.' Discuss.

Helpful hints: Remember the importance of structuring the essay properly.

- You need an introduction which shows you understand the parameters of the question.
- The points in your middle paragraphs should have a specific focus, relevant to the question set, and should be supported with factual information.

■ Your conclusion should validate your judgement, without simply repeating what you have said before.

The question singles out 'economic improvements': therefore you must focus on this issue. Do not dismiss this area, even if you think it is relatively unimportant. Illustrate the nature of the upturn in the economy, and give some precise details (perhaps taken from chapter 12). Also, you must explain the connection between the growth in the economy and the failure of fascism, pointing out the assumption in the quotation that people only turn to fascism in times of slump. Once you have dealt thoroughly with economic factors in fascism's failures, you can look, more briefly, at the other factors. Do you agree that economic improvements constitute the primary reason for fascism's failure? You do not have to agree, of course, and indeed you may think that economic factors were of only minor – or perhaps of overwhelming – importance; but you must comment explicitly on this issue.

Further reading

K. Lunn and R. Thurlow (eds), *British Fascism* (Croom Helm, 1980) – excellent collection of essays.
Richard Thurlow, *Fascism in Britain* (Blackwell, 1986) – the best single-volume history.
Robert Skidelsky, *Oswald Mosley* (Macmillan, 1975) – the standard biography.

Part Two

Warfare and welfare, 1939–56

15 1940: myth and reality

Time chart

1939: 3 September
Britain and France declare war on Germany: 'Phoney War' until May 1940

1940: 3 May
British troops forced out of Norway
7 and 8 May
Norwegian debate in the Commons
10 May
Churchill replaces Chamberlain as Prime Minister
May–June
Dunkirk evacuations
22 June
France surrenders
10 July–15 September
The Battle of Britain; followed by bombing raids on London and other cities

Britain declared war on Germany on 3 September 1939. Chamberlain's government expected immediate bombing raids from the German *Luftwaffe*. About 3 million people were therefore evacuated from areas perceived to be of high risk; 140,000 people were sent home from hospital, to make way for war casualties; and millions of shrouds and coffins were made ready. In addition, a blackout was instituted: all street lights were extinguished and cars were forbidden to use headlights. As a result, deaths on the roads doubled in September. But there were no raids or war casualties. This was the period which has become known as the 'Phoney War'. Contemporaries called it the 'bore war'. At first, Hitler was busy defeating Poland, and it was not until the spring that he moved westwards. Then, in 1940, Britain felt the full force of the war, inaugurating a period which has generally been interpreted as this country's 'finest hour'. But was 1940 such a glorious period? According to some historians, especially Clive Ponting, the accepted version of 1940 is more myth than reality. This chapter examines these issues.

The conventional version of 1940

There are several components to the traditional image of 1940. The most important are as follows:

- In May 1940, after weak government from Neville Chamberlain, the nation awoke to face the most dire situation in the whole of its history. **Winston Churchill** was called upon by the people to be their leader, and they could not have made a better choice, for he proved also to be their saviour. The photograph by Cecil Beaton of Churchill in 1940 (Figure 15.1) encapsulates something of his defiance and resolution.

PROFILE: *Winston Churchill*

Born in 1874, **Winston Churchill** did badly at Harrow but made a name for himself as a soldier and a war correspondent. He entered Parliament in 1900 as a Conservative but soon moved over to the Liberals and, before the First World War, held the offices of President of the Board of Trade, Home Secretary and First Lord of the Admiralty. During the war he resigned after the failure of the Gallipoli campaign in Turkey and served for a time in France, before returning as Minister of Munitions. He rejoined the Conservatives in 1924 and was Chancellor of the Exchequer in 1924–9. By this time he had held almost all the major offices of state except the premiership. But the 1930s were his 'wilderness years'. He opposed Indian reform, he championed the cause of Edward VIII and he stood out against the appeasement of Hitler. Before his stand on appeasement was vindicated, many considered him to be not only a diehard imperialist and a warmonger but a has-been. He was Prime Minister in 1940–45 and again in 1951–5. Among his many awards and distinctions was the Nobel prize for literature in 1953. When he died in 1965 he was the first person outside the royal family to be given a state funeral since the Duke of Wellington.

- Churchill proved an indomitable war leader who inspired the nation by his rousing oratory. All thoughts of a compromise peace were banished: even when Britain's only ally, France, had pulled out of the war, Churchill insisted that Britain would fight on alone until Germany was defeated.

Churchill in the House of Commons, 4 June 1940

'I have, myself, full confidence that if all do their duty, if nothing is neglected, and if the best arrangements are made, as they are being made, we shall prove ourselves once again able to defend our Island home, to ride out the storm of war, and to outlive the menace of tyranny, if necessary for years, if necessary alone. At any rate, that is what we are going to try to do ... We shall not flag or fail. We shall go on to the end. We shall fight in France, we shall fight on the seas and oceans, we shall fight with growing confidence and growing strength in the air, we shall defend our island, whatever the cost may be, we shall fight on the beaches, we shall fight on the landing grounds, we shall fight in the fields and in the streets, we shall fight in the hills; we shall never surrender.'

R. James (ed.), *Churchill Speaks* (1981).

Figure 15.1 Winston Churchill in September 1940. The 'saviour of the nation'?

The British were at their best during the war. This was a 'People's War', and the people maintained high morale even in the face of suffering and hardships: they were bloody but unbowed. They could take

ALL BEHIND YOU, WINSTON

Figure 15.2 David Low's version of the People's War, published on 14 May 1940. But was this propaganda or reality?

whatever the Nazis threw at them. Class differences faded away: all were in it together: never had Britons been more united. The cartoonist David Low was generally irreverent, but in the cartoon in Figure 15.2 he depicted a resolute and determined British people lined up behind their leader.

The fruits of this policy were immediately apparent. The British Expeditionary Force (BEF) was cut off on the beaches of Dunkirk, but the men were rescued by the valiant efforts of hundreds of little fishing boats and ferries, producing the headline 'Bloody Marvellous' in one newspaper. Later in the year the RAF won the Battle of Britain, putting an end to Hitler's succession of victories and preparing the way for his final defeat. 'Never in the field of human conflict,' said Churchill, 'was so much owed by so many to so few.'

141

One might expect that the traditional view, being the one which Churchill's government itself put forward in 1940, would be overstated. After all, Britain was fighting for its life; hence the emphasis was on survival not the pursuit of objective truth. In short, the government's propaganda machine had to insist that political leadership was superb and that morale was high. The job of the historian, however, is to disentangle truth from propaganda and to debunk the myths and exaggerated reputations of the past.

Conventional views challenged

Churchill's appointment as Prime Minister

We have seen (in chapter 11) that a good case can be made for appeasement. Neville Chamberlain knew that Britain was too weak to aid Hitler's victims in eastern Europe, and in this he was quite correct. The Poles, despite gallant resistance, were easily overrun in September – especially when the Soviets, temporary allies of the Nazis, invaded from the east. But Chamberlain did not prove a good war leader. He formed no agreement with the trade unions; his cabinet was, for the most part, composed of men without fighting spirit; and ministers made a series of over-optimistic speeches, insisting that Germany was on the verge of economic collapse. Furthermore, when Hitler invaded Norway in April 1940, Britain did badly in its first engagement with the enemy. As a result, Chamberlain was heavily criticised in the Commons on 7 and 8 May: when a vote was held the government's normal majority of over 200 fell to only 81. Chamberlain soon resigned, to be replaced by Churchill on 10 May.

In retrospect, many have recalled that Churchill was so popular and universally respected that he was the inevitable choice as premier. But this was not the case. Churchill, rather than Chamberlain, had been responsible for the unsuccessful Norwegian campaign, and he was lucky not to receive some of the flak. Admittedly his reputation stood high in 1940: after all, he had criticised appeasement consistently, arguing that Hitler could not be trusted, and events had proved him right. But he was certainly not everyone's choice as Prime Minister. An opinion poll in April 1940 revealed that Anthony Eden (Foreign Secretary in 1935–8 and Dominions Secretary in 1939–40) was supported by more people than Churchill; and when Chamberlain realised he could not survive, he called a meeting with both Lord Halifax, the current Foreign Secretary and a former Viceroy of India, and Churchill. The effective choice thus lay between these two men, but Halifax made excuses and turned the position down. Chamberlain would have preferred Halifax, the King would have preferred Halifax, and Labour's leaders would have been equally happy to work in a coalition with Halifax. Therefore Churchill was lucky: he got the job by default.

There was nothing fated about his rise to the premiership, and indeed many expected him to be a failure as Prime Minister. A civil servant has recalled that the thought of Winston as Prime Minister 'sent a cold chill down the spines of the staff at 10 Downing Street ... Our feelings were widely shared in the Cabinet Office, the Treasury and throughout Whitehall ... Seldom can a Prime Minister have taken office with the Establishment so dubious of the choice and so prepared to find its doubts justified.' A junior minister, R. A. Butler, described Churchill at this time as 'the greatest adventurer in modern political history ... a half-breed American'.

Churchill's impact and oratory

Churchill did indeed help to instil a sense of urgency into the government machine, but this was also caused by the state of the war. Hitler invaded Holland and Belgium on the very day Churchill took the reins of government, and in June the French surrendered, leaving Britain to fight – not alone, as is too often said, but with the support of its colonies and Dominions. Britons felt badly let down by the French, but arguably it was the French who had reason to feel aggrieved. After all, Britain sent only nine divisions to the continent, forming no more than 7 per cent of allied forces there; in addition, the RAF was retained for home defence. Things might have been very different (better or worse!) if Churchill had given full backing to his French allies.

Publicly Churchill insisted that Britain would never surrender. But, behind the scenes, there were several men in his cabinet who wanted to pull out of the war if reasonable terms could be obtained from Hitler. Indeed Churchill himself acknowledged that there might come a time when Britain would have to make peace. According to Chamberlain's diary, he said that 'if we could get out of this jam by giving up Malta and Gibraltar and some African colonies he would jump at it'. Yet he did insist that Britain would have to fight first, thereby winning Germany's respect – and so perhaps his willingness to countenance compromise was merely a tactical ploy, at a time when his authority within cabinet was insecure.

Churchill's oratory itself is one of the great features of 1940. Many were moved to tears by his words, and some believed that he transformed his listeners, instilling in them some of his own enormous self-confidence. According to the American Ed Murrow, Churchill 'mobilised the English language and sent it into battle'. Yet not everyone was impressed.

Admittedly he was capable of rousing purple passages – which have now passed into English literature – but his speeches also tended to be very long and, frankly, boring in places. They were also often delivered with a slurred accent, which led many to think that he had been drinking too much. (And Churchill did drink a lot. Franklin Roosevelt once called him a 'drunken bum'!) There is also some evidence that he did not intend his speeches to be broadcast over the radio, so unconcerned was he about them, and that they were therefore delivered by an actor, Norman Shelley (who played Larry the Lamb or perhaps Dennis the Dachshund – the issue is still debated – on the BBC's 'Children's Hour'). Whether Churchill inspired the British people, and if so to what extent, is still an open question. Churchill himself, not known for any false modesty, insisted that the British people were the lion: he was merely fortunate enough to deliver its roar.

The British people – unity and resolution

Were the British people really united in 1940, with high morale and defiant resolution? There is plenty of evidence that they were not. For instance, on 24 June 1940 there was at Euston station 'a queue of Rolls Royces and liveried servants and mountains of trunks': the rich were making their way to Liverpool en route for the safety of the United States. It was found next month that at least three MPs had fled the country. At this time Cecil King of the *Daily Mirror* wrote in his diary that 'the country is already reconciling itself to the idea of a Nazi conquest'. The cabinet soon decided that the numbers of those killed in air raids should not be published as they would be bad for morale. Nevertheless, an intelligence report in October noted that 'the morale of Londoners has deteriorated. There is less of "We can take it" and an inclination to say "This must stop at all costs".'

How can we possibly be sure of the morale of tens of millions of Britons in 1940? People obviously reacted differently to their experiences in the war, and it would be quite unrealistic to expect uniform morale, high or low. In general, people seem to have made the best of things, experiencing defiance, depression and also a good deal of indifference. It is also worth remembering that Britain suffered relatively little from bombing raids. Around 1,000 people were killed in the first three days of the Blitz on London, in August 1940, and in all 30,000 had been killed in 1940–41. But probably 30,000 Germans were killed in two days – 13 and 14 February 1945 – by allied raids on Dresden; and, in total, over half a million Germans were killed by allied bombers.

The presence of a common enemy must have made Britons feel more united than ever before, but too much emphasis can be put on this. Class distinctions were certainly not totally eradicated: and, as George Orwell, once noted, the hardships of rationing were 'to put it mildly, tempered for anyone with over £2,000 a year'. He also noted that you could only get an important job if you talked with the right accent. Nor does the image of a united nation take account of the black market that flourished during the war or of looting or of the crime rate, which jumped in 1940 and remained high throughout the war.

Dunkirk

After the evacuations from Dunkirk, the British public was told that the men of the BEF had 'not come back in triumph, they have come back in glory'. Admittedly the army had been saved from disaster by being ferried across the Channel: 338,000 men were saved (including 140,000 Frenchmen). But the venture was not as glamorous as the government's propaganda machine and the press portrayed it – 30,000 soldiers were taken prisoner by the Germans, and even those rescued lost all their equipment. In private Churchill called Dunkirk 'the greatest British military defeat for many centuries'. Furthermore, only 8 per cent of the men were saved by the 'gallant little ferry boats'; the rest, more prosaically, were rescued by the Royal Navy. No journalists had been present at Dunkirk, otherwise they might have reported how some officers deserted their troops in order to get aboard the earliest boats.

The Battle of Britain

Hitler had won a series of easy victories until he turned to Britain. He decided that the RAF would have to be destroyed before he could embark on 'Operation Sealion', the invasion of Britain. Around 700 British fighter planes (Spitfires and Hurricanes) had to face about 800 German fighters and 1,000 German bombers, but it was the British who emerged supreme, causing the invasion to be abandoned.

The RAF's victory was indeed momentous. But it has too seldom been realised that the British had several key advantages. First of all, Hitler's plans were extremely muddled: he began by bombing airfields and radar stations, and had he continued to do so, instead of bombing cities, the result might have been different. As it was, radar gave the British an important advantage. Furthermore, Britain's planes were much more manoeuvrable than Germany's, which had not been designed for attacks of this type. In fact no German plane could carry enough fuel to fly over British soil for more than about 25 minutes. Nor is it often remembered that the two most successful RAF pilots were a Czech and a Pole – or that the RAF wasted much of its expertise by insisting that office jobs must be undertaken by fully trained pilots. Finally, the extent of the British victory was deliberately exaggerated by the government. The date of

15 September was celebrated as Battle of Britain Day: but only 60 German planes were shot down that day, not the 185 reported. (In general the British exaggerated their successes by around 250 per cent, the Germans by 450 per cent.)

Conclusion

Was 1940 Britain's 'Finest Hour'? Undoubtedly the British made a real difference to the Second World War by resisting the Nazis. Had they capitulated, then the course of history would undoubtedly have been different – and, given the character of Hitler, would surely not have been improved.

Opinions of Churchill vary. No one can judge the precise effects of his oratory, and no one can be sure what would have happened if he had not been Prime Minister. Perhaps a compromise peace would have been made, for good or ill. But most historians believe that, despite his faults, he proved an inspiring and effective war leader in 1940. His enormous – and quite irrational – confidence in himself and in Britain and its empire made him the man for the job. Under his leadership Britain survived in 1940 when the odds against survival seemed great. Of course his importance has been exaggerated by some, as have the unity and resilience of the British people. Similarly, Dunkirk and the Battle of Britain have been glamorised, whereas most of the participants knew full well that war is never glamorous. It is easy to debunk the romantic and unrealistic image of 1940, but it may be that a more sober and historically accurate appraisal of 1940 leaves its pivotal role in twentieth-century history substantially intact.

Nevertheless there seemed no hope, by the end of the year, that Britain would be able to defeat Germany, even if Germany could not defeat Britain. Indeed it was apparent that Britain would be unable to carry on the war without the aid of the USA. The war was exacting a high economic and financial toll (see chapter 18). Britain was paying the price for its defiance of the Nazis.

Tasks

1 Study the photograph of Churchill by Cecil Beaton (Figure 15.1) and answer the following questions:

   a What character traits are conveyed by Churchill's pose and facial expression?

   b It might be thought that this portrait is 'artless', that Churchill has briefly stopped working for the cameraman to take a 'snap'. But what evidence is there that this is a carefully composed photograph? (Consider the room and the focus of the camera lens as well as the way Churchill is depicted.)

2 Read the extracts from Churchill's speech of 4 June 1940 on page 140 and answer the following questions:

   a How confident does Churchill seem of (i) survival and (ii) ultimate victory?

   b Why does he several times refer to Britain as an island?

   c Do you consider this passage to be effective oratory? Are all sections of the speech equally effective? Explain your answers by reference to the language Churchill uses.

   d What emotions do you think he was trying to arouse in his listeners? Might it have been unwise for Britons to feel fully confident of victory?

3 Study Low's cartoon (Figure 15.2) and answer the following questions:

   a Churchill is at the head of the group, followed by Chamberlain, Attlee and Bevin. But how does Low create the impression that all the figures were of equal status? Does he suggest that Britain was essentially a classless society?

   b What message is Low trying to put across in this cartoon?

   c How do you think the shape of the group reinforces the message?

   d To what extent do you agree that 'all' in Britain were 'behind ... Winston' in May 1940? Use the information of this chapter, and any other information you have, to formulate and to explain your answer.

Further reading

Paul Adelman, *Britain: Domestic Politics 1939–64* (Hodder and Stoughton, 1994) – an 'Access to History' title, clearly and crisply written.

Clive Ponting, *1940: Myth and Reality* (Hamish Hamilton, 1990).

Angus Calder, *The People's War* (Cape, 1969).

Robert Blake and Wm Roger Louis, *Churchill* (Oxford University Press, 1993).

16 The Beveridge Report: 'a time for revolutions, not for patching'?

In December 1941 the government published a long and weighty White Paper, containing 299 pages of small print and 45 statistical tables, *Social Insurance and Allied Services*. It might have been expected to produce a yawn of indifference from the public. Yet in fact it created a sensation. The 7,000 copies available at London's Stationery Office sold out on the morning of publication, and in total a massive 635,000 copies were bought during the war. No government publication has ever aroused such interest or received such a favourable reception. Its author, **Sir William Beveridge**, decided that the time was ripe for fundamental changes in British society: 'a revolutionary moment in the world's history,' he insisted, 'is a time for revolutions, not for patching'. He had therefore produced a blueprint for banishing poverty from British society. This chapter seeks to assess whether the Beveridge Report was indeed revolutionary. What changes did it seek to bring about, and what degree of continuity was there between its proposals and the welfare provisions of the past?

PROFILE: *Sir William Beveridge*

Born in 1879, **William Beveridge** had a lifelong interest in social issues, especially unemployment and poverty. He worked as a civil servant in 1908–19, helping to draft the 1911 National Health Insurance Act, before becoming Director of the London School of Economics. He was made Master of University College Oxford in 1937 and was drafted into government service in 1940. Ministers, who found him overbearing and arrogant, made him head of a committee on social insurance to keep him out of their hair. In fact, he did most of the committee's work himself and wrote the Report far more quickly than anyone anticipated. Immediately he became a popular celebrity, winning a by-election for the Liberals in 1944. Thus the rather crusty and pompous academic became, almost overnight, the celebrated 'People's William'. Beveridge died in 1963.

Social services before 1942

Pre-Second World War

Social welfare before Beveridge rested on a series of measures designed to provide against unemployment, accident and old age. The most significant were as follows:

- *1908, Old Age Pensions Act*. People aged 70 and over were entitled to a small pension, providing their income from other sources fell below prescribed levels. The pensions were financed from taxation.

- *1911, National Health Insurance Act*. This provided compulsory health insurance for all workers, aged 16–70, who earned less than £160 a year: each worker could claim sick pay during illness and was entitled to free treatment from a general practitioner (GP). The costs were borne by a fund – administered by insurance companies or trade unions, not by the state – which was created by flat-rate contributions from the employer, the worker and the government. The Act also provided for insurance against unemployment in the building, engineering and shipbuilding trades. Unemployed workers could claim benefit for 15 weeks in any year. This legislation marked an important change; but not all workers were insured, no dependants were included and medical provisions did not cover hospital treatment.

- *1920–21, Unemployment Insurance Acts*. The first of these extended the provisions of the 1911 Act to cover far more groups of workers, indeed virtually everyone earning less than £250 a year. The second extended the period during which benefit could be claimed to two periods of 16 weeks in any year. The unemployed could thus claim 'uncovenanted benefit' (commonly known as the 'dole'), after the benefits to which insurance entitled them had expired. The Unemployment Fund was therefore given powers to borrow from the Treasury. In addition, further legislation authorised extra payments for the dependants of those out of work.

- *1925, Old Age Pensions Act*. This increased national insurance contributions in return for a pension to bridge the gap until pensions could be claimed, at the age of 70, under the 1908 Act. It also provided allowances for widows and their dependent children.

These were the main changes introduced between the wars. Clearly, the central government was taking a much greater responsibility for social welfare, so that the nineteenth-century Poor Law and its workhouses became defunct. In general, more people than ever before could claim benefits. For instance, health insurance was extended to those earning up to £250; by 1939 19.2 million people (about 54 per cent of adults) were covered. Expenditure by central and local government on social welfare schemes rose significantly, from 5.5 per cent of national income in 1913 to 13 per cent in 1938. Indeed some historians have judged that by 1939 Britain had the most comprehensive set of social services in the world, however inadequate they might seem by later standards.

Yet there were several glaring problems:

- Poverty still remained. Social investigations showed this beyond doubt. Probably about one-third of all working-class families were at or below the poverty line. Unemployment or intermittent employment, low wages and large families were pinpointed as the prime causes of poverty.

- The system was far from comprehensive. Insured workers would receive free treatment from a GP, whereas their wives (unless insured themselves) and their children would not. Children at school would at least receive medical inspection, but nothing was done for those under school age. In addition, no hospital treatment was available under the state system, though some hospitals would provide means-tested treatment; and furthermore, many voluntary and municipal hospitals were dependent on charitable donations for their survival. In general, the provision of health care across the country was far from uniform and did not reflect need. Indeed provision was sometimes poorest where the need was greatest.

- The benefits were often means-tested. In the 1930s unemployed workers had to undergo a humiliating means test on the whole household, which sometimes meant that parents had to rely for support on their children – with a consequent break-up of families. By 1939 there were no less than 18 different means tests in operation for benefits conferred by seven different ministries.

- The whole 'system' – if such it can be called – was complex and confusing. Indeed it was a bureaucratic nightmare. Hence it is not surprising that there were anomalies. For instance, an insured man who was unemployed could claim an allowance for dependants, whereas if he were sick he could not.

The Second World War

The war made the reform of the system a necessity. The conflict was portrayed as a People's War, and therefore the government had to show that the people were benefiting in tangible ways. In 1940, therefore, free milk was introduced for all schoolchildren, and in 1941 the household means test was abolished. Hospital treatment was also reformed. The *Luftwaffe's* bombs fell impartially on those with private insurance and those without, and the old system could not cope. As a result, the government instituted the Emergency Hospital Service (EHS): henceforth all hospitals would lay aside beds for war casualties, the costs to be paid by the Treasury. It was almost as if hospitals were being temporarily nationalised.

Most people believed that at the end of the war the old patchwork of social provisions would have to be regularised and, in some measure, extended. Beveridge was the man chosen to bring order out of chaos.

Beveridge's proposals

Beveridge's main aim was to eliminate 'Want' (i.e. poverty), which was one of five Giants – along with Disease, Ignorance, Squalor and Idleness – that had to be slain. His scheme rested on three assumptions:

1 a national health service would be set up to ensure adequate health care
2 family (or child) allowances would be paid to all parents
3 there would be full employment (defined as around 3 per cent unemployment).

The basic means for eliminating poverty was to be an insurance scheme: every worker would make flat-rate contributions (supplemented by amounts from the employer and from the Treasury) and be able to claim a uniform rate of benefit. Such proposals, of course, sound familiar: they were based on existing insurance schemes, but Beveridge proposed to extend them in important ways. These included the following:

■ All benefits were to be administered by a single Ministry of Social Security.

■ Similarly, insurance contributions (for health, employment, accidents, pensions, etc.) would be unified as well: there would be one standard weekly payment. In this way a more efficient administrative structure would be provided, Beveridge aiming to 'eliminate a good deal of waste inherent in present methods'.

■ Furthermore, his scheme would not be selective (limited to certain categories of workers), like so many interwar schemes, but universal. Everyone was at liberty to take out private insurance, but only in addition to, and not instead of, the state scheme. Insurance only works if enough people participate, and so this compulsory scheme was expected to be the most effective form of all. (His assumption of full employment was also vital here: if there were mass unemployment, too many people would be claiming benefit at the same time, and so the insurance fund would run dry.)

▨ Since everyone was paying contributions, everyone would have the right to draw benefits, thus eliminating means tests. Hence 'benefits' would become 'entitlements', and receiving them would not be perceived as demeaning.

The end result of these proposals – providing that children's allowances were paid and mass unemployment removed – would be the elimination of Want. In short, the Beveridge proposals would comprise a safety net 'from the cradle to the grave' – from maternity benefits to death grants.

Beveridge wanted to eliminate actual poverty, and so he insisted that benefits should be at subsistence level (*i.e.* they should be adequate to cover people's basic needs), but he did not intend that state provisions should be generous. A safety net is not the same as a hammock! He certainly did not wish to discourage thrift or hard work: he was a staunch opponent of what he called the give-away 'Santa Claus state' and what others were calling the 'welfare state'. The government, he insisted, while establishing a national minimum, 'should leave room and encouragement for voluntary action by each individual to provide more than that minimum for himself and his family'. Prudent, responsible people would make further provision against a rainy day or retirement.

The reactions to Beveridge

A crusty and rather patrician figure became, almost overnight, a popular celebrity, the 'prophet of peaceful social revolution'. Beveridge was a hero tackling five Giants single handed (see Figure 16.2). Note how the figure of Beveridge had to be named: soon that would not be necessary. Also remarkable is how an extremely complex set of policies was being simplified and personalised, in a way that everyone could grasp.

There was a chorus of popular pro-Beveridge approval (which extended even to far-away Nigeria, where local nationalist leader Azikiwe called for a 'Beveridge plan right now'). *The Times* called the Report a 'momentous document' and thanked its author for his 'masterly exposition of the ways and means whereby ... poverty can be speedily abolished altogether'. From the opposite end of the political spectrum, the left-wing *Tribune* judged that Beveridge had laid down the conditions 'in which the tears might be taken out of capitalism'. The plan seemed to show that the poor need not always be with us. It was debated in the Commons, in universities, in trade unions and in the streets. A report of churchmen, while regretting that Beveridge had not included sin along with his other Giants to be slain, dubbed it 'practical Christianity'. There was a sustained call for the wartime coalition to implement the report at once.

TACKLING THE FIRST GIANT

Figure 16.2 The 180,000-word Beveridge Report reduced to a single image. The cartoon is captioned: 'WANT is only one of the five giants on the road to destruction' – The Beveridge Report.

Critical views were muted, but they did exist. They too assumed that Beveridge would mark revolutionary changes, though ones which were undesirable. Right-wing industrialists believed that employer contributions to the scheme would hamstring British industry; and some thought that, without the fear of falling into poverty, the working classes would settle down to an unproductive life living off benefits.

Revolution or patching?

George Orwell wrote early in 1943 that the great topic of the day was the Beveridge Report: 'People seem to feel that this very moderate measure of reform is almost too good to be true.' Commentators were indeed getting carried away and making unbalanced judgements. This was partly due to the circumstances of the war. With the recent victory at El Alamein in North Africa and the good news from the Eastern Front, the tide of war had finally begun to turn in the allies' favour, and so the Report was seized upon as a symbol of the better society all hoped would emerge out of the horrors and deprivations of war. But it was also due to Beveridge's talent for successfully courting publicity. He was a man who enjoyed the limelight and ensured that he got it, partly by the use of emotive rhetoric. Having insisted at the beginning of the Report that this was a time for revolutionary changes not patching, he later added, more soberly, that his scheme was 'in some ways a revolution but in more important ways it is a development from the past'. It might even be said that the Report was indeed an example of 'patching', even if of an extensive and ingenious kind.

Beveridge's proposals were built squarely on the legacy of the past, and in particular on the insurance proposals of Lloyd George's 1911 Act. In essence he was merely making universal previous provisions, and regularising them into a coherent administrative structure. Admittedly he hoped to see extra provisions, such as children's allowances, but there was, by 1941, an overwhelming consensus in favour of such measures. The significance of Beveridge's work therefore lies mainly in this competent and tidy-minded synthesis of the disjointed schemes which existed before the Second World War. It does not lie in the originality of his ideas. José Harris, Beveridge's biographer, and others have shown that many people had similar notions to those Beveridge was putting forward. The war, with its mingling of the classes and its stress on fair shares for all, had led to a greater awareness of poverty in Britain and a greater determination to tackle it. Small wonder, therefore, that the Beveridge Report received such a welcome response: it told people what they wanted to hear.

In addition, it should be noted that the Beveridge proposals were in fact far less practical than many people assumed. For instance, he called for benefits at subsistence level, but he never really devised a means of assessing real minimum needs, which must obviously vary with age and personal circumstances. The social scientist Seebohm Rowntree urged Beveridge to accept the principle that claimants should receive a flat-rate benefit plus their actual rent – but without success. Yet a subsistence allowance which fails to take account of variations in necessary expenditure is surely a contradiction in terms.

His ideas were also less 'generous' than was widely believed. It is true that Beveridge insisted that the insured could claim benefits as of right, without the need for a means test; but he realised that means-tested 'national assistance' would be needed for those who had failed to make enough contributions to qualify under the insurance scheme. A safety net would have to be drawn beneath the safety net! Yet little publicity was given to this aspect of the Report. Beveridge also believed that if pensions at the full rate were introduced at once, the insurance fund could not cope: better, therefore, to phase them in over 20 years. Yet the press lavished attention not on such issues but on eye-catching calls for the creation of a comprehensive national health service ('to ensure that for every citizen there is available whatever medical treatment he requires, in whatever form he requires it') and for the maintenance of full employment. Yet these proposals were merely 'assumptions', without which the plan to abolish Want could not work. Beveridge did not specify how unemployment could be prevented, and he did little more than piously call for the creation of some sort of health service. Precise health reforms had to be worked out after the war, when Aneurin Bevan was Minister of Health. Key decisions had still to be taken – and fierce battles fought (see chapter 21).

Beveridge's use of old-fashioned language (as with 'Want' instead of 'Poverty') may show that intellectually he was, to some extent, living in the past. Certainly he planned for families consisting of an employed father and a non-employed mother: he was keen for working women to return to the home after the war, to ensure 'the adequate continuance of the British race'. Nevertheless, while reflecting the past, his Report also looked to the future: but should his proposals be described as 'revolutionary'? In other words, would they completely change the pattern of inter-war provisions? Or did they merely extend and improve the previous pattern, in which case perhaps the term 'reformist' or 'evolutionary' should be used? The matter is one for debate. The other point that should be kept in mind is that Beveridge's report was only a plan. The key issue, perhaps, is not the novelty and rigour of his paper proposals but whether his scheme would be implemented and – most important of all – whether poverty could indeed be eliminated.

Task: note-taking

You may find it useful to take notes from this chapter by arranging your material into two main sections:

■ aspects of the Beveridge reforms which are clearly linked to what had gone before, i.e. *continuity*

■ aspects which suggest *change*, even revolutionary change.

You might want to arrange your 'continuity' and 'change' material in columns side by side. This work will require you to select material from different parts of the chapter. This will help you to avoid merely copying out an abbreviated version of the text and will encourage you to *think* about the material. Doing this will help the material stick in your mind. Remember that it is important to have done your hard thinking *before* tackling an exam question on this topic.

Further reading

John Stevenson, *British Society, 1914–45* (Penguin, 1984).
Paul Addison, *The Road to 1945* (Cape, 1977) – a seminal work on wartime politics.
José Harris, *William Beveridge* (Oxford University Press, 1977).

17 The changing role of women: the Second World War

The Second World War tested Britain's resources even more than the 1914–18 conflict. Now Britain was in danger not merely of defeat but of invasion and conquest. As a result, there was a greater mobilisation of resources – including people – than ever before. This was indeed 'Total War'. Whether they liked it or not, women were much more intensely involved in the Second, than in the First, World War. The bombing of British cities in fact killed more women than men, and women had once more to leave the home and enter the workforce. Might this second mobilisation of women have greater and more permanent effects than the first?

Women in the workforce

Phoney War

The early part of the conflict, from September 1939 to April 1940, was the Phoney War. People's lives were relatively little affected, though large numbers of people were evacuated to safer areas of the country: these included primary school children and their teachers, together with mothers and children of pre-school age. At first Chamberlain's government called for women voluntarily to give up their existing work and register for war service; but after six months of war half of those who volunteered were still unemployed. Of the first 30,000 to enrol in the Women's Land Army in August 1939, many were back in the dole queue once their training was complete. The employment of married women was as unpopular as it had ever been, and cynics decided that government policy was merely a ploy to hasten female redundancy.

Women's war work

In May 1940 the real war began, and Churchill's government infused new urgency into the war effort. Minister of Labour Ernest Bevin took active steps to mobilise the workforce for the successful prosecution of the war. Nevertheless he was loath to treat women in the same way as men. He wished to use voluntary means as much as possible, even though female unemployment stood at 300,000 by the end of 1940. Yet when it became clear that another 2 million workers were needed in British industry, he reluctantly accepted that women should be conscripted. From December 1941 women aged 20–30 had to register and be available for direction into war work. The system was subsequently extended to cover virtually all women from 18 to 51.

Women were again, as in 1914, substitutes for men who went off to fight. At the start of the war there had been about 5 million women in paid employment; by 1943 there were 7.2 million. This was just under half of the total adult female population. But it has been estimated that, if voluntary work is taken into account, as many as 80 per cent of married and 90 per cent of single women were working in some capacity outside the home. Official figures for female unemployment in 1943 stood at only 24,000. Particularly significant was that the marriage bar vanished overnight, and even working mothers were rapidly accepted into the workforce. The government welcomed women into the factories – as shown in the poster in Figure 17.1; hence nurseries were set up to allow women with young children to work. By 1944 there were some 1,500 nurseries, compared with only 100 in the First World War. One woman remembers how she was assured that a newly provided nursery, such as had been condemned by the experts in the 1930s, would make her son more intelligent and socially conscious.

What sort of work did women tackle? On the Home Front they undertook a wide variety of jobs. They worked in munitions factories, they welded ships, they worked on the railways, in vehicle manufacture, in the gas and water industries, as well as in more clerical jobs than ever before. Some women found that their old skills matched new requirements: for instance, textile workers now made uniforms and parachutes rather than civilian goods. There was also 'dilution', as in the First World War, so that unskilled workers could undertake different parts of skilled jobs. In addition, many women were trained – at government training centres – to undertake skilled work.

Difficulties and discrimination

Women's contribution to the domestic workforce was undoubtedly important. But the female lot was far from being an altogether happy one. It is true that there were more nurseries than ever before, but in fact there were far fewer than were needed, so that the majority of under-5s were not catered for. Nursery hours, generally 9 a.m.–4 p.m., were unsuitable for industrial shift work, and their cost, at 1 shilling (5p) per child per day, was also prohibitive. Wartime propaganda highlighted women's role in the war: such publicity was good for morale and emphasised the unity of British society. The truth of the matter, however, was

Figure 17.1 *As in the First, so in the Second World War: ZEC's poster welcomes women into the workforce.*

WOMEN OF BRITAIN
COME INTO THE FACTORIES
ASK AT ANY EMPLOYMENT EXCHANGE FOR ADVICE AND FULL DETAILS

more humdrum. Many women disliked their war work. It tended to be monotonous, poorly paid and to allow insufficient time for traditional home-based occupations such as shopping, which was often a lengthy process as a result of wartime shortages. Women also felt discriminated against in the small number of apprenticeships open to them.

The end of the war and the revival of feminism

Surveys revealed that most women expected to lose the jobs they had gained as a result of the wartime emergency. One young married woman insisted that 'You can't look on anything you do during the war as what you really mean to do; it's just filling in time till you can live your own life again.' Surveys revealed that three-quarters of single women expected to give up work when they got married. These attitudes showed remarkable continuity with the 1920s and 1930s, and most historians have judged that the end of the Second World War followed the pattern of the First. Penny Summerfield has written that women were needed in the factories and the services in 1941–3, and indeed 'everywhere in the build-up to D-Day' in 1944, but 'then nowhere after 1945'.

There is much truth in this view. Official figures show that 37.4 per cent of all women were in paid employment in 1951, compared with 34.2 per cent in 1931. The Second World War, like the First, had proved to be an exceptional period of little long-term significance. Most women's war work had been so tedious that they were pleased to return to 'normal' life; in addition the government, through its postwar social legislation, encouraged women to return to the home and breed children. Sir William Beveridge in his famous Report of 1942 insisted that British housewives 'as mothers have vital work to do in ensuring the adequate continuance of the British race and of the British ideals of the world', and in 1945 the Family Allowances Act sought to stimulate large families by paying a small weekly sum of money to mothers for every child after the first. The population duly complied after 1945, as women began to marry earlier and have more children than before 1939.

Yet the post-1918 trends were not entirely reproduced. First, since demobilisation was slower after 1945 compared with 1918, women remained in the labour force for longer. Indeed employment shortages after 1945 meant that women continued to work in heavy industry. But the government withdrew its grants for nursery provision, and by the end of the decade there was pressure on women to vacate 'men's' jobs. When redundancies were necessary, trade union officials reminded employers of the wartime agreement that women 'shall be regarded as temporarily employed'. The less identified a particular job was with traditional 'women's work', the more likely were women to be laid off. Certainly women stood little chance of staying on for long in the armed forces.

A more long-lasting legacy of 1939–45 was a decisive breach in the marriage bar. In 1951, when the percentage of all women in work was little changed from prewar figures, over twice the number of married women were in work as 20 years earlier (22, rather than 10, per cent). This was the most important long-term gain (or, to use a more neutral term, change) for women from the Second World War.

Another notable legacy came within the walls of the Palace of Westminster. Towards the end of the war the lady Members' room – the so-called 'Boudoir' – stirred itself into activity. Women within the Labour Party saw the war as offering new opportunities. Edith Summerskill pressed for the return of 100 women MPs – party affiliation was secondary to gender – at the next general election. In the event, there were 87 female candidates in 1945, 24 of whom were successful. This was far from being a phenomenal increase, but it showed that the war had led to some gains and that it held out the prospect of more.

Conclusion: post-1945 trends

The effects of the Second World War on female employment patterns – and, more generally, on women's place in society – were far from revolutionary. Feminists have deplored the fact that it was not more liberating. The war, like the earlier 1914–18 conflict, was seen as an exceptional time, so that a woman's place was still essentially in the home. If she worked, then her earnings were thought to be in addition to the wages or salary of the male householder. Few believed that a woman could possibly be the family's main breadwinner. Beveridge's welfare state proposals were based on the assumption that the average family unit comprised an employed father and a non-employed mother.

In the years after 1945 the traditional view of woman as the home-maker has proved remarkably resilient, a view encouraged by much commercial advertising. Such images confounded the extra work taken on by women in the war. The 1950s, like the 1930s, saw a pervasive 'cult of domesticity', again emphasised in advertisements. The gates of heaven were supposed to open for the mother bought a new household gadget by her husband, as in the illustration shown in Figure 17.6. The fact that this decade saw more married women working probably owed a great deal to the needs of the economy, which was switching from traditional heavy industries: employers often considered women more adept than men at the repetitive tasks demanded by light industry. Certainly they could be paid lower wages.

Education also continued to fit women for their male-designed roles. The 1944 Butler Education Act, passed by the wartime Parliament, extended secondary education to all, but girls attending secondary modern schools

Figure 17.6 *Advertising in the 1950s emphasised that a woman's place was in the home. In fact, washing machines and other labour-saving devices made it easier for women to go out to work.*

had a curriculum biased towards domestic duties. Such schools often provided furnished rooms wherein girls might learn the essential skills of housewifery. One critic, Dame Kathleen Ollerenshaw, claimed that the Act had been designed by men for boys.

Nevertheless the Education Act was also an engine of change. It outlawed the sacking of women teachers who married, while the provision of good-quality education, especially in the grammar schools, widened women's horizons. By the early 1960s nearly a third of undergraduates were female, and the professions saw a steady, though slow, increase in the number of women entrants. It may be said, therefore, that the Second World War had produced profound, if indirect, effects on the position of women in British society.

The war affected women more than men, and it played its part in the gradual changes that have occurred in women's roles in society. Many of the changes that occurred after 1945, including the Equal Pay Act of 1970 and the Sex Discrimination Act of 1975 may have owed much to the psychological effects of the war on women. Yet with events which are so recent, and for which we are able to see so many varied and diverse factors and causes, it is wise not to be dogmatic – especially when generalising about the lives of over half the population of Great Britain.

Contemporary history is always a minefield, and this is especially true of 'women's history'. Some may say that changes in the position of women in society have been too slow; others that they have been truly revolutionary. Some deplore them, others praise them. Is there a special female mentality which is essentially different from the male and which therefore defines the role – or roles – in society which women should have? (For that matter, is there a male mentality?) Much depends on this issue. Pundits are ready with a confusion of answers; but historians are likely to say that the debate is far from over and that the 'answers' are themselves of historical significance.

It is not easy to be scholarly and judicious and impartial on these issues: that is perhaps the disadvantage of women's history. The great advantage is its endless fascination. Hence it is even harder than usual to be indifferent.

Role play

You will notice how interpretations about what women did in the Second World War are affected by ideas – and often by prejudices – about what should have happened. Always try to spot the ideological point of view, or bias, not only of your sources but of the historians you read – including the author of this book, who is a mass of prejudices, though he tries hard not to let them show!

A role play, set in May 1945, about the effects of the war on women and about whether there should be a return to pre-1939 patterns of employment, should prove valuable in bringing out a variety of viewpoints and preconceptions.

Tasks

1 Read the extract from *The Times* on page 179.

 a Explain the meaning of the phrase 'rugged individualism'.

 b How far do you think the old interpretations of 'democracy', 'freedom', 'equality' and 'economic reconstruction' were characteristics of Britain in the interwar years?

 c Use your knowledge of the circumstances of the time to explain why these new ideas were current in 1940.

2 Read the extract from J. B. Priestley on pages 179–180.

 a Suggest reasons why this extract probably made an effective broadcast.

 b What further information would you need before you could make a final judgement on its effectiveness?

 c Put into your own words the differences between the 'property' and the 'community' outlooks which Priestley identifies.

 d What do you think Priestley's political stance was? Explain your answer.

3 Study the cartoon 'Here you are' (Figure 19.1).

 a What exactly is the wounded soldier offering with his left hand?

 b How would you describe the mood of the soldier? Refer specifically to his facial expression and to his words in the caption.

 c In what ways had Britain lost the 'victory and peace' which had been won in 1918?

4 Read the broadcasts by Churchill and Attlee on pages 183 and 184.

 a What do you find impressive in each speech and what unimpressive? Comment on both content and manner of presentation.

 b Draw up a list of the policies (either stated or implied) of each man.

 c Explain how voters might have been influenced by each speech, given the circumstances of 1945.

5 Study the two Low cartoons shown in Figures 19.2 and 19.3 and answer the following questions:

 a Do you find 'On the higher level' an adequate representation of the differences between Labour and Conservative policies? Refer specifically to the alternatives held by 'The Thinker'. How might a thoughtful Conservative have responded? (You may not fully understand all the details in the cartoon: the witch, for instance, is a malicious-looking Lord Beaverbrook.)

b Put into your own words the political message Low is trying to put across in 'On tour'. In particular, explain why Churchill is lined up with the six other figures on the ledge.

c How far do you think that Low was accurately depicting the campaign issues in these two cartoons, and how far was he merely indulging in pro-Labour propaganda?

6 Use these sources to explain why Labour ran a more effective campaign than the Conservatives in 1945.

Further reading

Peter Hennessy, *Never Again: Britain 1945–1951* (Cape, 1992) – an excellent book, scholarly but readable.

Kevin Jefferys (ed.), *War and Reform: British Politics during the Second World War* (Manchester University Press, 1994) – an invaluable collection of source material: chapter 6 covers the 1945 election.

Robert Pearce, 'David Low and the 1945 Election', *History Review*, no. 21, March 1995.

20 Why did Britain withdraw from India in 1947?

Time chart

1917: Montagu Declaration on India's future

1919: Montagu-Chelmsford Constitution: Indians allowed to control some ministries in the provinces

1928: Appointment of the all-white Simon Commission

1935: Government of India Act: provincial self-government

1939: Viceroy declares war on behalf of India

1942: 'Quit India' campaign
The Cripps offer, rejected by Congress

1945: New Labour government, which attempts to secure Indian agreement to the transfer of power

1947: February
Attlee announces time-limit for withdrawal; Mountbatten replaces Wavell
15 August
Transfer of power to India and Pakistan

British rule in India began in the middle of the eighteenth century and was fully established by the middle of the nineteenth, when the crown took over administration from the East India Company. Henceforth there was direct British rule over two-thirds of India, while the other third remained under the rule of the traditional Princes. India was certainly the most important part of the whole British Empire. Comprising about a fifth of the world's population and covering some 1.8 million square miles (20 times the size of Britain), it seemed a tangible, and reassuring, sign of Britain's greatness in the world. But after the Second World War Labour's Prime Minister, Clement Attlee, insisted that British rule must end, and quickly. On 15 August 1947, amid violent communal riots between Hindus and Muslims, British rule ceased, and two new successor states – India and Pakistan – were formed. This was a momentous change, directly affecting around 400 million Asians and encouraging decolonisation elsewhere.

This chapter asks why British rule ended. How far was withdrawal the goal of previous British policy, and to what extent was a reluctant imperial power expelled by nationalist forces? What effects did the Second World War have, and what role was played by economic factors? We must also examine key individuals: on the Indian side, Gandhi, Nehru and Jinnah; and for Britain, Attlee, his ministers and the Viceroy appointed in 1947, Lord Mountbatten.

British policy before 1945

Many Britons in 1947 claimed that Indian independence was the culmination of their rule in the subcontinent: it was the goal for which they and their predecessors had been patiently working for over 100 years. By 1947 their work of training and modernisation was complete, so that withdrawal was the fulfilment, not the defeat, of their imperial mission. Such an interpretation seems convenient – all too convenient – from Britain's point of view, but there is some evidence to support it. Britons had long been claiming that they were **trustees** for the local inhabitants; and, ever since 1917, constitutional reform, giving Indians a larger share in government, had been on the political agenda.

In 1917, when Indian loyalty needed to be won during the First World War, the Secretary of State for India, Edwin Montagu, declared that Britain's policy was 'the gradual development of self-governing institutions with a view to the progressive realisation of responsible Government in India as an integral part of the British Empire'. There was much that was vague in this statement, particularly the time-scale. Yet it was highly progressive, holding out the promise of self-government within the Empire. It was followed up by the Montagu-Chelmsford Constitution in 1919. This gave Indians greater representation in the Viceroy's central government in Delhi, though no real power there; and, more important, it gave Indian politicians in provincial governments control of certain ministries, though others (especially the key portfolios of law and taxation) were reserved for white officials.

In 1929 British policy entered a new phase. The Viceroy proclaimed that India would eventually achieve Dominion status (and thus be on a par with Australia, Canada, New Zealand and South Africa); and in 1935 another constitution was introduced. Now Indians were to have control of provincial governments, running all departments, while at the centre local people were to take charge of a number of ministries, once a federation between British and Princely India had been formed. Thus there was to be self-government in the provinces and power-sharing at the centre.

A pattern towards the devolution of greater and greater measures of self-government may thus be discerned. Perhaps the transfer of power in

1947 should be seen as the culmination of an evolutionary process which had begun much earlier.

Yet criticisms can be made of this view:

▨ Several important figures did not intend that complete self-government would result from these reforms. For instance, the Secretary of State for India, Lord Birkenhead, wrote to the Viceroy in 1925 that it was 'inconceivable' that India would ever be fit for self-government.

▨ British policy-makers wanted to win over the Indians by timely constitutional reform, but at the same time they wanted to retain British control. Hence they conceded the very least which they thought the Indians would accept. Often they miscalculated, and several times, in the 1920s and 1930s, Indians launched civil disobedience campaigns.

▨ In 1928 Britain appointed an all-white committee (the Simon Commission) to draw up constitutional proposals. This racial exclusivity showed little sympathy with, or understanding of, Indian aspirations.

▨ The 1929 statement on Dominion status was hardly a breakthrough: after all, Dominion status had been implicit in the 1919 Montagu Declaration. The 1935 Act may have promised that Indians would have some power in the central government, but the Princes never agreed to come into a federation, and probably the British knew they would refuse. The 1935 Constitution seemed more radical than it really was: this was because old-fashioned imperialists like Winston Churchill criticised it so extensively. In reality, India was still a very long way from real self-government, as **Gandhi** recognised.

▨ The British insisted that seats should be reserved for Indian minorities, and in particular for Muslims. Thus there were separate (or 'communal') electorates. Some have insisted that the British were trying to emphasise the differences between Indians, and especially between Hindus and Muslims: for the greater these differences, the less would Britain be faced with a united opposition and the easier it would be for Britain to continue to rule. Was Britain's policy 'divide and rule'?

The Second World War

Britain declared war on Germany on 3 September 1939. On the same day the Viceroy, without even consulting Indians let alone securing their agreement, declared that India too was at war. This tactless action showed how far India was from self-government. Local politicians felt slighted: they believed – and especially those who were ministers in provincial governments – that they had been badly treated. **Nehru**, the leader of the Indian National Congress, insisted that Indians would

PROFILE: *M. K. Gandhi*

Mohandas Karamchand ('Mahatma') Gandhi was the leading nationalist figure in India between 1919 and his death, from an assassin's bullet, in 1948. Originally, as a middle-class, British-trained lawyer, he had been a supporter of the Raj; but a turning-point came when, before the First World War, he championed the cause of Indians who were discriminated against in South Africa. His weapon against British rule in India was the non-violent civil disobedience campaign, together with occasional personal fasts. These tactics led to his imprisonment for a total of 11 years. The British were unsure whether he was a shrewd politician or a saint. He became a world-renowned figure, the symbol for many of India's struggle to be free. He resigned from the Indian National Congress in 1934 but still took a full part in the events and negotiations that led to Indian independence. Replying to British charges that his 'Quit India' campaign was irresponsible, given the circumstances of a world war, and would produce chaos, he replied, 'I tell the British, give us chaos. I say in other words, leave India to God.' He did much to minimise the communal tension and riots that scarred the transfer of power. Albert Einstein said at his death that future generations would scarcely be able to believe that such a one as Gandhi ever walked the earth.

PROFILE: *J. Nehru*

Jawaharlal Nehru came from a wealthy Indian family and was educated at Harrow and Cambridge University. Like many others he was outraged by the Amritsar massacre of April 1919 (when General Dyer ordered his troops to fire on an unarmed crowd, killing 379 and wounding nearly 1,000: Dyer was dismissed from the army but he was not put on trial). Thereafter Nehru became an implacable opponent of British rule, spending a total of 3,251 days in British gaols. He led the National Congress for long periods, and in 1947 he became the first Prime Minister of India, a post he held until his death in 1964.

support the war effort only if two conditions were met: important posts in the central government should be given to them; and Britain should promise to concede full self-government immediately the war was ended. When neither condition was met, Indian governments resigned in the provinces. Shortly afterwards a nationwide civil disobedience campaign was launched, designed to make Britain 'Quit India'.

PROFILE: *M. A. Jinnah*

Mohammed **Ali Jinnah** studied law in Britain in the 1890s and, though a Muslim, soon became a moderate member of the Indian National Congress, opposing separate electorates for Muslims and working hard to achieve Hindu–Muslim harmony. He was alienated by Gandhi's civil disobedience campaigns, and seemed to have given up politics altogether in 1930–35, when he lived in Britain. But he returned in 1935 as leader of the Muslim League. He contested the provincial elections under the 1935 Constitution but fared badly, winning only a quarter of reserved seats. He was willing to work alongside the Congress in provincial administration, but Nehru saw no need for cooperation – a decision for which he was later criticised. Jinnah became implacably opposed to Congress, insisting that it was seeking to establish a Hindu Raj. He seized his opportunity during the war, collaborating with Britain as the Congress withdrew support. In 1945 the Muslim League, thanks largely to Jinnah, won 90 per cent of the seats reserved for Muslims. He became Governor-General of Pakistan in 1947 but died a year later.

To the British, civil disobedience, coinciding with India's vulnerability to a Japanese attack, was further evidence that Indians were not ready for self-government. The Viceroy reported to London that he was 'engaging here in meeting by far the most serious rebellion since that of 1857, the gravity of which we have so far concealed from the world for reasons of military security. Mob violence remains rampant over large tracts of the countryside.' Over 60,000 were arrested, and the government admitted that police had killed more than 1,000. British rule had not ended, but it was in perilous danger of breaking down. This was one reason why, in 1943, an experienced soldier, Lord Wavell, was made Viceroy. The only ray of comfort was that, as the Hindus left government and moved towards implacable opposition, the Muslims, led by **Jinnah**, began to cooperate loyally.

Political initiatives failed to improve the situation. In 1942 Prime Minister Winston Churchill, who had been so thoroughly opposed even to the moderate reforms in the 1935 Constitution, was under pressure from the United States to reach an agreement with Indian nationalists. He therefore sent Stafford Cripps on a mission to India, promising self-government at the end of the war in return for Indian support in the meantime. But the proposal was turned down, perhaps because Churchill insisted on the 'Pakistan option': according to the offer, Muslims at the end of the war were to have the right to form their own separate state if they so wished. Perhaps, therefore, Churchill had wanted the deal to be rejected, in the anticipation that British rule would thereby continue. The outcome was that Muslim hopes of a separate state were boosted. While Gandhi called on the British to quit India, Jinnah began to favour the slogan 'Divide and Quit'.

The end of British rule: 1945–7

Attlee's government came to office in 1945 having pledged, in its manifesto, to give India responsible self-government. However, it was not so easy to achieve this aim. First, Attlee had to convince Indians that, at long last, Britain was about to leave. That was a difficult task. Second, he had to devise some means of leaving, and that proved almost impossible.

Sequence of events

In August 1945 a general election was held in India. Congress won a huge majority of votes among the non-Muslim communities, while the League – fighting for a separate Muslim state – also did extremely well. This deadlock meant that Attlee could not rely on Indians to devise their own constitution, for while Jinnah wanted a Pakistan, Gandhi and Nehru were adamant that the unity of India had to be preserved at all costs.

In February 1946 Attlee sent out a three-man Cabinet Mission to secure agreement on an independence constitution. When it was clear that there was still stalemate between Congress and the Muslim League, the mission put forward its own scheme, allowing Muslim provinces considerable autonomy while at the same time maintaining India as a single state. This plan won considerable support, but talks broke down over the composition of an interim government and over the possibility of future constitutional change. Jinnah returned to his call for a separate Pakistan, and in August the League, taking a leaf from the Congress book, began civil disobedience. Communal tensions between Muslim and Hindus soon reached boiling point. Violence began in Calcutta, its scale dwarfing even the Amritsar massacre. Soon there was virtual civil war in East Bengal and the Punjab. By the end of 1947 hundreds of thousands – perhaps half a million – had been killed.

Indian politics were deadlocked and confused; and, amid escalating violence, Wavell devised a plan for Britain to leave India province by province, handing over power to whichever party was in control. But Attlee decided that this would produce chaos or anarchy; and it would also blacken Britain's image in the eyes of the world. Instead, on 20 February 1947, amid an economic crisis at home, the Prime Minister announced that Britain would leave India by June 1948 at the latest. He hoped that the urgency of a time limit would focus the minds of the Indian politicians and force them to come to an agreement. At the same time, he announced that Lord Mountbatten, the King's cousin and a former Commander-in-Chief in south-east Asia, was to be the last Viceroy.

Mountbatten was an excellent choice. Not only did he add a touch of dignity to the last phase of British rule, he was also affable and friendly. He managed to establish excellent personal relations with the local politicians. (So did his wife, Edwina, who had an affair with Nehru!) But, even so, he found it very difficult to secure Congress–League agreement. Nevertheless the deadline had its effect. Very reluctantly, Gandhi and Nehru saw that the partition of India was the only solution. 'If we cut off the head,' remarked Nehru philosophically, 'we will get rid of the headache.' Attlee prepared to wield the axe, as in the cartoon by Vicky shown in Figure 20.4.

Mountbatten then brought forward the date for withdrawal to 15 August 1947, to avoid total administrative breakdown, and the final arrangements for the transfer of power were hastily improvised. Voting took place to see which provinces would join Jinnah's Pakistan, and the Punjab and Bengal were both divided. The result was that the new

Figure 20.4 *'The Partition of India': the diminutive Attlee wielded the axe decisively and quickly, but more than one stroke was needed, as Pakistan formed two discontinuous groups of provinces.*

JUDGMENT OF SOLOMON?
22nd May, 1947. Mr. Attlee is trying to find a solution to the Indian Problem.

Pakistani state comprised two groups of provinces (present-day Pakistan and Bangladesh) separated by 1,000 miles of Indian territory. Similarly, the Princely states had to opt for either India or Pakistan – with problems that rumble on to the present day in Kashmir, whose Hindu Prince ruled over a predominantly Muslim population.

Attlee had wanted to secure a defence treaty with India, to safeguard British military interests in the area. This was not achieved. But at least the final independence celebrations were dignified; and, despite the earlier antagonism, relations between Britain and both India and Pakistan were good. Both agreed to join the Commonwealth, and so wanted to maintain links with Britain. Many historians, therefore, have praised the actions of Attlee and Mountbatten. On the other hand, a slower pace of withdrawal might perhaps have led to a more orderly transfer of power and to fewer deaths, as Hindus and Muslims frantically tried to move to the Indian or Pakistani sides of a disputed border.

Conclusion

After this brief survey of events, we have to return to the issue of why the British left in 1947. Several pertinent questions have to be asked and (far more difficult!) answered.

1 *What was the significance of constitutional changes before 1939? Had British policy-makers been planning to transfer power?* The answer must surely be that they had been planning to transfer a measure of power, but only in order to reconcile Indians to further British rule. Certainly there had been no intention, before 1939, to transfer power as early as 1947. Nor was there any sign that, by 1947, British work was complete. Indeed communal tensions seemed, to some imperialists, to demand continued British rule, as did the indisputable fact that the mass of Indians were poverty-stricken. Hence it is hard to find much evidence to support the interpretation that the transfer of power marked the 'fulfilment' of British rule.

2 *How important was the Second World War?* In key respects the 1939–45 period was absolutely vital for the concession of independence:

■ British prestige slumped in Asia, as the Japanese captured colonies like Singapore, Malaya, Hong Kong and Burma.

■ Hitler's conquests and extreme racial beliefs meant that imperialism – even of the British variety – was no longer respectable. The British Empire was ideologically on the defensive, and Britain had to take account of the fact that its ally, the USA, was anti-imperialist in sentiment.

■ Britain was exhausted by its war effort: it had been drained of wealth and could no longer afford to coerce rebellious colonial citizens, certainly not on a large scale.

■ The 'Quit India' campaign had made India virtually ungovernable.

3 *Did nationalists force Britain to leave?* For a time, it looked quite possible that they might do so, and they certainly made it very difficult for imperial forces to remain. Indeed, Wavell noted in his diary on 31 December 1946 that 'we have lost nearly all power to control events', and he doubted that the police, or even the army, would remain loyal for long. The following month there were mutinies in the Royal Indian Navy in Bombay and Karachi and in the Royal Indian Air Force in Bombay. By 1947 nationalists were divided among themselves and had ceased to exert real pressure, but the omens for the continuation of the Raj looked extremely bleak.

4 *How important were economic factors?* At one time, India had been very important for the British economy; but this was no longer the case by 1947. India had long ceased to be an important market for British cotton goods. It was expensive to defend India, and famine just after the Second World War meant that Britain was expending scarce reserves on famine relief. Hence there were no compelling economic arguments against transferring power. Might continued rule of India have been perceived as an economic liability?

5 *Why did Labour leaders decide to pull out?* Traditionally, Labour had sympathised with the aspirations of Indian nationalists. This was especially true of Attlee and Stafford Cripps, and so the imperialist wing of the cabinet (led by Bevin) was overruled. But the situation also seemed to necessitate withdrawal. British rule had virtually collapsed, and the weakness of its economy meant that it did not have the strength to reimpose control, while international opinion would have been highly critical of such efforts. Furthermore, public opinion at home would have been opposed to widespread coercion. Chancellor of the Exchequer Hugh Dalton judged that not one Briton in 100,000 cared 'tuppence' about India, so long as British people were not being 'mauled about'. Attlee and Mountbatten may have played a crucial role in determining both the timing of the transfer of power and the form that it took; but the two men believed that, in pulling out, they were merely recognising the inevitable. Whether a Conservative government led by Winston Churchill would have been as realistic is, of course, another matter.

Tasks: essay questions

'The withdrawal from India in 1947 was the fulfilment of long-term British aims.' How far do you agree with this view?

Helpful hints: This is a straightforward title based on a quotation with which it is possible to disagree. Examiners often use this tactic. Remember to answer the precise question set and to do so directly – you are not asked what caused the withdrawal but to comment on a specific interpretation about that withdrawal. If your immediate reaction is to disagree with the quotation in the question, your argument will be all the stronger if you examine those aspects of British rule which *do* appear to support this interpretation – for example, dealing with the concept of trusteeship and the interwar constitutional reforms. Bear in mind that the timing of the withdrawal and the form it took (with partition) were certainly not part of any *long-term* plan.

If you think that the 'fulfilment' interpretation was of little or no importance, spend the next part of your essay explaining why: get on to the other factors that influenced events in 1947, Indian nationalism, the Second World War, etc.

Further reading

John Darwin, *Britain and Decolonisation* (Macmillan, 1988) – a perceptive account.

Brian Lapping, *End of Empire* (Collins, 1985) – provides a good narrative: if possible, you should also see the videos of the television series.

Lord Wavell, *Viceroy's Journal* (Oxford University Press, 1973).

21 Were Attlee's governments of 1945–51 really 'socialist'?

Time chart

1945: July
Labour win the general election

1946: Bank of England, coal and civil aviation nationalised
National Insurance and National Health Service Acts

1947: School-leaving age raised to 15
Nationalisation of electricity and the railways

1948: Nationalisation of gas
National Assistance Act
End of British rule in Palestine

1949: Nationalisation of iron and steel

1950: Labour narrowly win general election

1951: April
Resignation of Bevan over NHS charges
October
Labour narrowly lose general election

Labour won the 1945 general election with an overall majority of 146 seats. Thus the party had political power for the first time in its history. It also had a detailed programme of reforms and a determination to produce a new, fairer society. 'There was exhilaration among us,' Hugh Dalton, Labour's Chancellor recalled, 'joy and hope, determination and confidence. We felt exalted, dedicated, walking on air, walking with destiny.' This chapter examines the achievements of the Labour Party, between its victory in July 1945 and its defeat, by a rejuvenated Conservative Party in October 1951. We are thus concerned with the general – and perennially important – issue of change and continuity, and in particular with whether the changes Labour introduced amounted to 'socialism'. This also brings in the historiographical debate about the nature of Labour's achievement. Several historians (like Trevor Burridge and Ben Pimlott) have emphasised the degree of reform achieved by Labour, which in their view amounted to some form of socialism or social revolution; others (like Kenneth Morgan) have agreed that Labour made a big difference but have interpreted its policies in a non-socialist way; and a third group (including Paul Addison) has stressed the degree of continuity between Labour and its predecessors.

What is socialism?

First, we must define *socialism*, since without this we cannot possibly judge whether Labour introduced it or not. The only problem is that no generally accepted definition exists. The term has been used too often and by too many people with widely differing views – some deriving their inspiration from Karl Marx, some from the Sermon on the Mount, some being convinced democrats, others authoritarians, some hoping to achieve change quickly and others gradually. Hence it is only possible to identify different shades of meaning:

1 Some insist that 'socialism' means the opposite of 'capitalism'. To them, it is an entirely new form of human society. Instead of private ownership there should be public ownership of the means of production, or at least of the 'commanding heights' of the economy. In 1918 the Labour Party adopted a new constitution, containing, as Clause 4, a commitment to 'the common ownership of the Means of Production and the best obtainable system of popular administration of each industry and service'. Under public ownership, socialist cooperation would replace capitalist competition; and there would be a classless, rather than a class-based, society – one of fairness and equality, in which human beings could achieve their full potential.

2 Others, adopting a 'softer' definition, do not equate socialism primarily with economic change at all, though they often insist that a sector of the economy should be publicly owned and that government should 'manage' the economy to prevent exploitation. Nor do they stress complete equality. Instead they emphasise the importance of democracy and freedom, which by their very nature will lead to inequalities. Socialists of this school wish to see a more equal, more fair and more public-spirited society: they are thus reformist rather than revolutionary.

The first definition may be called *Marxist* and the second *Social Democratic*. These are the extremes – the poles – of a spectrum of socialist thought. In between there are many different shades of socialism. How did Labour fare between 1945 and 1951 when measured against these definitions?

Foreign and imperial policies

Little need be said about Labour's external policies, partly because it is so difficult to define the contents of a socialist foreign policy, certainly in the circumstances of 1945–51.

Presumably true socialists should, ideally, have fostered universal brotherhood. All left-wingers would have agreed on this, though not on the means of achieving it. A minority of socialists were convinced pacifists, and some believed that a socialist Britain should cooperate wholeheartedly with the Soviet Union, which had called itself socialist ever since the Bolshevik revolution of 1917. Left-wingers with this outlook were profoundly disappointed with the foreign policy adopted by Attlee's governments. In their opinion, Britain should not have opted for alliance with capitalist America, and Bevin at the Foreign Office should not have adopted such a truculent and aggressive line towards the Soviet Union.

It is easy to see what left-wing critics of the government meant. The wartime alliance of Britain, the USA and the USSR soon broke down after the defeat of Germany, and by 1951 Britain was firmly in the American (and thus capitalist) camp. (For further details of foreign policy, see pages 212–214.) On the other hand, Attlee's foreign policy can also be defended. Stalin's Soviet Union may have been socialist in rhetoric, but it was hardly so in reality, and it was perceived as a threat to the security of the West. Alliance with the United States made sense, increasing British security and thus making possible the achievement of socialism at home.

It is easier to judge Labour's imperial policies on socialist criteria. Certainly the liberation of India from colonial rule made socialist sense. Socialism, Labour spokesmen insisted, meant brotherhood regardless of race; and many were proud that, with the admission of India and Pakistan (and Ceylon in 1948), the Commonwealth ceased to be an all-white club. Yet Labour's record is, in many ways, equivocal. British forces (as we saw in chapter 20) had little choice but to leave India in 1947, while they left Palestine in 1948 unable to contain feuding between Jews and Arabs. In other colonies there was no early withdrawal, only the continuation of colonial rule. Complex situations made it virtually impossible to apply distinctly 'socialist' policies.

Domestic policies

Labour's record on socialism must stand or fall primarily by its domestic record. Despite deep-seated economic problems, stemming in particular from the legacy of war, and also a series of financial crises, Attlee's first administration (1945–50) turned out to be great reforming government – 347 Acts of Parliament were passed. But were these measures distinctly socialist and did they introduce socialism, in part or in full, into Britain? We must examine two areas of Labour's work in particular: its nationalisation measures; and its welfare reforms.

Nationalisation

In its manifesto Labour committed itself to an extensive programme of nationalisation. The following were taken into public ownership:

    1945 – the Bank of England
    1946 – coal industry and civil aviation
    1947 – public transport (railways, docks and inland waterways, and
             road haulage) and electricity
    1948 – gas
    1949 – iron and steel

Henceforth the public sector accounted for about 20 per cent of the economy. Such measures undoubtedly seem socialist, whatever definition is chosen. This was public, not private, ownership, and it gave Labour the means of creating a more equal and more just society. For instance, the government was able to improve conditions down the pits, thus lowering the appalling accident rate which had scarred interwar history (see page 48). It also meant that rural electrification (which private suppliers had not found cost-effective) could proceed apace.

However, key facts detract from the idea that the nationalisation programme was socialist. These include the following:

▓ Most of the industries taken into public ownership were public services or loss-makers. State control could therefore be justified on grounds of efficiency – indeed this is how Labour did justify its takeover. Socialist principle did not seem involved. Profitable private industry was left largely untouched.

▓ The government's administration of the industries did not involve any workers' control or participation in management decisions. Each industry was run by a public corporation dominated by people mainly of capitalist outlook and conviction. For instance, a former mine owner, Lord Hyndley, became Chairman of the new National Coal Board. The former Governor of the old private Bank of England became the new Governor of the state Bank of England. Was this the 'best obtainable system of popular administration and control' promised by Clause 4? The result was that the 'Us' and 'Them' attitude persisted, and so industrial relations were not greatly improved.

■ Large amounts, totalling £2,700 million, were paid in compensation to the previous owners. Few complaints were made by beneficiaries that the sums were too low, leading to a conclusion that they were probably too high. Certainly the nationalisation programme did not lead to any redistribution of wealth, which some (especially Marxist) socialists would have liked to see. It may well have made the rich richer.

■ As the 1940s drew to a close, many members of the government were losing faith in nationalisation. There was a fierce debate over whether to take the iron and steel industry into public ownership; and as a result the measure was pushed through hesitantly and was incomplete when Labour left office, preparing the way for privatisation under the next Conservative government.

Labour undoubtedly created a 'mixed economy' in Britain. Its Acts of nationalisation took the country closer to socialism, in the sense of state ownership of the economy, but they did so without conviction. Few expected that further measures of a similar type would follow. As a result, it was possible for Labour's critics to insist that it had merely introduced a form of 'state capitalism' rather than true socialism.

The welfare state

Labour's other great claim to being socialist lies in its programme of welfare reforms. There was no attempt here to create an equal society: the aim was the socialist (or Social Democratic) goal of achieving greater equality and social justice. The following series of measures helped to produce the welfare state:

■ 1945, the Family Allowances Act, giving a weekly allowance to the mother for each child after the first. This Act had been introduced by the 1945 caretaker government, but Labour began payments in August 1946.

■ 1946, the National Insurance Act, establishing a compulsory and comprehensive insurance scheme covering unemployment and sickness; it also provided for old age and widows' pensions and for maternity and death grants. All would pay the same, flat-rate, weekly contribution, and all would receive the same amount in benefits. Since all were insured, all could claim benefits as of right, without the need for a means test. The Act was based upon the Beveridge Report, and it came into effect in July 1948.

■ 1946, the National Health Service Act, providing medical treatment, in hospital and from a general practitioner (GP), free at the point of need. Dental and optical treatment was also included. Under this Act Britain's hospitals were nationalised, while GPs were encouraged to move from 'over-doctored' areas to regions with a shortage, thus ensuring equal provision for all (though private practice was allowed to continue). The new service came into operation in July 1948.

■ 1947, the school-leaving age was raised to 15. In addition, an Emergency Training Scheme produced an extra 25,000 teachers during the lifetime of the government.

■ 1948, the National Assistance Act, providing lump sums or weekly payments for those who, despite other legislation, had fallen below the poverty line. These benefits, not being based on insurance, were means tested.

■ The Minister of Health, Aneurin Bevan, insisted that, because of post-war shortages of materials, priority should be given to council houses, four of which should be built for every one private construction. He also laid down that council houses should be of good quality, with an average of at least 1,000 square feet (93 square metres) of space, a 25 per cent increase on interwar averages. In total just over 1 million new houses were built in 1946–51 (in addition to 16,000 'pre-fabs'), no mean achievement in view of the circumstance of the time, though fewer than were needed.

How socialist were these social reforms? Points can be made from contrasting perspectives:

Anti-socialist

■ Labour's plans were built upon the Report of Sir William Beveridge (a Liberal), and so were based upon the insurance principle. There was nothing socialist about this. After all, insurance had grown up in Britain with the growth of capitalism. Equal contributions from all, regardless of wealth, was hardly going to bring about an equal society. Some said that the insurance levy constituted an unfair poll tax: far better to pay benefits from graduated income tax.

■ The fact that all could claim benefits would aid those richer individuals who did not need help. Indeed middle-class people would perhaps prove more skilful in claiming what was now on offer.

■ The new National Health Service (NHS) did not eliminate private medicine: indeed (as an incentive to encourage the hospital consultants to participate in the new scheme) there were to be private patients (in 'pay beds') in NHS hospitals.

■ Labour may have raised the school-leaving age, but it did nothing to produce equality in education. The public school system remained, and in state education Labour accepted the 1944 Education Act, which instituted the '11 plus' exam and the division of children into grammar and secondary modern schools. Only in opposition did Labour begin to favour the more egalitarian comprehensive system.

Pro-socialist

▨ Labour did far more than merely implement Beveridge. For instance, Beveridge believed that new old age pensions should be phased in gradually, whereas Labour introduced them at once.

▨ Similarly, Bevan had to plan a National Health Service from scratch. Admittedly he had to compromise over private medicine, but this was the only way he could get the NHS up and running quickly. His socialism was practical, and he saw the need to be flexible. As it was, he had a tremendous battle with the doctors' union, the British Medical Association, before it would accept the new scheme.

▨ Only a universal insurance scheme could overcome the need for a means test. That some richer people would receive benefits was a price worth paying for this.

▨ Admittedly the scheme was based on insurance, but this made sound sense. Labour's socialism was not doctrinaire: the new ministers were practical men prepared to use whatever tools capitalist society had provided. They did not outlaw private medicine or private education, because to do so would infringe important liberties; but they were fundamentally improving the quality of life and were helping to bring about equality of opportunity in Britain.

Resignation of Bevan

A variety of contrasting verdicts can be given on Labour's socialism. Perhaps, in order to reach a definite verdict, we need to consider the closing stages of Attlee's period in office. By 1948–9, when a substantial programme of reforms had been implemented, ministers were considering a new programme to set before the electorate. Contrasting opinions were held by Herbert Morrison and **Aneurin Bevan**. Morrison believed that consolidation was now necessary: better to ensure that previous reforms were working well than to plunge headlong into further change. His aim was to win over more middle-class voters. On the other hand, Bevan wanted more changes, including further measures of nationalisation. Aiming to bring about a fundamental reorganisation in society, including a redistribution of wealth, he sought to appeal to the working classes. The two men seemed to personify different aspects of Labour's 'socialism': Bevan was a Marxist, committed to a 'hard' definition of socialism; Morrison was a socialist in the 'softer', Social Democratic sense.

PROFILE: *Aneurin Bevan*

Nye Bevan, one of 13 children, worked down the pits in South Wales, before entering local government. He became a Labour MP in 1929 and made a name for himself as one of the leading left-wingers in the party. He was expelled in 1939, for advocating cooperation with the communists but was readmitted the following year. During the war he was a leading critic of Churchill (who called him 'a squalid nuisance … the most mischievous mouth in wartime'). Many thought Attlee was taking a great risk in making him Minister of Health in 1945, but he proved a great success. He was Minister of Labour in 1951. To his supporters, he was a visionary socialist and a brilliant orator, despite a stutter. His critics thought him ambitious and irresponsible. At the 1950 election, the Conservatives made much of his statement that Tories were 'lower than vermin'. Bevan died, aged 62, in 1960.

Figure 21.2 *The extreme moderation of the majority of the Labour cabinet of June 1950*

23rd April, 1951. Mr. Bevan resigns from the Labour Government.

Figure 21.3 Vicky's comment on Bevan's resignation and its effects on the Labour government

Undoubtedly Morrison was the more representative figure in the Labour cabinet. Cummings' cartoon (Figure 21.2) – portraying the shock and anger directed against the man who dared mention Karl Marx at a 'socialist get-together' – is not entirely a caricature, especially in the circumstances of the cold war in 1950, though it does minimise the extent to which the silver-tongued Bevan could argue his case. It was Morrison who won the battle to minimise the importance of further measures of nationalisation in the 1950 election.

Further evidence of Bevan's minority position came in April 1951. At a time when defence expenditure was rising steeply, in view of the Korean War, the new Chancellor, Hugh Gaitskell, decided to introduce charges for false teeth and spectacles. Bevan believed that the socialist principle of a free health service was being compromised. He threatened to resign and, when neither Gaitskell nor the cabinet would budge, he did resign. Labour's ship of state, as in Vicky's cartoon shown in Figure 21.3, was being pulled apart – with Morrison in the larger portion. But, of course, neither side could keep afloat, and Labour duly lost the 1951 election.

Conclusion

Labour's achievements after 1945 were substantial. The National Health Service was set up, and this must surely be accounted one of the most beneficial reforms ever instituted by any government: the demand for its services in the first year (with 187 million prescriptions being written and 8 million pairs of spectacles dispensed) showed the pent-up demand for decent health care which had not been satisfied by the previous arrangements. Furthermore, a system of social security was instituted, generally without a means test; a substantial number of industries were taken into public ownership; and in addition there was full employment and no depressed areas. Poverty was substantially reduced, housing was improved and equality of opportunity undoubtedly increased.

Some historians, notably Paul Addison, have insisted that the war years were the vital period of change. By 1945 there was a consensus about future policy between the parties, which it fell to Attlee to implement. But several criticisms can be made of this perspective: there were differences between Labour and Conservative, despite a seeming identity; wartime plans, and even the Beveridge Report, did not amount to a blueprint; and there is a big difference between drawing up ideas and actually implementing them, especially at a time of economic and financial crisis.

Many historians have praised Labour's reforms. Peter Hennessy calls Attlee's government the 'most hyper-achieving peacetime administration' this century; and Kenneth Morgan believes it brought the Labour movement 'to the zenith of its achievement as a political instrument of humanitarian reform'. But should we accept the judgement that Labour was socialist in these years and that there was a social revolution?

Clearly socialism did not come about, if by socialism we mean our first definition, the Marxist version. Nye Bevan's vision of socialism was not realised. He believed that the imposition of charges in the NHS broke a vital principle. Nor was he happy that only a small portion of industry had been nationalised. Bevan had believed in the superiority of public enterprise, as opposed to private profit-making. Council houses, for instance, would be of better quality than jerry-built houses erected for a quick profit; similarly public medicine within the NHS would be superior to private medicine. Eventually, he believed, everyone would want a council house, while private medicine would wither away. Clearly this did not happen – though, in a mere five years, it could not be expected to happen.

Bevan's socialism, important for a time, was defeated. Morrison's vision, the Social Democratic variety, prevailed. But we are left with an impor-

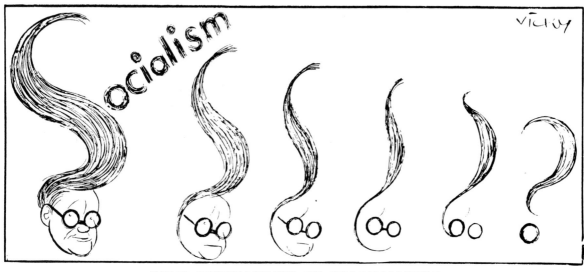

"THE INEVITABILITY OF GRADUALNESS"
—In memory of Sidney Webb.

Figure 21.4 Was Herbert
Morrison a socialist?

tant question. Was this really socialist in any meaningful sense, at least by 1950–51 when consolidation was Labour's watchword? Could Morrison, a right-wing member of a left-wing party have equally well been a left-wing member of a right-wing party? In its 1951 manifesto Labour failed to call itself socialist. Vicky's cartoon (Figure 21.4) marks a convenient end to this chapter. The question mark encourages us all to make up our own minds.

Task

The question 'How socialist were the Labour governments of 1945–51?' is one of the most discussed questions of modern British history. One reason for this is that, like many historical questions, it is also part of a debate about the present, in this case, what the present Labour Party should be like. It would be helpful to read some of the books on the reading list before building up a summary as suggested below:

1 a What definitions of socialism are there? Write at least two in your own words. Label them A, B (etc.).
  b According to your definitions, what kind of socialist was:
   i Aneurin Bevan?
   ii Herbert Morrison?
   iii Clement Attlee?

2 a Draw up two columns (or more, depending on how many definitions you have written in answer to **1a**). Label the columns A, B (etc.).

Look through this chapter and try to place all the various actions of the Labour government – in foreign policy, economic and social legislation – in the appropriate column.

b Are there any problems in carrying out task **2a**? Why do these occur? Is there confusion between what was done, how it was presented and what the Labour politicians thought they were doing?

3 What is your final conclusion to the question at the head of this chapter?

Further reading

Kevin Jefferys, *The Attlee Governments* (Addison Wesley Longman, 1992) – a good starting-point.

Robert Pearce, *Attlee's Labour Governments* (Routledge, 1994) – an 85-page essay.

Peter Hennessy, *Never Again* (Cape, 1992).

Kenneth Morgan, *Labour in Power* (Clarendon Press, 1984).

Paul Addison, *The Road to 1945* (Cape, 1975).

22 The Suez Crisis of 1956: a turning-point in British foreign policy?

Time chart

1947: National Service Act
The Truman Doctrine and Marshall Aid

1949: The North Atlantic Treaty Organisation set up

1952: Overthrow of King Farouk of Egypt

1954: October
Britain agrees to withdraw troops from the Canal Zone within 20 months
November
Nasser replaces Neguib as Egyptian leader

1955: Eden replaces Churchill as Prime Minister
USA and Great Britain agree to help finance the Aswan High Dam

1956: June
British troops withdraw from Egypt
July
Western aid for Dam is withdrawn after Nasser received Soviet weapons
29 October
Israeli forces invade Egypt
31 October
British and French bombers destroy Egyptian air force
6 November
Sea-borne invasion of Egypt; mission aborted after run on the pound

In 1882 Gladstone had invaded Egypt to safeguard the Suez Canal, in which Britain was a major shareholder, and thus ensure safe passage for British and other ships travelling to the East. The mission succeeded brilliantly, except for the fact that Gladstone was subsequently unable to withdraw. Britain remained in control of Egypt, which was in effect a British colony. In 1936 a treaty recognised Egyptian sovereignty, but still British troops remained guarding the Suez Canal. Only in 1956 did they leave, and then another Prime Minister, Anthony Eden, authorised another invasion. But this one was a failure, indeed a fiasco. This chapter examines the controversial Suez Crisis. Was it a turning-point in British foreign policy?

In order to answer this question we must put the crisis into the context of what came before and what went after. Did the events of 1956 mark a major departure from previous foreign policy? Also, did Suez produce great changes in foreign policy after 1956? If the answer to both these questions is 'Yes', then we may be certain that the crisis did indeed mark a turning-point.

Foreign policy 1945–55

Britain's status

There were several distinct features to British foreign policy after the Second World War. Perhaps the most obvious was that, despite the draining away of wealth and resources in the war, there was no fundamental reappraisal of foreign policy: successive governments were determined that Britain should remain a Great Power with worldwide influence. The Foreign Secretary, Ernest Bevin, told the House of Commons on 19 May 1947 that 'We regard ourselves as one of the Powers most vital to the peace of the world, and we still have our historic role to play'. In this year the National Service Act prepared for peacetime conscription, which continued throughout the 1950s. It was indeed unthinkable to most people that Britain would not play a leading role in world affairs.

Anti-communism

The main threat to world peace was perceived to stem from the USSR. Despite initial hopes that the wartime alliance could be continued into peacetime, British politicians soon decided that Stalin had ambitions to dominate much of Europe. These fears were confirmed in February 1948, when a communist coup took place in Czechoslovakia. No one thought of 'appeasing' Stalin: after all, such a strategy towards Hitler in the 1930s had signally failed. Hence there had to be a policy of firmness. Aggression had to be resisted whenever possible, and Britain had to remain strong militarily.

But how could Britain maintain a traditional world role, involving resistance to Soviet expansion, now that its power had diminished? The following features provide an explanation.

Truman Doctrine

Truman promised that the United States would 'support free peoples who are resisting attempted subjugation'. Such an open-ended commitment was a new departure in American foreign policy. It was followed up, a few months later, with Marshall Aid: the Americans made sizeable sums available to those countries whose impoverishment meant that they might fall prey to communism. Britain received $2.6 billion.

1 The American alliance

British politicians put a strong emphasis on what they (but not the Americans) called the 'special relationship' between Britain and the United States. Attlee's government did its utmost to prevent the Americans retreating into isolation, as they had done after 1918, so that they might lend their might to the defence of Europe against Soviet imperialism. The first success came in 1947 when President Truman stepped in to defend Greece and Turkey as British troops withdrew. The **Truman Doctrine**, issued in March 1947, was exactly what the British government wanted to hear.

The second success came with the North Atlantic Treaty Organisation (NATO) in April 1949. The United States, Canada, Britain and nine European nations agreed to regard an attack on any one of them as an attack on them all and to respond accordingly. Such a collective security pact was entirely foreign to American traditions of avoiding entangling alliances, and Ernest Bevin deserves a good deal of the credit for organising it.

British politicians and officials had done much to entice the Americans into agreeing to defend Europe. Yet alliance with the world's greatest superpower could not be an alliance between equals, and some believed that Britain was losing its independence in foreign affairs. In 1950 Attlee followed the lead of the USA by sending troops to fight in Korea, while American airfields in East Anglia meant that the British government did not have effective control over nuclear weapons on its own soil.

2 The nuclear strategy

Alliance with the United States could lead to dangerous dependency. This is one reason why the government built its own nuclear weapons. The Americans refused to share the technology, despite the fact that British scientists had done much to develop the new process during the Second World War; so Attlee's government decided to go it alone. The first British atomic bomb was successfully test-exploded in October 1951, and in 1955 the go-ahead was given for the manufacture of hydrogen bombs. Since Britain was in range of Soviet bombers, British nuclear weapons could well act as a deterrent; but they were also a relatively cheap means of ensuring that Britain's voice would be important in world affairs. In conventional forces, Britain was dwarfed by the superpowers, but nuclear weapons could perhaps bridge the gap between British aspiration and power.

3 The Empire and Commonwealth

British authority in the world could also be boosted by the Empire and Commonwealth. The days of the dependent Empire seemed numbered, especially since India and Pakistan became independent in 1947, followed the next year by Ceylon and Burma. But in its place was arising a new multiracial Commonwealth which, because of its size, population and raw materials, was potentially very powerful indeed. Leadership of the British Commonwealth might be another way for Britain to maintain a seat at the 'top table'.

4 Europe

Besides being an ally of the United States, a nuclear power, and leader of the Commonwealth, Britain was also a European nation. Moreover it was the leading nation in the Organisation for European Economic Co-operation, which was set up in 1948 to administer Marshall Aid. Thus Britain had a key role in Europe, which might further buttress its position as a major force in world affairs.

Assessment

Politicians, arrogantly assuming that the rest of the world needed wise British guidance, were determined to fight a long rearguard action to preserve Britain's status in the world, despite the decline of its wealth and economic power. A variety of policies, including the nuclear strategy, was available to shore up Britain's status as a major world player. But it was its place in various combinations of powers which would best ensure its continued importance. Winston Churchill put this well in a speech on 9 October 1948. He said that, among the free nations, he discerned three great circles: Europe, the British Commonwealth and Empire, and the English-speaking world, including the United States:

> 'These three majestic circles are co-existent and if they are linked together there is no force or combination which could overthrow them or even challenge them … We are the only country which has a great part in every one of them. We stand, in fact, at the very point of junction, and here in this Island at the centre of the seaways and perhaps of the airways also, we have the opportunity of joining them all together. If we rise to the occasion in the years that are to come it may be found that once again we hold the key to opening a safe and happy future to humanity, and will gain for ourselves gratitude and fame …'

Quoted in R. James (ed.), *Churchill Speaks* (1981).

This was a grandiose conception, showing the 'imperialist mentality' (or 'superiority complex') of so many Britons. But did the 'majestic circles' theory – and Britain's multifaceted foreign policy – make practical sense? What would happen if an issue drove a wedge between Britain and its American, Commonwealth or European supporting structures? This was exactly what the Suez Crisis did.

The Suez Crisis

Origins

Tension had been escalating for several years in Egypt, as nationalists demanded that Britain withdraw its 50,000 troops and quit the Canal Zone. Negotiations were held, but no agreement satisfactory to both sides was reached. The situation was made worse when the Egyptians came off badly in the Arab–Israeli war of 1948–9. The Egyptians and their allies had expected an easy victory when they invaded the new state of Israel; and there was a tendency to blame the British, who had left Palestine in May 1948, thus permitting the formation of Israel. Things became much worse in 1952. At the beginning of the year a clash between British troops and Egyptian police led to extensive riots in Cairo, and in June the monarch who had been tolerating the British presence, King Farouk, was overthrown by a military coup. The following year a republic was proclaimed. Yet instead of further confrontation with the British, there was, surprisingly, agreement.

Britain's Foreign Secretary, **Anthony Eden**, regarded the Middle East as of vital strategic importance, not least because of its valuable oil reserves. His strategy was based squarely on friendship with the kingdoms of Iraq and Jordan, but he was on the lookout too for other allies. If the issue of the Suez Canal could be settled amicably, then perhaps Egypt could take on this role. Hence in 1954 Eden promised to evacuate all troops from the Canal Zone by June 1956, while, in return, the Egyptian government of **Colonel Gamal Nasser** recognised Britain's right of re-entry if there were an external threat. Eden insisted on this compromise with Egypt, despite the misgivings of the Prime Minister, Winston Churchill, then aged 80, and a backbench revolt of Conservative MPs. Anglo-Egyptian relations thus seemed set fair, especially since both Eden and Nasser soon became politically more dominant. Eden took over from the ageing and ailing Churchill in 1955, while Nasser became President of Egypt in 1956. Yet in fact there was soon to be fierce confrontation.

PROFILE: *Anthony Eden*

Anthony Eden became a Conservative MP in 1923, at the age of only 26, and entered government in 1931. He served as Foreign Secretary in 1935–8, before resigning in protest against Chamberlain's foreign policy, and especially his conciliation of Italy. He gained a perhaps undeserved reputation as an opponent of appeasement. He was Foreign Secretary again in 1940–45 and seemed to be Churchill's obvious successor as Conservative leader. But it was only in April 1955 that he became Prime Minister. Some believe that, by then, his health was too poor to allow him to succeed: a gall-bladder operation in 1953 had nearly killed him and he had suffered from stomach ulcers for several decades. By 1956 he was dependent on prescribed drugs, which may have affected his judgement. Was Suez an aberration in an otherwise distinguished career, or did it reveal his fundamental inability to cope as premier? Eden resigned the premiership in 1957. He became the first Earl of Avon and lived to the age of 79.

PROFILE: *Gamal Abdel Nasser*

Born in 1918, **Gamal Nasser** trained at the Cairo Military Academy and entered Egypt's army, where he formed a secret organisation dedicated to the overthrow of the government. He engineered the coup of July 1952 which caused King Farouk to abdicate. The following year General Neguib became Prime Minister, but in 1954 Nasser accused him of seeking absolute power and replaced him. He became President of Egypt in June 1956 and so had the power to introduce far-reaching reforms, the most prestigious of which was the building of the Aswan High Dam, which was designed to use the Nile to irrigate 2 million acres (over 800,000 hectares) of land, to provide a steady supply of water and generate hydro-electricity. Money to build the dam was forthcoming from the United States, Britain and the World Bank. But Nasser had struggled for a long time against foreign control in Egypt and did not want to become a lackey of the West. In 1955 he began to buy arms from the Eastern bloc, after which American funding was cut off. The Suez Crisis made Nasser into an Arab hero, and he remained President of Egypt until his death in 1970.

The crisis

Nasser was in a very difficult situation. The ending of American aid meant that the High Dam project might have to be abandoned. But instead he seized upon an alternative source of revenue. He decided, just one month after the withdrawal of the British garrison, to nationalise the Suez Canal Company, previously in British and French hands. Existing investors would be compensated, but henceforth the canal tolls could be used to pay for the dam. A crisis had arisen in Anglo-Egyptian relations.

Eden decided that firm action had to be taken. The Prime Minister saw clear (but quite unrealistic) parallels with the 1930s: if only Hitler's ambitions had been checked in 1936, when he remilitarised the Rhineland! Nasser might well use his control of the canal to bully Britain with the threat of cutting off its trade, and hence, reasoned Eden, his thumb had to be removed from 'our windpipe'. Furthermore, if Nasser was left unpunished, British prestige in the Middle East would plummet. The United States government, whose cutting off of aid had precipitated the crisis, made it plain that it was against intervention. But Eden, who regarded the Middle East as Britain's sphere of influence, was determined to act independently: President Eisenhower might not like it, but with an election due shortly he would surely not make trouble. Secret plans were soon laid with the French and the Israelis. It was decided that Israel would invade Egypt; this would pose an obvious threat to the canal; and Britain and France would therefore have a good excuse to intervene and retake the canal. This daring strategy was not revealed to the whole cabinet, much less the House of Commons; and when Israel invaded at the end of October, Eden lied to Parliament, insisting that he had 'no foreknowledge'. The ends would justify the means – if, that is, the invasion plans worked out satisfactorily.

The failure

At first all went well. The Israeli invasion on 29 October 1956 was followed by an Anglo-French ultimatum that both sides had to cease fighting and withdraw 10 miles clear of the Canal Zone. Israel, of course, complied, and Egypt did not. Then, on 31 October, British and French bombers struck Egyptian airfields, destroying virtually the whole of the Egyptian air force.

So what went wrong? First, everything now slowed down, as the Anglo-French invasion force had to sail 900 miles from Malta for landings scheduled for 6 November. In the meantime the force of world opinion made itself felt. The debate in the House of Commons became violent, and divisions were mirrored in the country, as we can see from the

Figure 22.3 *A mass demonstration against the Suez adventure in London, November 1956. No longer was Britain seen to have moral right on her side.*

demonstrations that were held in Trafalgar Square, London, on 4 November (Figure 22.3). A portion of the population believed that Britain did not have justice on its side.

Internationally too there were outspoken criticisms at this throwback to old-fashioned imperialism. The Soviet Union condemned Britain and France – and then, under cover of the crisis, sent its tanks and troops to crush anti-Soviet demonstrations in Hungary. There seemed little to choose, some said, between Britain's actions and Soviet Russia's. Even the Commonwealth failed to back Britain, and the Indian leader Nehru was outspokenly critical. In the United Nations, only Britain's veto blocked a call from the Security Council for an immediate ceasefire. Most important of all, the United States was hostile. The British felt aggrieved at this. What about the 'special relationship' (and the strong pro-Jewish lobby in America)? But, in fact, Eisenhower, who guessed that Britain and France had colluded with the Israelis, was furious that this underhand and aggressive subterfuge had gone on without his approval. He was in no mood to rescue the Europeans, and at the start of November American pressure fuelled a run on the pound, so that 15 per cent of Britain's gold and dollar reserves quickly disappeared.

On 6 November Anglo-French forces landed in Egypt, occupying 20 miles of the canal very quickly. But the Chancellor of the Exchequer, Harold Macmillan, convinced Eden that Britain faced financial ruin, and so the mission was aborted at midnight. Eden still hoped that Britain, with troops occupying part of the canal, would be in a good bargaining position; but Eisenhower insisted on a complete withdrawal before he would give Britain, and its ailing currency, any financial support. At the end of the month the cabinet (without a sick Anthony Eden) decided to withdraw unconditionally.

Britain had suffered a humiliating defeat. Its prestige was damaged in the Middle East and throughout the world; the relationship with the United States was harmed; and, on the other side, Nasser became a hero in the Arab world. Few expected Eden to survive, and he did not, resigning in January 1957.

Conclusion

Was Suez a turning-point? First of all, there is no doubt that it represented a departure from previous policy. Admittedly the venture bore the imprint of several familiar British concerns, including its abhorrence of appeasement and determination to remain a major world power; but it ignored the vital importance of the US alliance. Nor did it show the professionalism which, on the whole, had characterised British foreign policy since the war. Indeed the affair seemed remarkably amateurish. How could Eden have expected world opinion to swallow the notion that Anglo-French forces were merely separating two warring combatants in Egypt? And why did he put at risk his pacts with Arab states, not to mention the relationship with the USA, by such a rash military venture? His Suez policy simply did not make sense. It was an aberration, a throwback to the heady days when Britannia had ruled the waves.

Yet we must also determine whether the crisis fundamentally altered the future course of British foreign policy. Suez certainly affected the British public, bringing home to them the degree to which their nation had declined since the days when the despatch of a gunboat would keep the 'natives' in order. Britain's 'self-image' would never be quite the same again. However, the political implications of the crisis should not be exaggerated. Eden may have resigned, but in 1959 the Conservatives, now under Macmillan, won a third successive general election victory. Nor was Britain's basic foreign policy strategy significantly altered.

Perhaps policy *should* have been rethought! After all, Suez seemed to show that:

- nuclear weapons were no use in a crisis
- the United States was not a reliable ally
- Commonwealth nations would not necessarily support Britain
- the European connection was of no great significance: Europe had not supported the venture, and Anglo-French relations were harmed by what the French saw as its premature ending.

Yet after 1956 Britain pursued a very familiar course in world affairs. It continued with its nuclear strategy. In 1957 the first British hydrogen bomb was exploded, and in the same year the White Paper on Defence assigned a more prominent role to nuclear weapons in defence strategy than ever before. Nor had the conception of the three interlinking circles changed. The 'special relationship' with the USA was repaired, Macmillan and President John F. Kennedy establishing a rapport. Similarly, British politicians lost no opportunity to indulge in imperial rhetoric, and the Commonwealth Prime Ministers' conferences were important ceremonial occasions. Finally, Britannia prided herself on being European, and in 1961 Britain applied to join the European Economic Community (EEC) (see chapter 28 for further details).

Politicians wanted Britain to have a finger in three pies, an arrangement requiring considerable digital dexterity. Revealingly, Britain's first application to join the EEC was turned down because, with its Commonwealth and American concerns, it was not committed enough to Europe. Was Britain, in an effort to preserve its power, diminishing its real influence in the world by failing to focus its available resources?

In short, the pre-Suez strategy was still intact. The crisis of 1956 thus had few lasting effects on British foreign policy. Suez marked a new departure but was not a turning-point.

Tasks

This chapter argues several controversial points: that the Suez venture was a departure from previous policy, that it did not affect future foreign policy substantially and, finally, that Britain's three-pronged foreign policy was not a viable one. You may accept these views, but – initially at least – you should be sceptical. This activity asks you to look at events from a different perspective. You should gain practice in arguing *against*, as well as with, the grain of what you read in a textbook. History, after all, is about reasoned argument. In the activity below make sure that you cite evidence to support the argument.

Write a list of points you would make to argue:

a That Eden's action in invading Suez was, in many ways, following a traditional policy (there is some evidence for this in this chapter).

b That the Suez Crisis did affect future British policy. (After all, there were no repetitions of Suez. The invasion of the Falkland Islands in 1982 was much better planned, and took place with American support.)

c That the overall strategy – of putting Britain's eggs in three baskets, rather than one – was sensible. Is it realistic to insist that Britain should have disengaged itself from the wider world and ceased to have Great Power pretensions?

Further reading

Alan Farmer, *Britain: Foreign and Imperial Affairs, 1939–64* (Hodder and Stoughton, 1994) – a good introduction, setting Suez into a wide context.

D. Reynolds, *Britannia Overruled* (Addison Wesley Longman, 1991) – a stimulating and scholarly account.

C. J. Bartlett, *The Special Relationship* (Addison Wesley Longman, 1992) – looks at Anglo-American relations.

Part Three   The contemporary era, 1956–79: national decline or readjustment?

23 British economic performance, 1956–79: relative decline and its causes

In this chapter we return to economic performance, a vitally important theme which has been of momentous importance in recent history. The aim is to assess how the British economy performed and to ask why it declined, not in absolute terms, but in relation to its competitors.

Chronological survey

The British economy has been undergoing relative economic decline at least since the 1880s. Some degree of decline has been inevitable, given that Britain's natural resources and population could not match those of certain rivals. By 1939 Britain stood fourth in the 'league table' of economic powers, behind the USA, Germany and the Soviet Union. Further relative decline seemed extremely likely, especially because of the Second World War, in which, according to a Treasury estimate, Britain lost about a quarter of its prewar wealth. Yet other economies, such as the German and Japanese, suffered even more, and the Labour administration of 1945–50 encouraged an export drive: the wartime slogan of 'We can take it' now became 'We can make it'. Exports grew by 77 per cent in this period, and by 1950 Britain's share of world manufactured exports stood at about 25 per cent, at least 4 per cent higher than in 1938. Nevertheless in the early 1950s there were signs that Britain's lead over its rivals was declining sharply. Things began to go wrong with the start of the Korean War in 1950: many thought that this heralded the start of a third world war, between the democratic West and the communist East, and so it was no time for timid rearmament. Britain therefore devoted more resources to military spending, with a consequent falling off of exports; and in addition the **terms of trade** began to move against Britain.

Furthermore, Europe and Japan, both in receipt of American aid, experienced a spectacular recovery from the effects of the war. Britain's lead therefore began to be whittled away, especially since the devastation in Europe and parts of Japan meant that new – and thus the latest and most productive – equipment was installed; whereas Britain still had its rela-

KEY TERM:

Terms of trade

This term means a comparison – or the ratio – between the cost of a given volume of imports and of a given volume of exports. In the 1930s manufactured goods, which Britain exported, fetched high prices on the world market, whereas raw materials, which Britain imported, tended to be relatively cheap: and therefore the **terms of trade** were in Britain's favour. But the opposite was the case in the 1950s: raw materials cost high prices, and manufactured goods fetched low ones.

tively antiquated industrial plant. There were thus advantages in starting from scratch, instead of having to muddle through with old machinery. Britain's output increased by 15 per cent in 1952–6; but France's grew by 20 per cent and West Germany's by 38 per cent.

The years 1956–64

There was continued growth during this period, and on the surface all seemed to be going well. There was a rising standard of living and an average growth rate of about 3 per cent. Moreover, unemployment was low and inflation was never higher than 5 per cent. Britain recovered remarkably quickly from the financial problems that marked the Suez Crisis (see page 219).

On the other hand, there were also problems. There was often a balance of payments deficit, and wages tended to rise faster than industrial production. This was the era of 'stop-go' when the economy lurched forward: expansion (as in 1953–5 and 1958–60) was followed by stagnation (1955–8 and 1960–62). European countries were much more economically stable. Furthermore, in 1962–3 unemployment touched 800,000, and the electorate was becoming aware that Britain's record was poor compared with that of its competitors.

The years 1964–79

Labour came to power in 1964, its leader, Harold Wilson, promising that Britain would grow strong by masterminding the 'white heat of a scientific revolution'. He aimed to increase production by a quarter in five years, and certainly statistics for consumption showed a remarkable increase. But there were immediate problems, including a large deficit on the balance of payments and a dock strike. In 1967 the pound was devalued from $2.80 to $2.40. British exports were now cheaper, and so in theory more competitive, but the trade gap widened. In 1972 the attempt to fix the value of the pound was abandoned, and it was free to 'float' in value. But this made no fundamental difference to the economy. Britain seemed to lurch from one crisis to another, so that politicians, instead of being able to follow consistent long-term policies, had to devote themselves to 'crisis management'.

One of the major problems was inflation (which jumped from 6 per cent in 1970 to 9 per cent in 1971), necessitating cutbacks in public investment and fuelling unemployment. Above all, perhaps, industrial relations were troublesome. This was certainly so for Edward Heath (Conservative Prime Minister, 1970–74). His industrial relations legislation (see page 287) met with stiff opposition from trade unions; and in 1972 more working days were lost in strikes (24 million) than in any year since the general strike of 1926. Half of this total was accounted for by a successful national miners' strike. The following year, in November 1973, the miners instituted an overtime ban in protest at the government's statutory pay policy; but Heath responded resolutely. He declared a State of Emergency, and in order to conserve coal most of industry was put on a three-day week. In February 1974, as the miners voted for an all-out strike, Heath called a snap general election on the issue 'Who governs Britain?'. Labour won a marginal victory. Heath's case for re-election was harmed by very poor trade figures and by high inflation, both of which were made much worse by a recent jump in the price of oil. War in the Middle East had led producers to restrict supplies and quadruple the price. Once again the terms of trade moved decisively against Britain.

KEY TERM:

Stagflation

The term **stagflation** was coined to describe a situation in which the economy is stagnant and yet inflation is high. In the past, inflation had been associated with times of boom, while stagnation had usually been marked by steady or falling prices. Now Britain's economic quandary seemed to break all the rules, and its very novelty made it doubly difficult to solve.

Labour was back in power from 1974, but there seemed no end in sight to Britain's economic woes. The country was suffering from **stagflation**.

Labour's first priority was to reduce inflation, which hit the unprecedented figure of 24 per cent in 1975. Sterling collapsed in 1976, and the pound fell to an all-time low against the dollar. In addition, unemployment stood at 1.5 million. With the Treasury (mistakenly) predicting a very high budget deficit, the Chancellor found it necessary to call on the International Monetary Fund for urgent loans, which were only granted on the condition that public expenditure was cut by £3,000 million over two years. This policy, together with the Social Contract (a voluntary incomes policy agreed with the Trades Union Congress) meant that inflation was brought down to 8 per cent. Finally, things seemed to be going well, and Britain was also beginning to enjoy the benefits of North Sea oil. Gas had been discovered in the North Sea in 1965, and 10 years later was supplying 90 per cent of Britain's domestic needs. Oil had been found in 1970. There was the enticing prospect of self-sufficiency in oil, and certainly Britain needed to import far less than its major rivals. The Scottish economy began to boom, with more jobs and higher wages. Aberdeen became the oil capital of the North Sea.

Yet in early 1979 the agreement with the unions broke down and there was a 'winter of discontent': 29 million working days were lost in strikes, and scenes of violent picketing were seen on television. Some ambulance drivers refused to carry patients to hospital and some local authority workers refused to bury the dead. In the spring another general election saw the return of the Conservatives, now under Margaret Thatcher.

Summary: absolute progress

It is all too easy to forget, amid the morass of economic problems, that there was any economic progress at all. In fact there was a good deal. By

1979 British industrial production was about 16 per cent higher than in 1970, 52 per cent higher than in 1960, 105 per cent higher than in 1950, and 430 per cent higher than in 1900. The postwar rate of economic growth was often higher than in the Victorian heyday.

Such progress was clearly visible in the standard of living. Surveys early in the 1970s showed that 96 per cent of British dwellings had an indoor toilet, compared with 80 per cent in 1951. Nine out of 10 homes had a vacuum cleaner, three out of four a refrigerator, two out of three a washing machine. In 1945 there had been one car on the roads for every 32 people in the population, while by 1973 the corresponding figures were one car for every four people.

Summary: relative decline

There are many illustrations of Britain's economic decline relative to its rivals. For instance, its share of world exports declined markedly, from about 25 per cent in 1950 to 16 per cent in 1960 and to 10 per cent in 1970. Also relevant is Britain's growth rate in the 1950s and 1960s, which was only about three-fifths of its rivals'. But most eloquent of all is Britain's falling position in the world's economic 'league table' of production per head of population:

    1961 – Britain was 9th
    1971 – Britain was 15th
    1978 – Britain was 18th (behind countries like Iceland and Finland)

Reasons for relative decline

How is Britain's relative decline best explained? Of course, some degree of decline, relative to its rivals, was only to be expected after 1950, but why did Britain fall so far behind rivals with similar resources?

Relative decline had been occurring for about a century before 1979, and a full explanation would involve a study not merely of the British but of the world economy. Furthermore, non-economic factors – including British politics and culture – also played a role. Therefore we should not be surprised either that the issue has spawned a massive amount of literature or that no consensus exists among commentators. In view of this, the rest of the chapter can offer no more than a brief introduction to the main explanations that have been put forward.

Industrial relations

Industrial relations in the postwar period have undoubtedly been poor.

Some regret that nothing was done to bridge the gap between management and workers, especially in the newly nationalised industries after the war (see page 202): hence 'Us' and 'Them' attitudes persisted. It was the miners who led post-1945 union militancy, just as they had in the interwar period, when the mines had been privately owned.

It can be argued that poor economic performance (and consequently low wages) caused poor industrial relations, but most commentators have argued that the frequency of strikes (the 'British disease') accelerated relative economic decline. Trade unions may have been responsible in several ways for harming industrial efficiency:

■ There were too many of them, so that a strike by one small union could paralyse a whole factory or industry.

■ Unions were often unwilling to see lower, and more realistic, manning levels. When foreign competitors were becoming increasingly efficient, overmanning in Britain, while retaining jobs in the short term, would lead to much higher redundancies in the long term.

■ There were too many 'restrictive practices' – too many petty rules about which part of a job should be done by which workers. A study of over 90 British engineering firms in 1968–74 showed that, on average, workers spent only 48 per cent of their time actually using machines. Other surveys showed that British workers had a far lower output than American or West German workers using the same equipment.

Poor management

Part of the blame for low productivity must lie with the managers, who failed to gain union acceptance of more efficient procedures. In addition, managers often paid themselves high rewards while urging restraint upon the shop-floor. Foreign observers often found that British managers had been poorly trained and were amateurish, particularly in their marketing techniques.

The politicians

Some blame should probably also attach to the politicians and their civil service advisers. They too were amateurish, and they had insufficient expertise to manage the economy properly (see pages 286–8 for a brief analysis of their policies).

Lack of investment

Many studies have shown that Britons had far inferior industrial machinery than their competitors abroad. For instance, it was estimated in 1978 that the average industrial worker in Britain was working with fixed assets worth £7,500, whereas in West Germany the corresponding figure was £23,000 and in Japan it was £30,000. Small wonder, then, that German and Japanese workers were producing so much more. According to this view, the problem was one of insufficient investment. It is not that Britons had little money to invest but that they tended to invest it abroad rather than at home.

Defence spending

Another factor was heavy British spending on defence. Some have said that there was a choice for Britain: it could try to remain a Great Power with worldwide defence commitments or it could reinvigorate its economic base, but it could not do both. Yet politicians failed to realise this. They took it for granted that Britain must maintain overseas bases, must have a nuclear deterrent and must play a full role in Western defence.

▓ Hence Britain regularly spent a higher proportion of its wealth on defence than did most of its rivals. In the 1960s Britain spent 6 per cent of its gross national product on defence, whereas the French spent 4.4 per cent, the West Germans 3.6 per cent and the Japanese only 1.1 per cent.

▓ Heavy spending abroad regularly pushed the balance of payments into the red, necessitating cutbacks in domestic investment.

▓ A large number of research scientists (40 per cent in 1956) were engaged in military projects when they might have been revitalising civilian industries.

The welfare state

Many have argued that the costs of the welfare state harmed investment in industry.

▓ Certainly spending on the National Health Service (which had reached over £5,000 million a year by 1975) was much higher than predicted. Furthermore, employers' national insurance contributions ate into company profits and acted as a disincentive for them to take on more workers.

▓ Perhaps the cushion of the welfare state encouraged a 'dole mentality' among the British people: individuals no longer had to use their initiative to meet their own needs and therefore ceased to use – or very soon to have – any initiative. The rest of society – in other words industry – supported them. But how could British industry compete effectively with this lead weight tied round its neck?

▓ According to this theory, the key period for decline was 1945–51, when the welfare state was completed. Yet other countries, whose economies outstripped Britain, often spent more on social services. Healthy and secure people often make the most productive workers. Perhaps therefore it is the low, rather than the high, level of social spending in Britain which accentuated decline.

British culture

Some have argued that an 'anti-enterprise culture' developed, conditioning Britons to despise industry. Britain was pictured as a 'green and pleasant land' rather than 'the workshop of the world', and as a result engineering and manufacturing were considered suitable careers only for those unable to enter the 'professions' (law, medicine, finance or teaching). Such a view has been criticised as vague and impressionistic, but it raises several important issues:

■ The public schools, which had originally served the children of wealthy Victorian entrepreneurs, concentrated on teaching the classics and sport. They taught their pupils to be 'gentlemanly' (so that they always 'played the game' and always lost), and thus unfitted them for the role of thrusting entrepreneurs.

■ More generally, there was a lack of top-class technical and scientific education.

■ Perhaps the 'permissive society' (see chapter 26) explains Britain's poor economic performance. The British people decided that man could not live by gross national product alone: they wanted to enjoy life, not dedicate themselves to work. Though some have deplored such an attitude, seeing it as a sign of moral decadence, others have praised it as eminently sensible.

■ The British may have been fatally complacent. After all, there were obvious signs of increasing affluence to disguise what was happening. In addition, British history (or, rather, the glorious version taught in schools) may have been partly to blame: the British expected success as, somehow, their right and did not realise, until it was too late, that they had to get their hands dirty and struggle. Was Britain too traditional a society to compete effectively? Perhaps a country less imbued with imperial traditions would have realised more quickly the advantages of joining the European Community.

Conclusion

Single-cause explanations of Britain's relative economic decline will not do: instead, we must employ different perspectives. In 1958 a British engineer who had worked in the USA judged that in America there was a general atmosphere 'that nothing is impossible and most things are worth trying'. In contrast he found in Britain 'the attitude ... that most things are impossible and not worth trying'. Here we have a fine example of why Britain was in steep relative decline. But how difficult it is to explain the attitudes and atmosphere which the engineer sensed! Was the difference created by management or unions, or both? What part was played by government policies, by levels of investment, by the social security system, by education and culture? What seems certain is that all these factors had some effect and that, moreover, they interacted with each other to create an enormously complex web of causes.

Task: essay

'Why was Britain unable to avoid economic decline in the years 1950–79?'

There is no blueprint for essay-writing, but if you are ever stumped for a plan, you might like to think about: *Define; Describe; Explain; Analyse*.

   i In this case we first have to *define* what is meant by economic decline. It was not an absolute decline, it was a relative decline.
  ii Go on to *describe* this relative decline (and absolute growth). Describe the various ways governments tried to halt this relative decline. Always make sure your descriptions relate to the question, however, which will have an analytical focus. Here, for example, you are asked to *give reasons*, or *explain causes*. Factual material about decline must relate to reasons or causes.
 iii Then *explain* why there was a relative decline. The contributory factors are dealt with in turn on pages 227–230.
  iv Finally, your conclusion should *analyse* the underlying reasons given in the explanation paragraphs. Was the problem one of attitudes: of trade unionists, business leaders, educationalists, politicians? Or were the facts of the situation against Britain: old industrial plant, the costs of two world wars, stiff competition from the newly tooled-up Germany and Japan? Were the British too slow to adjust to the rapid changes of the postwar world and its economy?

Further reading

Alan Sked, *Britain's Decline* (Blackwell, 1987) – part one of this short book provides an excellent introduction to the economy.

Andrew Gamble, *Britain in Decline* (Macmillan, 1981).

Martin Wiener, *English Culture and the Decline of the Industrial Spirit* (Cambridge University Press, 1981).

B. W. E. Alford, *British Economic Performance, 1945–75* (Macmillan, 1988).

231

24 The Commonwealth Immigrants Act of 1962: the end of unrestricted Commonwealth immigration

Time chart

1948: British Nationality Act, confirms the right of Commonwealth citizens to come and settle in Britain

1958: Riots in Nottingham and Notting Hill, in which white youths attacked West Indians

1962: Commonwealth Immigrants Act, imposes restrictions on immigration into Britain from the Commonwealth for the first time

Britain is a nation of immigrants. From prehistoric times, the British Isles have witnessed successive groups of newcomers. The most recent influx came after the Second World War, when substantial numbers of citizens arrived from the British Commonwealth, especially from the West Indies and the Indian subcontinent. They had an automatic right of entry, which had been reiterated in 1948 with the British Nationality Act. It was an important feature of British imperial propaganda that the Commonwealth was a genuinely multiracial and multicultural institution and that all citizens, of whatever race, colour or religion, could come freely to Britain, the 'Mother Country'. Yet in 1962 the traditional 'open door' policy came to an end, and restrictions were imposed. This chapter examines why the Commonwealth Immigrants Act was passed.

Afro-Asian immigration

There was a substantial non-white population in Britain before the Second World War, especially around the ports. But it was from 1948 that large numbers of West Indians began to arrive. On 22 June 1948 the *Empire Windrush*, carrying 492 Jamaicans, docked at Tilbury, Essex; in

October the *Orbita* brought 180 to Liverpool; and the following year another 253 came on the *Georgic*. In the 1950s immigrants began to arrive from India and Pakistan (see Figure 24.1).

Figure 24.1 *Numbers of Commonwealth immigrants*

Period	West Indians	Asians	Totals (including others)
1948–53	14,000	4,000	28,000
1954	11,000	1,300	18,000
1955	27,500	7,600	42,700
1956	29,800	7,600	46,850
1957	23,000	11,800	42,400
1958	15,000	10,900	29,850
1959	16,400	3,800	21,600
1960	49,650	8,400	58,050
1961	66,300	48,850	136,000
Jan.–June 1962	27,000	43,000	83,700

In total, there were perhaps 350,000 non-whites in Britain by the start of 1962, around 0.7 per cent of the population.

They came for a wide variety of reasons. These may be conveniently divided into two basic types: 'pull' and 'push'. The 'pull' factors, attracting them to Britain, were:

■ Many immigrants had a romantic, glamorised (and totally unrealistic!) image of Britain. They had been taught at school to regard Britain as the Mother Country: the British monarch was their monarch; they learned English literature and history, and so they had a natural curiosity to come here.

■ There were severe labour shortages in Britain after the war, so jobs were readily available. Recruiting campaigns were run in the West Indies to attract workers to take up employment with London Transport and the National Health Service.

There were also 'push' factors, encouraging men and women to leave the lands of their birth:

■ There were traditions of migration or emigration in both the West Indies and the subcontinent. Restrictions imposed on entry into the United States in 1952 led many to come to Britain as a second choice.

■ There were economic problems at home, often including poverty, unemployment and a high birth rate. However, typical migrants were not unemployed and had above-average skills.

■ It was the spirit of adventure and the prospect of improving the lot of themselves and their families which led them to come to Britain, the same motives which had prompted Britons to emigrate a century earlier. This similarity is brought out in the cartoon by Cummings shown in Figure 24.2 (though of course the white migrant in 1855 would have a very different status in the colonies from that of the black migrant in Britain a century later).

Figure 24.2 *The same but different: white and black migrants.*

The movement to restrict immigration

Almost as soon as large-scale immigration began, there were calls for restrictions. A variety of complaints was made against the newcomers:

■ Some said they were lazy and would not work.

■ There were complaints that they were living on national assistance ('the dole') and making undue demands upon health services – and without having made any contributions, as native-born Britons had done. Backbench Conservative MP Cyril Osborne said that immigrants were attracted to Britain by the 'honey pot' of the welfare state.

■ Others said that the immigrants, far from being lazy, were willing to work for less money and for longer hours than other workers, and so were cutting wage levels and depressing the standard of living for all.

■ It was said that the immigrants were responsible for a disproportionate amount of crime.

■ There were also complaints at the customs of the West Indians and Asians and of their unwillingness to mix.

Two vital factors made tensions between black and white worse. One was that the immigrants settled in a relatively small number of towns and cities, and only in certain districts of those areas. This was only to be expected since black immigrants were discriminated against in housing. Not only was it perfectly lawful for landlords to stipulate 'No Coloureds' or 'No Blacks', but some landlords, like the notorious Peter Rachman, charged exorbitant rents for overcrowded accommodation. The second was that white British people had been conditioned by decades of imperial propaganda – which penetrated adult and children's fiction, school textbooks, films and the media – to regard non-whites as inferior.

Racism had long been a prop of the British Empire: indeed it would probably have been impossible for Britons to rule the colonies without the belief that the 'subject races' were in some way deficient and so needed white rule. Colonial peoples had long been thought of as being lower down the evolutionary scale from Europeans: at best they were children, at worst animals. Admittedly politicians now spoke in liberal terms of multiracialism, and the old Empire was rapidly being replaced by the Commonwealth of equal states; but deep-seated attitudes could not be altered with equal rapidity. Old habits of thought died hard. Hence irrational judgements were made about the 'dark strangers'. Above all, perhaps, non-white people were stereotyped, many whites refusing to recognise the individuality of blacks. When blacks committed crimes, therefore, the entire community was suspected of criminal tendencies. If some blacks were unemployed or relied on social security, all the rest were considered to be improvident wastrels.

The 1962 Act

In 1961 the Conservative government of Harold Macmillan introduced a Bill to restrict immigration. Henceforth there would be no right of unrestricted entry for Commonwealth citizens. The dependants of those already here could enter freely, and so could students who wished to study here. But everyone else would have to apply for a voucher from the Ministry of Labour. These vouchers were to be of three types:

- an 'A' voucher would be issued to someone coming for a prearranged, specific job
- a 'B' voucher would go to someone with special skills or qualifications which were in short supply in Britain
- a 'C' voucher would be issued to other applicants, though the numbers of such vouchers would be limited year by year.

In this way, said critics of the Bill, the government would be able to cut down, or eliminate, black immigrants (the great majority of whom could only apply for a 'C' voucher), while letting in white Commonwealth citizens, from Australia, Canada and elsewhere, with 'A' or 'B' vouchers. Certainly the governments in India, Jamaica and elsewhere complained about this scheme. While not mentioning race at all, the Bill was effectively racist.

The government was proposing to make a fundamental change with this legislation, one which would alter Britain's overseas reputation, and also its self-image as the imperial metropolis. It expected a fierce debate, and it got one. Strong and impassioned arguments were put forward on both sides.

Arguments for and against restrictions

Of the arguments put forward in a wide-ranging debate in Parliament and in the country, the following were especially important.

1 Numbers

▨ Britain was already a crowded island, said the pro-restriction lobby, with one of the highest population densities in the world. How ludicrous, therefore, to have immigration laws which would allow every member of the populous Commonwealth to come to Britain! In theory, one-quarter of the entire world's population could settle here.

▨ On the other hand, the anti-lobby believed that this was not the real motivation behind the Bill. They insisted that free entry had not produced problems of overcrowding in the past and would not do so in the future. If the government was so worried about the number of entrants, why did they give permission for substantial numbers of aliens (i.e. people from outside the Commonwealth) to live in Britain? Moreover, why were they continuing to allow unrestricted entry into Britain from Eire – especially since the numbers of Irish entering often exceeded those from the Commonwealth?

2 Jobs

▨ Although the great majority of immigrants found work, there would be trouble if the economy went into recession. A voucher system, however, could regulate the inflow to match job vacancies.

▨ Labour spokesmen insisted that the relationship between jobs and numbers was self-regulating. When job vacancies were fewer, there would be fewer people entering – for the simple reason that immigrants sought work in Britain. The smaller numbers entering in 1958 and 1959 reflected a downturn in the economy. The inflated numbers of 1961 merely showed a wish to 'beat the ban' which everyone was expecting.

3 Social tensions

■ The pro-legislation spokesmen insisted that tensions between black and white were running dangerously high. This had been seen in a number of incidents, especially in the riots that had taken place during 1958 in Nottingham (where there was violence after an alleged assault on a white woman by a West Indian) and Notting Hill (where 'Teddy boys' went on the rampage attacking West Indians and attempting to burn their homes). Furthermore, on 16 May 1959 a carpenter from Antigua, Kelso Cochrane, was stabbed while walking home from hospital in Paddington: he bled to death on the pavement.

■ However, others argued that social tensions were not excessive and that the way to deal with violence was not to penalise the victims but to punish the wrongdoers with the full force of the law. Judge Salmon was quite right, they said, to sentence nine white youths to four years' imprisonment after the Notting Hill outrages and to insist that justice must be colour-blind. In the cartoon shown in Figure 24.3 Vicky mocks the pretensions of the white hooligans to any cultural superiority over black immigrants. The implication is that such mindless chauvinism and hooliganism should not be allowed to determine immigration policy.

4 Social services

■ Some said that the immigrants were making unreasonable demands on the welfare state. After all, they had made no contributions to welfare funds.

■ Others said this was a prejudiced view. There was no evidence that immigrants were making undue demands. Indeed, as doctors, nurses and auxiliaries, they were helping to run the health services. In addition, immigrants, as colonial citizens, had made a contribution: Britain's wealth stemmed in no small measure from the exploitation of its colonies, while the part played by the Empire in producing victory in the Second World War ought not be forgotten.

5 Housing

■ Immigrants were criticised for concentrating in particular areas of a small number of towns. Moreover they were responsible for overcrowding and for producing slums; and when these slums were declared unfit for human habitation, the immigrants had to be

NOTTING HILL

"THEY JUST AIN'T CIVILISED—LIKE WE ARE . . . !"

Figure 24.3 'Teddy boys' in Notting Hill, London: racism was no longer respectable.

rehoused by the local council. Small wonder, then, that white Britons accused them of 'queue-jumping' council-house waiting lists.

■ The contrary viewpoint was that immigrants had to accept whatever housing they could get. They were forced into slums, and were not rehoused as often as they should have been. The answer to the problem of poor housing was to build more and better houses, not to make scapegoats of immigrants.

6 Racial prejudice

■ Although some of those who favoured restrictions hotly denied any racial prejudice, others, like Cyril Osborne, openly said that they did not want Britain to become a 'chocolate-coloured' society. They wanted to keep Britain white. Many (while insisting that, of course, they themselves were free from the taint of prejudice) admitted that other people were prejudiced. What, they insisted, was the point of denying this? Most people were prejudiced, and commonsense demanded recognition of this important fact. There was not a single example of a harmonious multiracial society anywhere in the world, certainly not in the United States, South Africa or Central Africa, where well-publicised problems existed. Why should Britain needlessly introduce racial problems?

■ The other side believed that racial prejudice was an evil which should not be pandered to and thereby encouraged. It was a sign of immaturity, bred from ignorance: people would grow out of it in time, once they realised that non-whites were not fundamentally different from themselves. A truly multicultural society was to be welcomed: it would add a refreshing variety to the traditional British way of life.

7 *The Commonwealth*

■ Many believed that the Commonwealth was essentially part of Britain's past. More important for the future was the European Economic Community, and the 'special relationship' with the United States. Above all, the notion of Britain as the 'Mother Country' was sentimental nonsense: perhaps there were close ties with the old (all-white) Commonwealth, but there could not be the same close affinities with the new Commonwealth (including Africa, India and the West Indies). Since the Commonwealth was a collection of equals, why should Britain, alone of Commonwealth nations, allow free entry? The very idea was imperialistic, smacking of a bygone age.

■ But opponents were profoundly worried by the effects which restrictions would have on the future of the Commonwealth, which they saw as a vital institution in world affairs and a beacon of multiracial light. Britain was proposing not just to restrict immigration but to cut back especially on black immigration: after this, how could anyone take seriously British professions of multiracialism? The Commonwealth would be dealt a severe blow.

The arguments were wide-ranging in 1961. Most commentators in the press judged that the opposition had the best of the tussle and that the Commonwealth Bill was indeed racist. But the government had two aces. The first was the fact that public opinion polls revealed substantial support, as high as 90 per cent, for restrictions. The second was that the Conservatives had a clear majority in Parliament. Hence the Bill became law in 1962.

The Government's motives

Government records make clear beyond a shadow of doubt that, in restricting immigration from the Commonwealth, ministers were concerned primarily with black immigration. Hence it was not the number of immigrants that was their primary concern, but their race. The politicians had been dismayed by the number of Afro-Asian immigrants arriving in the late 1940s, and from the early 1950s officials had been warily monitoring the situation. In fact, a Bill to restrict entry had been debated in cabinet in the mid-1950s, but had been thrown out because of ministerial deadlock. Some ministers had wanted immediate restrictions, and in particular Lord Salisbury (Lord President of the Council, 1951–7) was anxious about the effects of intermarriage on British racial stock. But other ministers had opposed restrictions, arguing that the furore abroad would make their jobs impossible. In particular, the Colonial Secretary, Alan Lennox-Boyd, would not have been able to form a West Indies Federation if the 'open door' were closed. Ministers were aware that legislation, however drafted, would appear racist, and they were not prepared to face the criticisms that would ensue.

What had changed by 1961? First of all, enthusiasm for the Commonwealth had begun to ebb. In addition, problems for the Colonial Secretary had lessened. The delicate negotiations needed to form a West Indian Federation were over – in fact, the Federation was well on the way to being scrapped as a failure! In addition, the riots of 1958, while making immediate legislation politically impossible, convinced several ministers that restrictions would have to come soon. Also, the riots made immigration a major media item. In the 1950s the Conservatives had been uncertain how the public would react to the end of the 'open door': now they knew it would be welcomed. There was another justification too. Press speculation fuelled a movement by immigrants to 'beat the ban' and make the passage to Britain while it was still possible to do so – and the increased number of arrivals provided further ammunition in favour of restrictions. Labour's leader, Hugh Gaitskell, promised to revoke the law, but such a commitment would not harm the Conservatives at the next election and might well rebound to their advantage. The new law would be branded as racist, but now the government was confident that it could ride out the expected storm of disapproval.

Hence we can see that there are many reasons to explain the Immigration Act of 1962. But the legislation was not the end of the controversy over immigration, as we shall see in the next chapter.

Tasks

a List as many reasons as you can for the restrictions imposed on Commonwealth immigration in 1962.

b Now try to classify each reason. Mark the 'preconditions', those longer-term causes without which the legislation would not have come about, L; the 'precipitants', the medium-term factors or events which made some form of restrictions extremely likely, M; the 'triggers', the short-term factors which determined the timing of the new law, S.

c Which do you think were most important – L reasons, M reasons or S reasons? Justify your decision, commenting on all three types of reason.

Further reading

Dilip Hiro, *Black British, White British* (Eyre & Spottiswoode, 1971) – wide ranging.

Colin Holmes, *John Bull's Island* (Macmillan, 1988) – an excellent textbook.

Edward Pilkington, *Beyond the Mother Country: West Indians and the Notting Hill White Riots* (I. B. Tauris, 1988) – very valuable for its use of oral testimony.

25 Race and politics in Britain, 1962–71

Time chart

1960: Formation of the Birmingham Immigration Control Association

1962: Commonwealth Immigrants Act

1964: October
Labour returns to power at the general election, but Patrick Gordon Walker defeated after a racist campaign in Smethwick

1965: January
Gordon Walker defeated in a by-election at Leyton
Race Relations Act, banning discrimination in public places

1968: February
Kenyan Asian crisis produces an emergency Commonwealth Immigrants Act
Race Relations Act bans discrimination in employment, housing and financial services
Enoch Powell's speeches on immigration in Walsall (February), Birmingham (April) and Eastbourne (November)

1971: Immigration Act, stopping all 'primary' immigration

The Commonwealth Immigrants Act of 1962 might have been expected to remove immigration from the political agenda. The government could now limit the numbers of Commonwealth citizens entering the country, thus removing one source of controversy. In addition, the Labour Party decided to accept the measure. Hugh Gaitskell, who had called the Act 'miserable, shameful and shabby', died in January 1963 and was succeeded by the more pragmatic Harold Wilson. The new leader believed that if limitations on the numbers of Afro-Asians entering were combined with a law against racial discrimination, the result would be a lessening of tensions. Roy Hattersley summed up this policy with the slogan 'Integration without control is impossible. Control without integration is indefensible.' But in fact immigration became a highly contentious issue, and in 1968 racial issues hit the political headlines when Enoch Powell made the most widely reported and debated speeches of postwar British history. This chapter examines the important theme of race and politics.

Labour's 'liberal hour'

Labour supporters hoped that the new government would inaugurate a new era of racial harmony. Hopes were pinned especially on Roy Jenkins (Home Secretary, 1965–7), who responded by insisting that black immigrants could not be expected to conform to the customs and traditions of white Britons. He wanted the immigrants to 'integrate' with whites, so that there would be a united nation, but he defined 'integration'

> *'not as a flattening process of assimilation, but as equal opportunity, accompanied by cultural diversity, in an atmosphere of tolerance'.*

To foster the all-important ingredient of tolerance he introduced legislation.

1965 Race Relations Act

Labour backbenchers had long been calling for legislation to curb racial discrimination. The Conservatives had argued that it was impossible to make people unprejudiced by Act of Parliament, but Labour insisted that government should make known its disapproval of prejudice and that, in certain instances, discrimination could be outlawed. In 1965 a Race Relations Act made it illegal to discriminate on grounds of race in public places (such as cafés, dance halls, hotels and cinemas). Two new bodies were also set up: the Race Relations Board, to handle complaints arising under the Act, and the National Committee for Commonwealth Immigrants (headed by the Archbishop of Canterbury), to promote contacts between the races in Britain.

Many were disappointed because the Act lacked strength and scope. It lacked teeth because a Conservative amendment had been accepted, making discrimination in public places merely a 'civil misdemeanour' rather than a criminal offence. Its extent was limited because it did not include discrimination in the key areas of employment and housing. In its defence, the government pleaded the lack of a workable overall majority and a dearth of concrete evidence of discrimination in the fields of jobs and homes. However, in 1966 another general election increased Labour's majority from five to almost 100, and in April 1967 an authoritative report made clear the extent to which racial discrimination was still occurring.

The PEP Report

The Race Relations Board and the National Committee for Common-wealth Immigrants had jointly commissioned Political and Economic Planning (PEP) to investigate discrimination. Its report showed, as one of the investigators put it, 'that in Britain today discrimination against coloured members of the population operates in many fields not covered by the existing legislation and that it operates on a substantial scale'.

The investigation was held in six areas of the country and involved not only questionnaires and interviews but 'situation tests'. A white Briton and a West Indian (with equivalent qualifications and needs) applied for the same job or the same flat – and so did a Hungarian, in order to test whether discrimination was caused by 'foreignness' rather than colour. The results were clear-cut. The Hungarian was treated unfairly, but not nearly so often as the West Indian. In housing the discrimination was particularly blatant because applications were limited to the minority of landlords who did not stipulate in advance 'No Coloureds' or 'Europeans Only'. Even so, the West Indian was turned away, sometimes politely and sometimes very impolitely, on two-thirds of the occasions when the white man was welcomed. Non-whites were also liable to be charged higher mortgage rates.

1968 Race Relations Act

Labour now went further than in 1965 and introduced a Bill to outlaw discrimination in housing, employment, the provision of goods and ser-vices, in trade unions and in advertising. It was to be enforced by the Race Relations Board; but again the legislation lacked teeth. First the Board would investigate a complaint, and – if it were satisfied that dis-crimination had occurred – would then set up conciliation procedures: only if the offender refused to undertake to desist from discriminatory behaviour could he or she be taken to the county court. During the first year of the new Act, only one offender was actually put on trial.

The failure of Labour's formula

Despite the two Race Relations Acts, Labour failed to bring about improved race relations. Why was this?

■ Some would say that the two Acts were not rigorous enough, others that they were impractical. Certainly it was extremely difficult to prove discrimination in real life (as opposed to 'situation tests').

■ Perhaps Labour's formula for better race relations, limiting the number of new entrants and at the same time forbidding overt discrimination against those already here, ignored human psychology.

By limiting the numbers entering, the government was branding Afro-Asians as undesirable. How would this encourage whites to integrate with blacks, or blacks with whites?

■ There were three further factors, as we shall see in the next section of this chapter: the electoral advantage that could be secured by playing the racial card, the Kenyan Asian crisis, and the intervention of Enoch Powell.

Race and politics

Smethwick

At the 1964 general election there was a national swing to Labour of 3.5 per cent. Yet in the West Midlands constituency of Smethwick there was a swing to the Conservatives of 7.2 per cent, and Labour's Patrick Gordon Walker, the shadow Foreign Secretary, lost the seat he had held since 1945. What was significant was the reason for the defeat – racial animosity.

Over the preceding years Gordon Walker (Secretary of State for Commonwealth Relations in 1950–51) had become Labour's leading expert on the Commonwealth. In 1961 he had led the attack on the Immigration Bill, insisting that the traditional 'open door' policy should be maintained. But his viewpoint was particularly unpopular in the Birmingham area, where an Immigration Control Association had been formed in December 1960. Its Secretary insisted that Britain was becoming 'the refuse heap of the world for the unskilled, the criminal, and the layabout'. People with this outlook deplored opposition to restrictions and, after the Bill had become law, insisted that it did not go far enough, especially because dependants were still allowed entry.

In his election campaign, Gordon Walker emphasised that the problems of Smethwick stemmed from inadequate housing and 'get-rich-quick' landlords who were exploiting immigrants; but his meetings were often interrupted, and he was a target for racial abuse. It was said that he had sold his house in Smethwick to West Indians; his wife was said to be black; his daughters had married black men; he was arranging for leper hospitals to be built in the town. Smethwick had succeeded Notting Hill as the focus for racial confrontation.

The Conservative candidate, Peter Griffiths, used very different tactics from Gordon Walker. He called for a complete ban on further black immigration and for the repatriation of those who had been unemployed for six months. Gangs of children were organised to parade the streets shouting: 'If you want a nigger neighbour, vote Labour.' Griffiths refused to condemn the words, insisting that they were a manifestation of popular feeling which democrats ought to take seriously.

When Griffiths took his seat in the Commons, he was condemned by Harold Wilson as a 'parliamentary leper'. Even so, his tactics had reversed the national trend against his party. Clearly the 1962 Act had not taken immigration out of politics, and there were votes to be won by playing the racial card. It was a lesson underlined in January 1965 when Gordon Walker lost a by-election in the seemingly safe Labour seat of Leyton. There were many reasons for his defeat, and the Conservative candidate refused to exploit race. Yet immigration was an issue nevertheless. Gordon Walker's meetings were interrupted with flour-bombs and calls of 'Send the blacks back' from racist demonstrators. Race may have made the difference between success and failure in a close contest. Who, henceforth, could afford to ignore the wishes of a large sector of voters?

The Kenyan Asians

There had long been friction between the African majority in Kenya and the more prosperous minority of Asian settlers. It seemed possible that the Asians might be expelled at independence, in December 1963, and so the British government agreed to offer British passports to Asian (and white British) residents. Soon, as predicted, the Kenyan government began to discriminate against Asians, and particularly those who had not accepted Kenyan passports. Many lost even their homes, and it is not surprising, therefore, that many decided to come to Britain. In the period from December 1967 to February 1968, 7,000 entered. Conservative right-wingers Duncan Sandys and Enoch Powell called for restrictions, and party leader Edward Heath warned of 'serious social consequences' if many more came. The *Daily Mirror* insisted that Britain 'now faces the prospect of an uncontrolled flood of Asian immigrants'. In total, perhaps another 80,000 had a legal entitlement to enter.

At this stage, the Conservative shadow cabinet formulated a new policy towards immigration. Tories wished to see the tightening of existing controls, the return of illegal immigrants, financial help for those immigrants who wished to return home; and they judged that Asian passport-holders from Kenya should be allowed to enter gradually, not all at once.

On 23 February 1968, the Labour government introduced an emergency Commonwealth Immigrants Bill, which was rushed through both Houses of Parliament and became law on 1 March. The government insisted that it was 'extremely reluctant' to interfere with the rights of British passport-holders to enter the country but that, in this case, it had to do so. Otherwise, the strain on social services would be too great. Hence only those passport-holders with 'substantial connections' with Great Britain – by virtue of their birth, or their father's or grandfather's – were to be admitted; and an extra 1,500 vouchers were to be made available for their use. Labour ministers had thus gone further than the Conservatives had demanded. There was no mention of race or colour here (any more than there had been in the 1962 Commonwealth Immigrants Act), but a clear distinction was nevertheless being made between British and Asian settlers wishing to leave Kenya.

Supporters of the measure believed that the government had taken regrettable but necessary action. Otherwise the furore over race and immigration was likely to continue, perhaps fuelling support for the National Front, an extreme right-wing group set up in 1967. As it was, opinion polls showed that the great majority of British people supported the government's action. Opponents, however, were disgusted that Labour had rushed such an overtly discriminatory Bill through Parliament. It seemed a case of the racist tail wagging the parliamentary dog.

Enoch Powell's speeches

While the Kenyan Asian issue was still raging, **Enoch Powell** made his first controversial contribution to race relations in Britain. He spoke at Walsall in February 1968, arguing that the annual admission of '40,000 or 50,000 actual or alleged dependants' was straining education provision, and he pointed in evidence to the daughter of a constituent who was the only white child in her class at school. That a wholly avoidable problem should now be magnified by the admission of large numbers of Kenyan Asians was, he averred, enough to drive one to despair.

The speech caused a stir. It also led to a search for the single white child. In fact, it turned out that there was no class in Wolverhampton which contained only one white child, though there had been a class which, through various circumstances, had contained a solitary white girl on one day. But it was his next speech, at Birmingham in April 1968, which created a sensation.

In his second speech Powell argued that the function of statesmanship was to provide against preventable evils – and that he could see storm clouds brewing for Britain because of the admission of immigrants. In 15 or 20 years, he insisted, maximising the totals, there would be 3.5 million Commonwealth immigrants and their descendants in Britain, and by the year 2000 there would be 5–7 million, one-tenth of the whole population, occupying whole towns and districts of towns. He also told the story

PROFILE: *J. Enoch Powell*

John Enoch Powell had a very successful academic career, at King Edward's School in Birmingham and Trinity College, Cambridge. He became Professor of Greek at the University of Sydney at the age of 25. He resigned to join the armed forces as a private when war was declared, and by 1944 he was the youngest brigadier, at 32, in the British army. After several years in the Conservative Research Department, he became Conservative MP for Wolverhampton South-West in 1950, holding the seat until 1974. From 1955 he served as Under-Secretary at the Department of Housing and then as Financial Secretary to the Treasury. He was Minister of Health in 1960–63 and Conservative spokesman on defence in 1965–8. He had a reputation for being a man of principle, resigning in 1958 in protest at what he considered to be inflationary financial policies. Though no time-server, he was certainly ambitious, and in 1965 he contested the leadership of the Conservative Party, coming a poor third behind Heath and Maudling. A loner in politics and exceptionally hard-working, Powell was not an easy colleague or companionable figure. Harold Macmillan moved him from the cabinet seat usually occupied by the Minister of Health because 'I can't bear those mad eyes staring at me'!

Powell was a man of strong convictions. At one time an ardent imperialist, he ended up an equally ardent anti-Commonwealth figure. He believed that taxation and expenditure should be kept low and that market economics would work best with minimum government interference. Some believe that the driving force in him was a romantic nationalism: this may explain his speeches on immigration, his opposition to the European Community and his position as a Unionist MP for South Down from 1974 to 1987.

of falling into conversation with a middle-aged man who worked for a nationalised industry:

> 'After a sentence or two about the weather, he suddenly said: "If I had the money to go, I wouldn't stay in this country." I made some ... reply, to the effect that even this government wouldn't last for ever; but he took no notice and continued: "I have three children, all of them married now, with family. I shan't be satisfied till I have seen them all settled overseas. In this country in fifteen or twenty years' time the black man will have the whip-hand over the white man."

I can already hear the chorus of execration [condemnation]. *How dare I say such a horrible thing? How dare I stir up trouble and inflame feelings by repeating such a conversation? The answer is that I do not have the right not to do so. Here is a decent, ordinary fellow-Englishman, who in broad daylight in my own town says to me, his Member of Parliament, that this country will not be worth living in for his children. I simply do not have the right to shrug my shoulders and think about something else. What he is saying, thousands and hundreds of thousands are saying and thinking – not throughout Great Britain, perhaps, but in the areas that are already undergoing the total transformation to which there is no parallel in a thousand years of English history.'*

Quoted in Bill Smithies and Peter Fiddick (eds), *Enoch Powell on Immigration* (1969).

Powell then relayed the story of a respectable street in Wolverhampton where, eight years before, a house was sold to a black person. Soon there was noise and confusion. The white residents moved out, leaving a single white woman, a widow and old age pensioner, whose husband and sons had been killed in the war. This woman was soon subjected to abuse from her black neighbours, who wished to buy her house and turn it into flats. Her windows were broken and excreta was pushed through her letter box. To cap it all, the woman wondered whether, due to her refusal to rent rooms to non-whites, she would be sent to prison under the new Race Relations Bill.

The answer to such problems, Powell insisted, was Conservative immigration policy: 'stopping, or virtually stopping, further inflow, and . . . promoting the maximum outflow'. But unless such statesmanlike action were taken now, there would be insuperable difficulties:

'Whom the gods wish to destroy they first make mad. We must be mad, literally mad, as a nation to be permitting the annual inflow of some 50,000 dependants . . . It is like watching a nation busily engaged in heaping up its own funeral pyre . . . As I look ahead, I am filled with foreboding. Like the Roman, I seem to see "the River Tiber foaming with much blood" . . . Only resolute and urgent action will avert it even now. Whether there will be the public will to demand and obtain that action, I do not know. All I know is that to see, and not to speak, would be the great betrayal.'

The speech produced intense interest and anger. Many immigrants felt insulted and believed that their time here might be limited. The press had a field-day, publicising the speech, debating its ideas and trying – in vain – to locate the pathetic old lady being victimised by her neighbours. (No one ever did find her; and Powell admitted that he had never met her.) Almost all newspapers condemned the speech, and so did almost all politicians. Indeed Heath sacked Powell from the shadow cabinet for the inflammatory tone of his remarks, which seemed calculated to inflame the situation and bring about the very eventualities he professed to deplore. There is no doubt that it was a rabble-rousing speech, despite the classical allusions. Powell received tens of thousands of letters of support; immigration officers at Heathrow made known their agreement with his views; and London dockers marched through the streets in protest at his dismissal. Furthermore, opinion polls showed support for him varying between 67 and 82 per cent.

Powell's motives for making the speech are not easy to assess. Was he being statesmanlike, voicing far-sighted views regardless of the cost to himself? Was he merely doing his duty as a constituency MP? Was he making a populist bid for power? Was he simply showing racial prejudice, and therefore sowing the seeds of hate, as in the cartoon shown in Figure 25.2.

Figure 25.2 Liberals were critical of Powell's speeches on race. Here he is depicted as sowing seeds which would produce a British Ku Klux Klan. The caption to the cartoon was: 'Where the seeds of the whirlwind have been sown, scarcely more than the first blades are yet above the surface.' (Enoch Powell)

It is much easier to decide the consequences of the speeches. Powell undoubtedly harmed his own career, especially because he was unrepentant. At Eastbourne in November he made another inflammatory speech, retelling stories of anti-social behaviour by black against white which he insisted were typical, and warning that time was running out for 'England's green and pleasant land'. He was never to hold another ministerial office. Yet once again the message for mainstream politicians was glaringly obvious: immigration could rouse the emotions of the public as no other topic, and the electors expected a further tightening of immigration controls. In 1970 the Conservatives were back in office, with Powell on the backbenches, and the following year they passed a new Immigration Act. This virtually ended all fresh immigration for settlement. Henceforth new arrivals were limited to the spouses or dependants of those already living here and to those who had a parent or grandparent born in the United Kingdom.

Tasks

1 Read carefully the extracts from Powell's speech of 20 April 1968 on pages 248–9 and answer the following questions:

   a Why do you think Powell was relaying the words used by his middle-aged constituent?

   b Why do you think that he so often told these anecdotes about other people?

   c Can you think of any change in British history comparable to the 'transformation' being brought about in areas where immigrants lived and worked?

   d Why do you think Powell used the image of a nation 'heaping up its own funeral pyre'?

   e What image of himself do you think Powell was trying to create by this speech?

2 a Study the cartoon by Garland (Figure 25.2). What message was the cartoonist trying to put across about Powell and his proposed policies?

   b What do you think Powell meant by 'the seeds of the whirlwind'?

3 Using the information in the **profile** of Powell on page 248, and any other information, explain what you think his motives were in making these speeches in 1968.

Further reading

Patrick Cosgrave, *The Lives of Enoch Powell* (Bodley Head, 1989).

Robert Pearce (ed.), *Patrick Gordon Walker: Political Diaries, 1932–1971* (The Historians' Press, 1991).

See also the books listed in further reading at the end of chapter 24.

26 The 'Swinging Sixties': changing moral standards

Changes in attitudes and behaviour were so great in the 1960s that, according to the journalist Bernard Levin, the decade 'saw an old world die and a new one come to birth'. Many people now look back on the 'Swinging Sixties' with a certain awe, as a time of unparalleled creativity, personal fulfilment and freedom. They applaud the fact that puritanical and hypocritical Victorian morality finally came to an end and that people had the courage to seek to change what was wrong in society. For these, it was the best of times. For others, however, it was the worst of times: they deplore what they see as the licence, self-indulgence and sheer mindlessness of the decade. This chapter examines the degree to which moral standards did alter and asks how the 1960s should be interpreted by the historian – as progress, as decadence or, simply, as value-free 'change'.

Preconditions

Commentators are too prone to characterise decades with a simple label: the 'Naughty Nineties', for instance, or the 'Roaring Twenties' and 'Hungry Thirties'. Such phrases can give only a simplistic, stereotyped view. Also, the characteristics associated with a decade generally have their roots in the preceding period. This is certainly true of the Sixties.

Many features of the 1950s prefigured the Sixties. These include the following:

■ The 'age of austerity' and rationing ended in the early 1950s. The 'age of affluence' had arrived, with steady economic growth and a higher standard of living. When Macmillan told the British people that they had 'never had it so good' in 1957, he was disguising important economic problems, but he was also stating a truth. He added that what had been the luxuries of the rich were now becoming the 'necessities of the poor'. As in the cartoon in Figure 26.1, his allies in the 1959 election were cars, television sets, washing machines and refrigerators. Some said that society was becoming far more materialistic. It was also becoming more hedonistic, and this search for pleasure included state-approved gambling. In 1956, to the dismay of the churches, Premium Bonds went on sale.

'Well, gentlemen, I think we all fought a good fight . . .'

Figure 26.1 *The 1959 general election: the Conservatives' allies in the affluent consumer society. The caption reads: 'Well, gentlemen, I think we all fought a good fight . . .'.*

■ The 'baby boom' of the postwar period meant that there were more teenagers than ever before in Britain. A 'youth culture' was created, due to the fact that school-leavers found it easy to get jobs. It has been calculated that in 1959 teenagers had £830 million to spend; and most of this went on buying records and record-players. This was an important period for the music industry. For the first time, in the 1950s, the 'top twenty' best-selling records were listed in the music papers. Small groups of five or six became more popular than orchestras of 20, and music – especially rock 'n' roll – began to be written just for the young. Bill Haley's film 'Rock Around the Clock' (1956) was regarded as a landmark: it was banned in some cinemas because its heady combination of pulsing music and dancing caused otherwise sane youths to lose control of themselves and begin tearing up cinema seats.

■ There was greater violence and dissent in society, the former being particularly associated with gangs of youths known as 'Teddy boys' (from their American version of Edwardian dress). There was also a greater use of drugs – especially cannabis – and in society as a whole,

253

but especially in the 14–21 age range, there was a greater incidence of crime. At the opposite end of the spectrum, however, there was a determination to prevent war and especially to avert a nuclear disaster. In 1958 the Campaign for Nuclear Disarmament (CND) was formed, organising well-publicised protest marches. People also voiced extensive criticisms of society. The mid-1950s saw the cult of the 'angry young man', who (like Jimmy Porter in John Osborne's famous play *Look Back in Anger*), while uncertain how to improve society, was perfectly clear about present ills.

■ There was now greater sexual realism in the arts, and in 1959 a new Obscene Publications Act was designed to stop the prosecution of reputable books, like D. H. Lawrence's *Lady Chatterley's Lover*, for obscenity. (Yet, paradoxically, the Director of Public Prosecution invoked the new law first against Penguin Books – for publishing *Lady Chatterley*! The prosecuting counsel handled the case badly – even asking whether the book was suitable for wives or servants to read – and the publishers were acquitted.) There was also a greater use of contraception, so that the number of children per family averaged 2.3 in the decade. Divorce was also becoming more common. Furthermore, Private Members Bills were introduced in 1953 and 1960 to make abortion easier to obtain: they failed to become law, but the topic was at least being debated more than ever before. Society seemed to be becoming more liberal in its attitudes. Similarly, in 1957 the Homicide Act abolished the death penalty except for murderers who killed police officers, who used firearms or who killed while committing burglary.

In retrospect, the 1950s seem an important decade of transition, combining both old and new: some lived mentally in the era of the British Empire and the 'stiff upper lip', while others called for change, and the faster the better.

The Sixties: social trends

In the 1960s Britain's economy continued to decline relative to its rivals; but unemployment remained low, rarely above 0.5 million, and affluence grew, with shorter hours of work and a steadily rising standard of living for most people. By the end of the 1960s around 8 out of 10 households had a television set (and some had new colour models), and a quarter of all spare time was spent watching. The number of cars on the road, which had doubled in the 1950s, doubled again in the Sixties. Another continuing trend was the high proportion of young people in the population. Youths not only had important spending power within the economy, they also received more education than ever before. Following the Robbins Report of 1963, there was an expansion of higher education. Many new universities were founded, including Sussex, Essex, York, Norwich, Warwick, Kent, Lancaster and Stirling, as well as 30 new polytechnics. Young people had never had it so good, but neither had they ever complained so much. There was in the Sixties a decline in deference and, generally, in respect for authority.

The Sixties: new legislation

Acts of Parliament did not create a new social culture in the 1960s but they reflected, and to some degree reinforced, the new ideas and values coming to the fore. Among the most important new statutes are:

- 1960, the Betting and Gaming Act legalised off-course betting and led to the rapid growth of betting shops, casinos and bingo halls.

- 1965, the death penalty was abolished for all types of murder.

- 1967, the Abortion Act made the termination of pregnancies of up to 28 weeks legal on four grounds: where continued pregnancy could harm the physical or mental health of the mother; where there was a possibility of a baby being deformed; where the mother had been raped; and where the baby would be born into undesirable conditions. By 1980 1 million legal abortions had been performed.

- 1967, the Sexual Offences Act decriminalised male homosexuality, providing acts were performed in private between consenting adults over the age of 21. Before this, practising homosexuals had run the risk of criminal prosecution – and of blackmail from those who threatened to expose them. (Lesbianism had never been recognised in law and so was unaffected.)

- 1968, the Theatres Act abolished the Lord Chamberlain's right to censor stage plays. The result was a series of plays featuring nudity and four-letter words. *Hair* was the first successful production to be mounted under the new dispensation; later in the decade Kenneth Tynan produced the equally controversial *Oh! Calcutta!*. A similar free-for-all existed in books: the failure to ban *Lady Chatterley's Lover* meant that almost anything could be printed, including, at the end of the decade, the notorious *Fanny Hill*. The censorship of films remained, but it was now much less stringent. In the 1950s the nude women at the Windmill Theatre had had to remain stationary; but now striptease shows were permitted. Sex was being exploited commercially as never before. In addition, standards on television earned the wrath of Mary Whitehouse, who began a 'Clean-up TV' campaign in 1964.

■ 1969, the Divorce Act made it much easier to end marriage. Hitherto the only grounds for untying the knot was the 'matrimonial offence' of one partner: generally this meant adultery – and often a willing couple would concoct evidence if none existed. But now divorce could be secured by the 'irretrievable breakdown' of the marriage, shown by separation for two years. In the early 1930s there had been almost 5,000 divorces a year; in the late 1950s there had been an average of 28,000; just before the Act there had been 55,000; but now the annual total exceeded 100,000. This did not mean that marriage was going out of fashion, only that re-marriage ('the triumph of hope over experience') was more popular than ever.

■ Also in 1969 the voting age was reduced from 21 to 18.

Insofar as these reforms were based on any consistent philosophy it was that acts were to be judged as good or bad, desirable or undesirable, not in themselves but as a result of their likely consequences. Would capital punishment deter murder? If not, it should be abolished, especially because the innocent had sometimes been convicted. Could the law prevent homosexual acts or stop abortions? If not, then the law should be changed so that homosexuals would not be persecuted and so that safe, as opposed to backstreet, abortions would be performed. Marriages were obviously breaking down in ever greater numbers, and so it should be possible to get a divorce relatively painlessly and quickly, without the need for one partner to be branded the adulterous 'guilty party'. British people were tending to believe not in absolute values, such as those traditionally taught by Christianity, but in relative, **utilitarian** ones.

KEY TERM:

Utilitarianism

Utilitarianism was the philosophy developed in the nineteenth century by Jeremy Bentham. It argued that actions should be judged 'good' insofar as they tended to produce 'the greatest happiness of the greatest number'. Hence legislation should be passed if it tended to maximise the pleasure, or reduce the pain, of the public.

The Sixties: new standards

The dominant ethos in the Sixties was one of youth challenging authority (including politicians, the church and parents). Thus there seemed to be a profound generation gap. Heroes now tended to be young rebels. This was true of sporting figures – such as the wayward George Best of Manchester United – and, especially, of pop stars. From 1962, The Beatles were worshipped almost like gods; and John Lennon decided in March 1966 that they were 'more popular than Jesus' (see Figure 26.2). In 1967, after the group stopped giving live performances, it issued 'Sgt Pepper's Lonely Hearts Club Band', whose album sleeve, reproduced in Figure 26.3, features the quartet, and their wax images, against a background of various twentieth-century figures, including the American singer Bob Dylan. The lyrics of several of the songs bore the imprint of LSD and other hallucinogenic drugs. Scarcely less popular or influential were The Rolling Stones, alluded to on the album sleeve.

Figure 26.2 *'Beatlemania': teenage fans welcoming The Beatles back from their spectacularly successful tour of the United States in September 1964. The words on the banner allude to the record 'A Hard Day's Night': notice the missing apostrophes.*

Figure 26.3 *'Psychedelia': the 'Sgt Pepper' album sleeve of 1967.*

The young were urged not to accept tamely what they were told but to find out for themselves. Spontaneity and free expression were demanded. At the basis of such thinking was a profound optimism about human nature, as shown in the song 'Woodstock' from 1969:

> *I don't know who I am*
> *But life is for learning.*
> *We are stardust,*
> *Billion year old carbon,*
> *We are golden,*
> *Caught in the Devil's bargain,*
> *And we got to get ourselves back to the garden.*

Such attitudes affected a whole spectrum of society, from Bishop John Robinson, who insisted in *Honest to God* (1963) that 'Nothing can of itself always be labelled as "wrong"', to satirical reviews such as 'Beyond the Fringe' and television programmes like 'That Was The Week That Was', and magazines like *Private Eye*, begun in 1962. Nothing now seemed sacred – not even male dominance. The Women's Liberation Movement became strong in Britain towards the end of the 1960s, and in 1970 Germaine Greer published her influential text *The Female Eunuch*. In all, the pompous were debunked, and so, for good measure, were the not-so-pompous. No one was exempt, certainly not the royal family or politicians. When someone asked on television when Harold Wilson was lying, the answer came: 'When his lips are moving'.

Above all, this ethos can be seen in music. Songs in the 1950s tended to stress a yearning for prosperity and respectability. In the 1960s prosperity had arrived for many, and it seemed that respectability was not needed. Song lyrics now spoke of revolt and dissatisfaction with 'too much of nothing'. Bob Dylan addressed pertinent words to the older generation, urging mothers and fathers to recognise that their sons and daughters were beyond their command, for the 'times they are a'changing'.

Manifestations of this new mood can be seen in many areas:

■ Standards of fashion were changing. Long hair for young men became almost obligatory, and jeans scarcely less so. It was no longer possible to be sure of people's social class by looking at their clothes. Mini-skirts were also a sign of the times. (Look at the striking differences between the 'New Look' of the 1940s and the fashions of 20 years later, as shown in Figure 26.4.) Topless dresses were banned, but 'see-through' was acceptable.

■ There was greater violence in society. Crimes – or at least reported crimes – increased in the Sixties. Hooliganism certainly grew. In the

a   b

Figure 26.4a *The 'New Look' fashion of the 1940s: Chancellor of the Exchequer Stafford Cripps disapproved because too much material was used.*
b *The briefer fashions of the 1960s. Cripps, the puritan, would still have disapproved.*

early part of the decade there was violence between the 'Mods and Rockers' (the former generally white-collar workers with a neat image and riding scooters, the latter working class with a tough image, leather jackets and motor-bikes). They clashed at seaside resorts – such as Clacton and Bournemouth in 1964 – on Bank Holiday weekends. Next came the 'Skinheads', with their 'bovver boots' and aggressive attitudes towards non-whites, hippies and homosexuals. There were also political demonstrations, which sometimes led to violence, especially against the war by the USA in Vietnam. In fact student demonstrations against a variety of ills, including their 'irrelevant' syllabuses, became commonplace, and there were 'sit-ins' at Sussex, Essex, the London School of Economics and elsewhere.

At the opposite extreme were the 'Flower People', preaching peace and free love, and using drugs like cannabis and LSD. In 1967, 50,000 held a three-day 'love-in' at Woburn Abbey, and the following year a smaller number attended a LEMAR (Legalise Marijuana) rally in Hyde Park. Some disposed of their shoes in order to establish direct contact with the life-forces emanating from Mother Earth. They also manifested a realistic concern for the environment – Joni Mitchell, a singer-songwriter, lamenting that they had 'paved paradise and put up a parking lot'.

■ In a period that stressed our innate creativity, there was an explosion of cultural production. Much of it, especially the music of performers whose talent was deep-rooted and whose dedication transcended the merely spontaneous, seems to be standing the test of time well. But inevitably there was much that was ludicrously bad, and not only in the field of popular music. John Cage's most famous and celebrated work of the decade was entitled 'Four Minutes, Thirty-Three Seconds': the pianist sits in silence, without even lifting the piano lid, for precisely that duration. The Tate Gallery exhibited a perfectly regular plank. And a sculptor once found that a stone, which he had been intending to carve, was taken away, exhibited and sold before he had even begun work on it! Bernard Levin has judged that it was 'a credulous age, perhaps the most credulous ever'.

■ An undoubted feature of the decade was a new sexual freedom. This was the 'permissive society'. Reliable methods of birth control – especially the 'pill', freely available on the NHS by 1969 – were tending to make sex recreational rather than procreational. Equally important, the development of antibiotics meant that venereal diseases like syphilis and gonorrhoea could be cured within weeks. Sex before marriage became more common and acceptable. In the 1950s, it seemed that Love and Marriage had gone together, in the lyrics of a popular song of the time, like a Horse and Carriage. But no longer: 'Let's spend the night together' was now a characteristic lyric.

■ It seemed difficult to get away from sex – and sexism – in the media. The sleeve of the Jimi Hendrix album 'Electric Lady Land', for instance, featured 21 nude models; and sex also sold newspapers. In 1963 the Profumo Affair shocked the nation: Minister of Defence, John Profumo, had been availing himself of the services of Christine Keeler, a prostitute who was also sharing her favours with a Russian diplomat. Thereafter the stories became more and more lurid, as the jaded national appetite was less easily shocked. Some said sex was being made into a new religion. That engaging and articulate social critic Malcolm Muggeridge wrote that 'The orgasm has replaced the Cross as the focus of longing'.

Assessment

The 1960s had much in common with both the late 1950s and the early 1970s. Yet it is the decade alone which is remembered as witnessing the birth of the 'permissive society'. This is because the Sixties have been subjected to myth-making: they have been presented as the summit of post-war idealism and progress, or, alternatively, as the nadir of decadence and decay.

The pessimistic view

Prophets of gloom complained of the debased standards they saw all around them. Some thought that this slippery slope to decadence was all a plot got up by the communists. The sight of a long-haired Mick Jagger caused A. K. Chesterton, of the League of Empire Loyalists, to wonder how a 'once sturdy race' could produce anything so 'stomach turning': Great Britain was becoming 'mini-Britain' and seemed likely to become 'minus Britain – an erasure, a political and historical void'. Muggeridge complained that the British were a race of gaderene swine:

> 'Curious sensation belonging to a dying civilisation – like living in a house which is falling down – roof collapses, floorboards give, rain comes in through the windows, but still some sort of shelter provided, and each new manifestation of decay, after initial shock, got used to.'

Yet, in fact, this was Muggeridge writing in his diary in 1950, and he had also been equally critical of the 1930s. His criticisms in the 1960s, and those of others, obviously owed much to temperament. The pessimist will always see the glass as half-empty, the optimist as half-full.

The optimistic view

Gurus of a brave new world were wholeheartedly in favour of the changes of the 1960s. Roy Jenkins said that the permissive society was really the 'civilised society'. But then he would, wouldn't he? He was the Home Secretary who furthered much of the new legislation. Such 'optimistic' judgements also reflect personality and taste.

Neither the optimistic/positive, nor the pessimistic/negative version provides a full enough picture to carry conviction. The Sixties were not the best of times or the worst of times.

A third view

Others see the Sixties as just another decade. Yes, there was an undoubted generation gap – but there always is. There were some who confidently expected a much improved world, and there were others who predicted the end of civilisation – but there are always media pundits who gain a name for themselves by exaggerated, one-sided judgements. The standards of many changed enormously, but the lifestyles of many more stayed pretty much the same. Certainly there were moral changes after 1945, and Victorianism was coming to an end; but this was a slower and more gradual process than the notion of the 'Swinging Sixties' may lead us to suppose.

Conclusion

In the 1960s there was, as we have seen, an extraordinary challenge to accepted ways of life, but there was also continuity. People talked of a sexual revolution, but not everyone was touched by it. Many who set out eagerly to find sexual liberation in the Sixties drew a frustrating blank. Surveys in the late 1960s indicated the tenacity of older standards, including a high regard for virginity at marriage. Most people probably adhered to monogamous, heterosexual relationships – at least to a similar degree as in the past – and many would scarcely have been aware of changing moral views had it not been for the media. Certainly many continentals still found the British attitude to sex stuffy and inhibited. (Revealingly, the condom was still known in Britain as the 'French letter', the diaphragm as the 'Dutch cap'.) In addition, a large number of middle-class students only played at being rebels: they grew their hair, had their sit-ins, experimented with drugs and sex – and certainly did precious little academic work – before settling down to the sort of respectability they had formerly scorned. Perhaps, indeed, their 'rebellion' had been no more than conformity with their peers. Many of their former heroes were likewise absorbed into the Establishment. The Beatles received the MBE in 1965. It was harder and harder to regard pop music as subversive when even the right-wing newspaper *The Daily Telegraph* began printing the 'Top Ten'.

The Sixties saw much that was trivial, much that was silly and naive, and much that was vicious. There was a good deal of hypocrisy and exploitation, not least in the fortunes made by those who sang about the evils of money. But there was also much that was noble, heroic and deeply serious. Of which decade is this not true? Let us not forget that there were approximately 55 million people in the United Kingdom, and so it is not surprising that evidence exists to support almost every view about behaviour and moral standards. But perhaps the only acceptable generalisation is that we should be very wary of generalising!

What conclusion may be given? We will all have our own ideas about the desirability of particular aspects of Sixties' culture, but such judgements may well tell us as much about ourselves as about the objects of our concern. It is true that many less hesitant judges, confident that values are absolute, may be prepared to venture a verdict for society as a whole; but the historian – or at least this historian – is content merely to chart what happened.

Class discussion: passing judgement on the 1960s

Most of the debate about the 1960s turns on *values*: what were the dominant values, the moral decisions, behind the legislation, the behaviour, the attitudes of the 1960s? And, having identified them, did these values represent a change from those of the 1950s and earlier?

A number of possible labels can be put on the values of the time:

- utilitarian (see page 256)
- libertarian – people should be free to do what they like provided no one else is harmed
- rebellious – people were determined to oppose old systems, values, leaders just in order to be rebellious
- permissive – more freedom should be permitted
- selfish
- silly.

You should divide into groups, taking one or more of the 'labels' above. Your task is to:

1 Look back over the events of the 1960s described in this chapter. Which of the value systems listed above lie behind each of them?

2 Decide whether people in the 1960s would have used different labels to those you have applied.

Report back your findings, and discover whether the class as a whole has reached an overall view about a decade which has probably divided opinion more sharply than any other in the second half of the twentieth century.

Further reading

Alan Sked, *Britain's Decline* (Blackwell, 1987) – the second section of the book focuses on morality.
Bernard Levin, *The Pendulum Years: Britain and the Sixties* (Cape, 1970).
Arthur Marwick, *British Society Since 1945* (Penguin, 1982).

27 Northern Ireland: origins of 'The Troubles'

Time chart

1922: Anglo-Irish settlement: Irish Free State set up, Northern Ireland remaining part of UK

1937: New Constitution for Eire

1949: The Republic of Ireland left the Commonwealth

1963: O'Neill becomes Prime Minister of Northern Ireland: beginning of reforms

1967: Formation of Civil Rights Association

1968: October
Demonstration in Derry produces violence: start of the conflict

1969: Provisional IRA is formed
August
British troops sent to Northern Ireland

In the late 1960s marches and demonstrations in Northern Ireland flared up into violence. Soon the whole province seemed to be engulfed, and British troops were sent in to prevent a civil war between Protestants and Catholics. Yet their presence did not improve matters. By 1976 about 1,500 people had been killed in 'The Troubles'. Thereafter violence was sporadic both in Northern Ireland itself and in mainland Britain until, in August 1994 a truce was signed and talks began for a settlement on the basis of an 'all-Ireland' policy. This ceasefire itself broke down early in 1996 while the search for a permanent settlement went on. But why did the violence begin in the first place? What caused 'The Troubles'?

The fundamental issue

We saw in chapter 5 that an Irish settlement had been achieved in 1922. The six Ulster counties with the largest number of Protestants remained part of the United Kingdom: they formed 'Northern Ireland', with representation at Westminster but also with their own parliament at Stormont, in Belfast. The remaining 26 counties, whose population was overwhelmingly Catholic, were given Dominion status as the 'Irish Free State', and so were free to run their own affairs, though retaining the British monarch as their head of state.

Yet this state of affairs fully satisfied nobody. Many Southerners wished for complete independence and republican status. Moreover, they hated the partition of Ireland and refused to recognise British control in the North. The settlement split the Irish Republican Army (IRA) into two factions: the Regulars (now incorporated into the Free State army) were willing to accept it, but the Irregulars refused to compromise. Only in May 1923, after a bloody civil war in which the government imprisoned 12,000 IRA activists and shot 77, was there peace. Southern Ireland had marginalised the IRA and Sinn Fein, its political wing, though no Southern politician accepted that partition would be permanent.

As for the population of Northern Ireland, there was no unity among them:

- Two-thirds were Protestants, who fully approved the new regime. They were thus 'Unionists' or 'Loyalists'. But, as only 30 per cent of the whole of Ireland, they felt vulnerable and beleaguered – a state of affairs which encouraged an aggressive mentality. They looked upon the Catholics in their midst as a Fifth Column for the IRA, a potentially disloyal element who could have no stake in a Protestant nation.

- The remaining third were Catholic. Not only did they have religious differences with the Protestants but they had a different outlook, reinforced by history, myth and tradition, which amounted to a separate national identity. Many of them were Nationalists, wishing to see a united Ireland controlled from Dublin.

Such differences produced riots on the streets of Belfast in 1920–22 which killed over 450. Thereafter feelings were kept high by the annual marches of the Protestant Orange Lodges and the Catholic Republican Clubs. In addition, there was very little mixing between the two groups: they had separate schools, separate housing estates and there was virtually no intermarriage.

There were thus two important unanswered questions challenging the future of Ireland:

- Could the two communities in Northern Ireland be reconciled, given that their aims and outlooks were fundamentally different?

- Would partition survive, given the ambitions of the Catholics in North and South to achieve reunion?

Gerrymandering

Deriving from the name of a Governor of Massachusetts, Elbridge Gerry, the term **gerrymandering** means the manipulation of constituency boundaries to maximise the effect of voting for a particular party. In Northern Ireland after 1923 the Protestants drew and redrew local government boundaries to prevent the Roman Catholics forming a local council. Even in Derry (which the Protestants called Londonderry), where there were almost twice as many Catholics as Protestants, the Catholics were kept out of power. Other devices used to the same end included plural voting: wealthy Protestants, with property or residential qualifications, could vote many times in the same election.

Politics in Ireland

Northern Ireland – discrimination against Catholics

The fundamental division between the majority of Protestant Loyalists or Unionists and the minority of Catholic Nationalists produced an inherently unstable mixture. It was made potentially explosive by political and socio-economic discrimination against the minority community.

Political parties in Northern Ireland did not divide along class lines, as they did in the rest of the United Kingdom: instead, they formed along the religious divide. Therefore the Loyalists, as the majority population, could never lose an election, and the Catholics could never win one. Every member of the Stormont Parliament between 1922 and 1968 was a Protestant. What is more, the Catholics were kept out of local government, even in areas where they formed the majority, by **gerrymandering**.

Catholics thus suffered severe political disadvantage. This made social and economic discrimination easy for the Protestant majority:

- Catholics found it more difficult to get jobs. This was particularly so in local government posts, which Protestant councillors would control. The Minister of Agriculture, Basil Brooke, insisted in 1933 that 'If we allow Catholics to work on our farms, we are traitors to Ulster'. (Brooke was Prime Minister of Northern Ireland from 1943 until 1963!)

- They also found it very difficult to get houses, especially council houses.

- They were often badly treated by the police (the Royal Ulster Constabulary) and by a new paramilitary part-time force set up to combat the IRA, the B-Specials, who were armed and overwhelmingly Protestant.

Discrimination against the Catholics was made worse by the poor state of the economy. Northern Ireland suffered far more from the slump in the 1930s than any other part of the UK. But whatever the reasons, Catholic fears that the 1922 settlement would work against them had proved all too true. Hence some looked for redress to the government in the South.

The role of Eire

The supporters of the settlement were in power for the first 10 years of the Free State's existence, but in 1932 Fianna Fail ('Soldiers of Destiny'), led by Eamon de Valera, came to power. The new government called for a united Ireland and insisted that the British Province in the north had no legal existence. But at the same time, de Valera began a process which made the prospects of reunion less attractive to the Protestants of the North:

- In 1937 a new constitution not only adopted the name 'Eire' for Southern Ireland but gave special recognition to the Catholic Church and replaced the British monarch as head of state by an Irish president.

- During the Second World War Eire was the only Dominion to proclaim itself neutral, and shortly after the war it became a republic.

However, de Valera did not encourage violence from the IRA, which he saw as a threat to his own government as well as to the British in the North. During the war he executed six members of the IRA, **interned** 400 and allowed two men to die on hunger strike.

KEY TERM:

Internment

To **intern** is to imprison without trial or sentence. It was used in Eire and later by the British in Northern Ireland to combat terrorism, especially when it seemed unlikely that juries would be willing to convict. The problem with such a measure is that innocent people may be imprisoned. The illiberal nature of internment can also be used as a propaganda weapon by 'freedom fighters'.

Prospects for peace

A final settlement?

In 1949 the UK government passed the Ireland Act. This did two things:

- It recognised the Irish Republic as independent.

- It insisted that 'in no event will Northern Ireland or any part thereof cease to be part of His Majesty's dominions and of the United Kingdom without the consent of the parliament of Northern Ireland'.

The partition which Lloyd George had implied might only be temporary seemed to have become permanent, and some hoped that the Irish Question had finally been settled. Certainly some sort of *modus vivendi* had emerged between North and South. Admittedly the Irish Republic continued to proclaim its right to rule the North, but it made no effort to make good the claim. In addition, many Catholics in the North – especially the younger, well-educated ones – accepted that partition was permanent and so pinned their hopes for a better future on peaceful change; and they were beginning to receive support from a section of the Protestant community. Another promising sign was that the new welfare state, with its family allowances, national insurance and free health treatment for all, was improving conditions in Northern Ireland and helping to produce greater equality between the communities.

The IRA

In 1956 the IRA began a campaign of violence in the North. But this achieved very little, largely because most Northern Catholics refused to give their support, and it was called off in 1962, after a total of 19 deaths. IRA leaders complained of the attitude of the public 'whose minds have been deliberately distracted from the supreme issue facing the Irish people – the unity and freedom of Ireland'. The Republic also clamped down on the IRA, once again using internment. Perhaps the Army might abandon the idea that force could end partition.

Political leadership

Further promising signs came with changes in political leadership:

- In the South de Valera retired in 1959 and was replaced by figures less hostile to the Unionists.

- In the North **Terence O'Neill** replaced hardliner Brooke as PM.

PROFILE: *Captain Terence O'Neill*

Terence O'Neill, born in 1914 and educated at Eton, served as a captain in the Irish Guards during the Second World War before entering Stormont in 1946. He held several important ministerial positions in the 1950s and became leader of the Ulster Unionist Party and Prime Minister in 1963. He was much more radical than his predecessor, being determined to improve both the economy of Northern Ireland, by instituting a large-scale building programme and pumping money into heavy industry, and the position of its Catholics. Perhaps Protestants and Catholics would be able to work together under O'Neill. But was there a pace of change that would satisfy both sides? What one group would criticise as 'too little too late' would anger the other as 'too much too soon'.

Another hopeful sign was that Wilson's Labour government was also pressing for reforms. For decades Westminster had turned a blind eye to Ulster, but now it was discovered that the relative economic backwardness of Northern Ireland was costing the Exchequer some £45 million in welfare payments. The British press also took a new interest, exposing discrimination against Catholics and dubbing the Province 'Britain's political slum'. The omens for the future therefore looked bright. Or might new initiatives disturb the uneasy balance in the North and revive the latent hostility of the two communities?

Onset of The Troubles

The failure of reform

Many Protestants in O'Neill's own party believed that reforms were too swift – and some, like the Reverend Ian Paisley, did not want change at all. Catholics, on the other hand, found the pace too gradual. There was certainly no transformation of their position. There were continuing problems in housing, employment and local elections. In Dungannon, in County Tyrone, the Protestant council was refusing to rehouse Catholics. In Derry 80 per cent of salaried employees of the city council were Protestant, and the majority Catholic population was still able to elect fewer councillors (8) than the minority of Protestants (12). This was a situation which had been tolerated before, but now it aroused greater indignation.

The civil rights movement

This was a period when civil rights were being demanded all over the world – especially in the United States, where Martin Luther King had led demonstrations against racial discrimination, and in Paris, where students took over their universities and threatened to unleash a revolution in 1968. People generally seemed to be exhibiting a new willingness to protest. In Ireland a Civil Rights Association (CRA) was formed in 1967, demanding the same standards of social justice as in the rest of the UK. It proved especially attractive to young, middle-class Catholics. In 1968 they organised a series of protest marches to demand equal rights, as shown in Figure 27.2. (There is no sign in this instance that the youthful protesters intended any violence. 'One Man, One Vote' was demanded in dozens of places throughout the world, though the religious message was more peculiarly Irish.)

Developments in the IRA

Northern Ireland stood at a crossroads around 1968. The demands of the Catholics might lead to a more equal, and ultimately more unified and cohesive, society. This in turn might have cemented Irish partition. How would the most militant Catholics, the IRA, react? Would they surrender their cherished dream of reuniting Ireland? This was clearly a period of crisis for the IRA.

In fact the Army split. In 1969, after violence had begun the previous year, the 'Provos' (the Provisional IRA), about 600 strong, broke away from the 'Official' movement and began a campaign of violent urban terrorism. They were determined to reject the road of integration in the North.

Figure 27.2 One of the smaller Catholic civil rights marches in 1968

Start of the violence

The first key event was in October 1968. A CRA demonstration in Derry, along a traditional Protestant marching route, was dispersed very roughly by the Royal Ulster Constabulary and the B-Specials. Similarly, a march from Belfast to Derry in January 1969 was broken up by the RUC in what was widely regarded as an act of blatant anti-Catholic policing. Riots and violent incidents then began to occur with regularity. Catholics erected barricades in the Bogside area of Derry in August 1969, while in Belfast Protestants attacked Catholics in the west of the city, killing 10, wounding 1,600 and causing damage to property estimated at £8 million.

The Cameron Report on the disturbances, published in September 1969, put the long-term blame on 'failure in leadership and foresight among political leaders on all sides'. It also singled out discrimination against Catholics as a prime cause of The Troubles. An investigation by the British judge Lord Scarman decided that:

■ The riots had not been planned, either by Protestant groups or the IRA.

■ They arose from a complex political, social and economic situation.

■ There were six occasions on which the police were seriously at fault for their tactics, though misconduct was the exception rather than the rule.

■ Communal tensions were running high: many Protestants believed that the Catholics were trying to end partition, and many Catholics thought that the police were their enemy.

Soon things went from bad to worse. O'Neill called a general election in February 1969: he needed a mandate to press ahead with changes and especially to reform local elections. But the result made the political situation more, not less, confused: there were no fewer than eight anti-Union parties and groups, gaining about 30 per cent of the votes, while the Unionist side split into pro- and anti-O'Neillites and Paisley's hardline Protestant Unionists. O'Neill soon resigned, but none of his successors was able to control events.

Escalation of violence

On 12 August 1969 the traditional Apprentice Boys' march in Derry degenerated into violence which spread to other towns. Thousands of people, mostly Catholics, were made homeless by fire in Belfast, and on 14 August six people were killed. The Provos were being faced on the streets by Protestant paramilitary groups. Two days later Westminster sanctioned the sending of troops from the mainland to contain the violence, and in particular to protect the Catholic minority. The cartoon shown in Figure 27.3 is a wry comment on this initiative. Does its humour show a lack of understanding of what divided the two communities and, particularly, of the degree to which 'Catholic' and 'Protestant' were political categories?

The British government also insisted on important reforms:

■ The B-Specials were abolished and the RUC reformed.

■ A fairer system of allocating council houses was devised.

■ Gerrymandering was stopped and election rules were changed so that all people were treated fairly.

■ Employment grants were given to set up new factories.

■ Furthermore, in 1974 the British insisted on 'power-sharing', so that for the first time the executive of Northern Ireland contained representatives from both communities.

Might this combination of reform and military firmness solve Ulster's problems? There seemed some hope at first, but not for long. The

Figure 27.3 *British troops were sent to Northern Ireland in August 1969: local Catholics and Protestants were divided by far more than denominational differences. The soldier is saying 'It's just as well they believe in the same God.'*

Provisional IRA portrayed British soldiers as an alien army of occupation, coercing the Catholics, and their case was given greater substance when, in 1971, internment was introduced and was used almost solely against Catholics. Official British reports admitted that internees were treated badly. Hence the impact of reform was very limited, and the strength of opposition meant that 'power-sharing' was short-lived. The IRA campaign of shootings and bombings continued.

'The Troubles' had undoubtedly begun. In 1968–70, 39 people were killed in Northern Ireland. In 1971 the first British soldiers were killed, in a death toll of over 170. In 1972 around 450 died, and this year saw another 'Bloody Sunday', troops killing 13 members of a civil rights march on 30 January. No one can be sure whether they were IRA members or simply peaceful demonstrators. Later in the year the IRA took reprisals by bombing the barracks of the Parachute Regiment in Aldershot. Amid fears of outright civil war, Heath's government decided on direct rule: the parliament at Stormont was suspended and a minister from Westminster was put in control of Northern Ireland. But no significant improvement in the situation came about. In July 1973, 20 bombs exploded in Belfast, killing 11 and injuring 120: this was 'Bloody Friday'. About 250 people were killed in the Province in this year, with similar totals in 1974 and again in 1975. In 1974 the reality of urban terrorism made itself felt in central Birmingham when 21 people were killed by an IRA bomb. The IRA were determined to have Ireland's troubles make an impact in Britain too. Violence went on and on.

Conclusion

It is extremely difficult to sum up the causes of The Troubles in Ireland. Certainly no full explanation can be given, since this would require insight into the minds and mentality of all those who participated in the generation of tension and its eruption into violence. But a simple causal framework can be constructed.

- First, there are the important preconditions, without which the violence would not have started. The settlement ratified in 1922 must be considered one of these. We may now be tempted to see it as a fatal compromise, though Lloyd George had done the best he could in almost impossible conditions. More fundamental, however, was the existence of two communities – both in Ireland as a whole and in Northern Ireland – with separate national identities. Hence we must trace the preconditions back well before 1922, to the British conquest. But the preconditions were generated in the period after 1922 as well, when a fatal neglect had done nothing to assuage differences between the two communities. Perhaps a golden opportunity had been missed.

  Such 'preconditions' are also 'causes' of The Troubles, but they did not lead automatically to them. They first had to be activated by the 'precipitants' of the violence.

- Among the precipitants or medium- and short-term causes must be considered the reforms of O'Neill, which raised Catholic expectations while, at the same time, arousing the fears of the hardline Protestants. (This is not of course to say that O'Neill was to blame. After all, moral responsibility should be judged by intention.) Also important were the initiatives taken by civil rights activists.

- The 'triggers' which actually sparked off the violence came with the actions of the RUC, the IRA and those involved with the demonstrations and riots of 1968–70. Some would perhaps say that these factors are the most important causes of The Troubles: without them, the tensions between the communities might have ebbed away. Certainly there were some hopeful signs that reform was producing beneficial change.

- So far we have explained, in some measure, why The Troubles started, but not why they continued. New factors also came into play, including the decision to send in the troops, which was a propaganda victory for the IRA. But surely the key factor is that the violence became self-sustaining. The barbarity experienced by one community seemed to warrant retribution, which the other community experienced as fresh barbarity. As Mahatma Gandhi is supposed to have said, 'an eye for an eye' and the whole world will be blind.

Task: role play – Northern Ireland, 1968 and 1975

Divide into groups of four. The four roles are:

A A middle-class Roman Catholic civil rights activist
B A hardline Protestant Unionist
C A moderate Unionist
D A member of the IRA.

1 It is 1968. What are the views of each of the four on:

  a civil rights for all Roman Catholics in Northern Ireland
  b a united Ireland?

2 It is 1975. What are the views of each of the four on:

  a rule from Westminster
  b British troops in Northern Ireland?

Although you will find that these groups generally have distinctive views, don't let your role plays degenerate into mere stereotyping. Remember that people within the same group would be expected to disagree among themselves about certain things. They would almost certainly give different emphasis. For example, one moderate Unionist might support a particular reform which another thought dangerous. Members of the IRA will have had furious debates about the value of bombing particular targets. Groups are made up different people. Allow your selection of evidence to reflect at least some differences *within* groups.

Further reading

Sabine Wichert, *Northern Ireland Since 1945* (Addison Wesley Longman, 1991) – an in-depth analysis.

D. G. Boyce, *The Irish Question and British Politics, 1868–1986* (Macmillan, 1990) – a wide-ranging account.

28 Why did Britain join the European Community?

Time chart

1951: Treaty of Paris establishes the European Coal and Steel Community

1957: Treaty of Rome establishes the European Economic Community

1961: Britain's first application for membership of EEC, vetoed by de Gaulle in 1963

1967: Britain's second application, also vetoed by de Gaulle

1970: Britain's third application, this time successful

1973: 1 January
Britain formally enters the EEC

1975: Referendum on continued British membership: two-thirds majority in favour of staying in

It may be that future historians, looking back upon Britain in the twentieth century, will single out 1 January 1973 as a vital turning-point. On this date Britain entered the European Economic Community (EEC). Will these chroniclers decide that the impact of the Community on Britain was harmful or beneficial – or both? Of this we cannot be sure. But we may be certain that they will chart the caution, hesitation and ambivalence with which Britons entered Europe. If entry was made so reluctantly, why was it made at all? This chapter seeks to provide some of the answers.

Traditional British attitudes

In the nineteenth century some Britons felt a deep kinship with the nations of Europe. For instance, Gladstone (Prime Minister on four occasions) once said that Britain was part of the 'community of Europe', and he believed sincerely in wholehearted cooperation with his continental neighbours. Probably more typical, however, was Lord Salisbury (Prime Minister three times). It is a myth that his policy in the 1880s and 1890s was 'splendid isolation': he knew that isolation from the Great Powers of Europe was dangerous, not splendid. On the other hand, he judged that Britain should not become an exclusively European power itself, since its major interests were overseas and especially in the Empire. Britain should therefore maintain friendly but formal relations with Europe, avoiding entangling alliances. It should only become fully involved in the emergency of war, to prevent one nation achieving a predominance which, sooner or later, might lead it to have designs on Britain itself.

One such intervention occurred in 1914. Britain joined the First World War, somewhat reluctantly, to prevent German hegemony. The nature of the conflict certainly justified the reluctance, and the mass slaughter on the Western Front produced an emotional recoil from Europe. After 1918 Britain was once more wary of intervention: as Austen Chamberlain (Foreign Secretary, 1924–9) put it, we should be 'semi-detached' from Europe, and the Foreign Office was adamantly opposed to a Channel Tunnel linking Britain with the continent.

Britons were conscious of being different from Europeans, and usually thought they were superior to them. (As we saw in chapter 4, the imperialist mentality continued into the interwar period.) Certainly there was something distinct about Britain, as George Orwell wrote:

> *'When you come back to England from any foreign country, you have immediately the sensation of breathing a different air. Even in the first few minutes, dozens of small things conspire to give you this feeling. The beer is bitterer, the coins are heavier, the grass is greener, the advertisements more blatant . . . There is something distinctive and recognisable in English civilisation . . . The English are outside the European culture . . .'*
>
> George Orwell, *The Lion and the Unicorn* (1940).

Orwell thought that the British were gentler and less intellectual than continentals, with an island race's typical insularity. He, and almost everyone else, not only recognised British differences but judged that they were well worth preserving.

The Second World War emphasised the fact that Britain was set apart from the continent. In the dark days of 1940 Churchill may have called for Britain and France to unite to form one nation, but this was only a vain attempt to keep France in the war. After June 1940, when the French – all too tamely, it was thought – made peace with the German aggressors, Britain stood alone; and if the second European civil war within a generation helped to bind Europe together, the experience emphasised Britons' feelings of separateness. Along with the Americans, they were the liberators of Europe, an outside force, not part of the European fabric. Britain was also set apart in that its economy, although weakened in the war, had not been devastated like mainland Europe's.

The European movement, 1945–57

After 1945, many Europeans felt that only real cooperation could help the continent to recover from the ravages of war, and that only political and economic integration could prevent further wars. There were several landmarks *en route* to the European Union:

- 1944, the leaders of Holland, Belgium and Luxembourg formed the Benelux Union to link their industries and trade.

- 1948, 800 delegates, forming the Congress of Europe, met at The Hague. The following year they set up the Council of Europe, which some looked upon as an embryo parliament.

- 1948, the Organisation for European Economic Cooperation (OEEC) was set up by 16 nations to coordinate Marshall Aid. The United States was thus boosting European integration.

- 1951, the Treaty of Paris set up the European Coal and Steel Community. It was expected that such an organisation would not only prevent Germany or France from secretly preparing for war but would boost economic growth. German coal would be complemented by French iron ore. It was agreed that the members would create one market for coal and steel, with no customs duties, and that there would also be a council of ministers, a parliamentary assembly and a court of justice. These arrangements were described by the Treaty as 'the first concrete foundations of the European federation'.

- 1955, an important conference was held at Messina in Sicily after the Benelux countries had called for a common market for all goods, not just iron and steel.

- March 1957, the Treaty of Rome was signed by six countries (France, West Germany, Italy, Holland, Belgium and Luxembourg), setting up the European Economic Community. There was to be a single market for all goods, with a common external tariff against imports from elsewhere, while the Six were to work towards the 'ever closer union' of their countries.

Britain's role

British politicians approved of the movement towards European integration. Churchill called for the creation of 'a kind of United States of

KEY TERM:

Federation

A **federation** is a grouping of several states, all of which control their own local affairs but which are subordinate to a central (federal) government for key general issues like defence. The USA, for instance, is a federation. The opposite of a federation is a unitary government, where a single parliament controls all aspects of a country's government. The UK was a unitary state in the 1950s, and hence the sovereignty (or ultimate control) of Parliament would be lost if Britain joined a federation. More acceptable to Britain would have been membership of a looser organisation, sometimes referred to as a confederation. (To complicate matters, such terms as 'federation' and 'confederation' were interpreted slightly differently in the rest of Europe.)

Europe'. In his view, Britons should be 'the friends and sponsors' of such an organisation but should not actually join. Britain, in his view, had three spheres of interest: the Empire/Commonwealth, the 'special relationship' with the United States, and Europe (see page 213), and so there could be no absorption within any European grouping. 'We are with Europe,' he said, expressing the ambiguity of Britain's position, 'but not of Europe.'

Attlee's ministers had similar ideas. They took a full role in the OEEC, in order to extract maximum benefit from Marshall Aid, but were against giving the Council of Europe any more than advisory powers. In 1951 Attlee refused to join the European Coal and Steel Community: no supranational body (i.e. one with the power to override the decisions of nation states) should be able to interfere with newly nationalised British industries. Bevin insisted that Britain was not 'just another European country' and that Parliament had to remain sovereign in British affairs. On the subject of European **federation**, he added, in inimitable fashion and with blissful ignorance of Greek mythology: 'If you open that Pandora's box, you never know what Trojan 'orses will jump out'!

The Conservatives criticised Labour's attitude to the Coal and Steel Community, and so, later, did the American diplomat Dean Acheson. He argued that Britain's failure to join was 'the great mistake of the postwar period'. With hindsight, we may perhaps be inclined to agree with this critical verdict; but at the time there seemed few advantages in joining. Certainly the Conservatives, who came to power in 1951, reversed their earlier judgement and did not apply for membership. Churchill told his cabinet that Britain should take no part in a European federation: Britain's first aim was the consolidation of the Commonwealth, second was its 'fraternal association' with the United States, while relations with Europe came third. Prime Minister-in-waiting Anthony Eden felt the same way. He judged that Britain's real interests lay beyond Europe, across the seas, in every corner of the world: 'That is our life'. It is not surprising, therefore, that the Conservatives did not take a full part in the Messina negotiations in 1955. Instead of attending himself, Foreign Secretary **Harold Macmillan** sent an Under-Secretary from the Board of Trade. Thus Britain did not sign the Treaty of Rome in 1957, and the EEC was formed without Britain.

Why did Britain not join? There are several explanations, apart from feelings of separateness:

■ Only a few Conservative ministers were unreservedly in favour. Many, like Harold Macmillan, were generally 'pro-European' but disliked the idea of a federal Europe, and some were set against.

PROFILE: *Harold Macmillan*

Harold Macmillan, who had first entered Parliament in 1924, became Prime Minister in 1957, after Eden's post-Suez resignation. He managed to turn around Conservative fortunes, so that they won the 1959 election, after proclaiming that British people had 'never had it so good'. The cartoonist Vicky parodied him as 'SuperMac', a name which in fact the public decided was a term of praise not abuse. He brought an image of Edwardian elegance and unflappability to politics though in private he was a nervous, tense man. His motto was 'Quiet, calm deliberation disentangles every knot'. His decision to apply for membership of the EEC in 1961 came as a shock to many. Certainly it had not been included in the previous election manifesto. Macmillan resigned as Prime Minister in October 1963. He accepted a peerage on his 90th birthday and died in 1986, aged 92.

■ The Commonwealth, now being expanded by the admission of Ghana, the first African state, seemed a far more important focus for British energies than Europe.

■ The pattern of Britain's overseas trade did not warrant membership. It was sensible for the Six to form a common market, since they traded predominantly in Europe; but Britain had more extra-European than European trade. Only a quarter of British exports went to Europe, while a half went to the Empire/Commonwealth, and so the adoption of the common external tariff would anger Britain's overseas customers and be against Britain's interests. Joining the EEC would therefore be bad for Britain: this was the stark verdict endorsed by the cabinet, not that much time was spent on what seemed a relatively unimportant matter.

Britain's applications

The first application, 1961–3

In 1957 the government – for good reasons – did not seriously consider joining the EEC. Yet in July 1961 Macmillan applied for entry. Labour leader Hugh Gaitskell was adamantly opposed: he judged that entry into the Common Market (as it was then generally called) would constitute 'the end of Britain as an independent nation ... the end of a thousand years of history, the end of the Commonwealth'. Why did such arguments no longer deter Macmillan and the Conservatives?

A number of new factors were having an effect in the early sixties:

■ The Commonwealth was not living up to expectations and was no longer quite such a focus of British thinking. Particularly galling was that Ghana had become a dictatorship. There was not enough unity among Commonwealth nations for Britain's liking. Significantly, at the same time as the application for EEC membership, plans were being adopted to limit Commonwealth immigration into Britain, despite the fact that member states would be offended (for further details, see chapter 24).

■ Perhaps Europe might be a better focus for British ambitions than the Commonwealth, especially now that Europeans themselves seemed to be playing down its political and federal implications. Could the EEC become a 'surrogate empire' for Britain? Certainly some old-fashioned imperialists preferred it because it was all-white.

■ On its own, Britain could never compete on equal terms with the superpowers (the USA and USSR), but as a member of the EEC it might well have greater power and status in the world.

■ Many Britons felt that there had to be a British national goal. Dean Acheson offended the government by insisting in 1962 that Britain had 'lost an empire but failed to find a role'. Clearly he had struck a raw nerve. Perhaps Europe might provide that role.

■ The Americans put a good deal of pressure on Britain to join the EEC (especially because a united Europe would be a more resilient barrier to the spread of communism than separate governments).

■ Successful entry into Europe might also boost the Conservatives' chances at the next general election. Certainly Macmillan's now ailing government, suffering from a series of disappointments and scandals, needed something to boost its fortunes.

■ In 1960 Britain had set up the European Free Trade Association (EFTA), with Norway, Denmark, Sweden, Austria, Portugal and Switzerland, as a rival to the EEC. This was preferable from Britain's point of view because it involved no common external tariff or supra-national institutions. On the other hand, EFTA performed poorly, especially because the combined population of the member states was relatively low.

■ Above all, perhaps, there were economic arguments in favour of entry. Trade with the Six was increasing very rapidly: trade with the Commonwealth was still more valuable, but only just. What was clearer was that while British wealth was increasing only slowly, that of the EEC members was growing with extraordinary rapidity. After 1955 Britain's annual economic growth rate of 2.8 per cent was dwarfed by that of Italy (5.4 per cent), France (5.4 per cent) and West Germany (5.7 per cent). Britain's share of world trade was also falling steeply (see chapter 23 for further details of British economic decline). Typically, only two days before the formal application, a financial crisis necessitated a mini-budget, in which interest rates were raised and a pay-pause was instituted. Membership of the thriving EEC might well stop such difficulties and decline – at least that is what was hoped.

There were thus a number of reasons for Britain's application. Edward Heath, leader of the British negotiating team, spoke positively of Britain's desire 'to become a full, wholehearted and active member of the European Community in the widest sense', but this was going too far. Many of the motivations behind the application were negative, stemming from doubts and fears, and there were a number of critics to whom the proposed entry was anathema. Even Macmillan had his doubts, and he insisted that if 'European unity would disrupt the long-standing and historic ties between the United Kingdom and the Commonwealth, then the loss would be greater than the gain'. He, like Churchill before him, believed in the 'three majestic circles' theory. Clearly, then, the application was tentative – which was one reason why it was turned down.

In January 1963 Britain's entry was rejected by the EEC. Five member states would have accepted Britain, but France's leader, General de Gaulle, exercised his right of veto. No one can be certain of his reasons. Was he getting his own back for the way Churchill had treated him during the war? Did he fear that Britain might upset France's secure position at the head of the Community (so that there would be 'two cocks in the hen run')? Publicly he insisted that Britain was too involved with both the Commonwealth (and would never give up cheaper Commonwealth food to buy dear French items) and the Americans (from whom Macmillan had recently agreed to purchase sea-to-air Polaris nuclear missiles) to become a committed European power. Britain in the EEC, as a French commentator put it, might well be an American Trojan Horse.

The second application, 1967

The rejection of Britain's application was a great blow to Macmillan, who resigned through ill health in October 1963, and to the Conservative Party, which lost the 1964 general election to Labour. The Labour Party had opposed entry into the EEC, despite having a number of ardent pro-marketeers within its ranks. But in 1967 this position was reversed: Wilson decided to apply, while a minority of Labour MPs were set against joining. He decided it was worth trying to join for exactly the same reasons as Macmillan. Indeed several of these motivations now had greater force.

■ The Commonwealth was less cohesive than ever before. In November 1965 a crisis erupted: the white settlers in Southern Rhodesia made a unilateral declaration of independence (UDI) to prevent black majority rule. Britain imposed economic sanctions, but many Commonwealth states insisted that troops should be sent in to quell the rebellion. Wilson's refusal to take such an action fuelled speculation that perhaps Britain itself would be expelled from the Commonwealth.

■ Wilson faced severe economic problems in the years before 1967. It could no longer be denied that the country was undergoing rapid economic decline relative to the members of the EEC. Something had to be done to stop the rot. 'If you can't beat them, join them' was part of the government's (hopeful) reasoning.

Yet the result was very similar to 1963. General de Gaulle again exercised his veto. Admittedly he did so rather more tactfully this time: Britain could have 'association', rather than full, membership. But the end result was exactly the same.

The third application, 1970–72

The Conservatives returned to power in 1970 under a new leader, Edward Heath, who was far more committed to membership than either Macmillan or Wilson. Heath was the first postwar Prime Minister to have no emotional ties to the Empire/Commonwealth, and by this time the Commonwealth was far less important for Britain. Trade with Europe very clearly exceeded in value that with the Commonwealth. In addition, Commonwealth states objected far less to this application than to the previous two, especially since there was to be a special six-year transitional period before the common external tariff came into force. A major obstacle to membership had thus been reduced; on the other hand, the main reason for applying – Britain's economic worries – remained as strong as ever.

Both the parties were divided on the issue of entry. But Heath's government insisted that

> 'our country will be more secure, our ability to maintain peace and promote development in the world greater, our economy stronger and our industries and people more prosperous if we join.'

Here was a chance of 'new greatness': Great Britain could become 'Greater Britain'. Of course membership would entail duties and obligations, but Heath insisted that there would be 'no erosion of our essential national sovereignty'. Presented in this way, all the advantages seemed to lie with entry, while the disadvantages were minimised.

Heath was optimistic – especially since, this time, there could be no veto from de Gaulle, who had retired in 1969 and had died the following year. The member states therefore scheduled the entry of Britain (and also Denmark and Ireland) for 1 January 1973, providing that their parliaments ratified the agreement. It was a close-run thing in the House of Commons. On the important second reading of the Bill, 39 Conservatives defied party whips and voted against entry, while 69 Labour MPs defied the party line that the terms were not good enough and had to be renegotiated. Heath secured entry by 301 votes to 284.

Britain had entered the EEC, but there was no wholehearted consent from the British people. Nor did the early years of membership help to solve Britain's problems. In June 1975 Labour held a referendum – the first in British history – on whether to stay in. It was not a time of calm deliberation. The politically astute Labour prime minister, Harold Wilson, only promoted the referendum in order to prevent further damaging splits in his party. The level of debate was low. Both pro- and anti-marketeers overstated their case: one side said it would be a disaster and an act of unparalleled madness to stay in, while the other side said it would be a disaster and an act of unparalleled madness to come out. In the end, 26 million people voted and there was a clear, two to one, majority in favour of remaining a member; but the result is perhaps best seen as the British people pragmatically deciding to give the Community a reasonable try. Probably the majority did not feel themselves to be Europeans. It would take time to forge the psychological bonds which could alone make the European Community a living force. What may, in the future, be interpreted as a vital turning-point did not seem like that at the time.

Further reading

Alan Farmer, *Britain: Foreign and Imperial Affairs 1939–64* (Hodder and Stoughton, 1994) – provides a good, clear starting-point.
John W. Young, *Britain and European Unity, 1945–92* (Macmillan, 1993) – a more detailed text.
Alan M. Williams, *The European Community* (Blackwell, 1991).

29 Consensus in British politics, 1956–79: myth or reality?

The vital issue of definition

'Consensus' is one of those annoying terms which – like many others in the language! – means different things to different people. Hence historians who disagree about whether consensus existed or not in the years from 1956 to 1979 may really be arguing not about what happened, and how best it should be interpreted, but about the meaning of the word. Such merely semantic arguments can be sterile and unrewarding, and the best way to avoid them is for the historian to define as clearly as possible what he or she means by the key terms. Otherwise those who debate may be at cross-purposes.

What does 'consensus' mean in the title above? It might mean something like 'general agreement within society about which political goals are desirable' or 'general agreement between political parties'.

Either is possible, but this chapter examines the second definition – agreement between politicians, not in society as a whole. This simplifies matters, but there are still ambiguities. Do all the political parties need to subscribe to this 'general agreement', even fringe groups like the Communist Party or the National Front? The author's answer to this is 'No': it is quite unrealistic to expect consensus from groups which do not subscribe to the basic principles of parliamentary democracy. Therefore we are concerned only with the parties represented at Westminster; and since only two parties achieved power in 1956–79, we will focus our investigation on Conservatives and Labour. On all the members of these parties? Labour had a vociferous left wing which was highly critical of its own leaders, let alone of the other party, and the same is true of the right wing of the Conservatives: if we concentrate on these groups, therefore, we will find very little consensus. Hence we will limit ourselves to the leading figures of the Conservative and Labour Parties, and in particular to the governments of the period.

Clearly we must look at political actions rather than rhetoric. Exaggerated criticism of opponents is part of the 'political game', and should not be taken too seriously. Actions speak louder than words.

Similarly, policies formulated while in opposition, but not subsequently enacted while in government, should not carry much weight.

We have now reformulated the somewhat vague question in the title of this chapter into a more precise and manageable form. We have to decide whether there was a consensus – in the sense of general agreement – between Labour and Conservative policy-makers in 1956–79. But (you are probably asking) exactly what degree of agreement or similarity constitutes consensus? This is the key issue, but it cannot be decided by any definition: the word 'consensus' simply will not admit of such a precise meaning. Therefore it is best, at this stage, to look at what happened during our period: then we can return to the issue at the end and use commonsense to decide whether or not consensus existed.

It is impossible here to do more than highlight specific aspects of the crowded period after 1956, so coverage will focus largely, though not solely, on the issues covered in more depth in chapters 22–8. But we must bear in mind that our conclusions might well be modified by further investigations.

Chronological framework of governments

1955–64: The Conservatives won the general election of May 1955 with an overall majority of more than 50. In January 1957 Macmillan replaced Eden as Prime Minister and won the general election in October 1959 with a majority of around 100. He was himself succeeded by Sir Alec Douglas-Home in October 1963.

1964–70: Labour won the general election in October 1964 with an overall majority of only four. Harold Wilson became Prime Minister. In March 1966 another general election increased the majority to almost 100.

1970–74: The Conservatives won in June 1970 with a majority of 30. Edward Heath was Prime Minister.

1974–79: In February 1974 Labour polled fewer votes but won four more seats than the Conservatives and so formed a minority government until another election in October, which secured an overall majority of only three. James Callaghan took over as Labour Prime Minister on Wilson's retirement in April 1976. In May 1979 the Conservatives, led by Margaret Thatcher, won an overall majority of over 40 seats.

Government policies

The constitution

Neither party made any major constitutional changes. There was talk of abolishing or fundamentally reforming the House of Lords, which would have divided the parties, but instead two relatively minor and uncontentious reforms were instituted:

■ The 1958 Life Peerages Act, which enabled peers to be appointed for their lifetimes only, thus diluting the hereditary element in the Lords. It also enabled women to become peers.

■ The 1963 Peerage Act, which enabled hereditary peers to renounce their titles.

There was greater disagreement over Labour's plans to devolve some authority on assemblies in Scotland and in Wales. Labour said this would appease Scottish and Welsh nationalists and so prevent the break-up of the United Kingdom; the Conservatives insisted it would hasten disintegration. Only after a hard-fought battle were Labour's plans accepted by Parliament, and then the Welsh people rejected them by four to one in 1979. In Scotland 51 per cent voted in favour, but the measure foundered as it was not supported by the required 40 per cent of those eligible to vote.

There were calls, especially from the Liberals, for the introduction of proportional representation (see page 132). Given that no government since the war had achieved a majority of the popular vote, the acceptance of this would have had profound effects on British political life. But Labour and the Conservatives – happy in the sixties and seventies to be alternating in office – refused to alter the 'first-past-the-post' system.

The economy

Most politicians judged that it was the standard of living which determined how the electorate voted, and so the economy provided an issue of fierce political debate. Normally the opposition did its utmost to 'rubbish' a government's record, while ministers generally issued dire warnings of the inadequacy – if not outright imbecility – of the shadow cabinet's proposals. But was there much difference between Conservative and Labour policies? Several pertinent points should be made:

■ No government, Labour or Conservative, was able to stem Britain's relative economic decline.

■ In the 1950s the press talked of 'Butskellism', policies accepted equally by R. A. Butler (Chancellor of the Exchequer, 1951–5) and Hugh

Keynesianism

The Cambridge economist John Maynard Keynes (1883–1946) had been the foremost critic of official financial and economic policies between the wars. He scorned the notion that the economy was a self-regulating mechanism and believed that government should intervene actively to keep the demand for goods high. From 1940 he became a Treasury adviser, and many came to believe that he had devised the means of maintaining both economic growth and high employment. Only with the inflation of the 1970s were his prescriptions seen to be inadequate.

Incomes policy

Normally wages are decided by 'free collective bargaining' between employers and unions, without state intervention. But because wage costs tended to push up the prices of goods and services, thus causing inflation throughout the economy, governments in the 1970s and after have often pursued an **incomes policy**, prescribing desirable levels of increases in pay. Labour, with its close connections with the unions, has tended to favour voluntary restraint, while the Conservatives under Heath used statutory means (*i.e.* Acts of Parliament).

Gaitskell (Labour's Chancellor in 1950–51 and leader in 1955–63). In theory the two men, and their parties, espoused different political philosophies, capitalism and socialism, but in practice they both favoured **Keynesianism**. They wanted to see a 'mixed economy', with both private and public sectors, and aimed to keep employment high. Butler and the Conservatives accepted almost all of Attlee's measures of nationalisation. For his part, Gaitskell did his best to drop Clause 4 from the Labour Constitution. Only the nationalisation of iron and steel was really contentious: nationalised by Labour in 1949, it was denationalised by the Conservatives in 1953 and nationalised again by Labour in 1967.

■ It was harder to maintain consensus after the 1950s, especially when unemployment and inflation both mounted. But the parties were equally baffled about how to cure these intractable problems. The Conservative and Labour Parties both, at one time, insisted that they would not have an **incomes policy** to decide pay rises, but both then changed their minds.

■ In 1970 Heath promised to intervene less in the economy: instead, he would allow 'market forces' to operate much more freely. Certainly he scorned the policy of propping up 'lame ducks', ailing industries which could not survive without government subsidies. However, in 1971 Rolls Royce, the makers of the famous cars and aero-engines, went bankrupt, and Heath decided to nationalise the firm. To have stood aside would have been too grave a blow to the economy and to national pride. He also subsidised Upper Clyde Shipbuilders, much as Labour had done earlier.

Industrial relations

Incomes policies and rising prices put a strain on industrial relations in the 1970s. The Conservatives endured a rash of strikes in 1970–73, especially from the miners; and for a time Labour seemed far better able to promote industrial harmony. The Conservative manifesto for the general election of February 1974, *Firm Action for a Fair Britain*, was very different from Labour's *Let Us Work Together*. Indeed the new Labour government in 1974 repealed the Conservatives' pay policy and their union legislation, the 1971 Industrial Relations Act (with its compulsory registration of unions, its provision for strike ballots and a cooling-off period, and its fines). There seems to be no consensus here. However,

■ Labour had itself proposed similar legislation, with its 1969 White Paper *In Place of Strife*, which it abandoned because of union hostility

■ Labour had similar problems with the unions in the early months of 1979, 'the winter of discontent' (see page 226).

Welfare state and education

Both Labour and Conservatives accepted the importance of the welfare state created after the Second World War. Welfare spending, particularly on the National Health Service, rose regardless of which political party was in power. There was some controversy over prescription charges: introduced in 1956, they were doubled in 1961; then Labour abolished them in 1965 but reimposed them in 1968. Not until the 1980s did anyone believe that the welfare state was under threat.

In its education policy, Labour came out firmly in 1964 for the comprehensive (as opposed to the grammar/secondary modern) system. There was no consensus on this issue. Yet Labour tacitly accepted the public schools, and both Labour and Conservatives fostered the expansion of higher education.

The Commonwealth

It was the Labour Party which conceded independence to India and Pakistan in 1947, thus creating the multiracial Commonwealth. But it was the Conservatives who presided over its expansion: despite the opposition of right-wing Tories, Macmillan realised that there was no sense in opposing the 'winds of change' blowing throughout Africa from the late 1950s. Similarly, the decline of enthusiasm for the Commonwealth affected both parties in the Sixties (see pages 279–282). There were differences of emphasis in their attitudes, but on the whole there was a bipartisan policy.

Foreign policy

This part of the book started with the Suez Crisis, when Labour condemned the Eden government's illegal and incompetent aggression. But thereafter differences between the parties dimmed, and their leaders often spoke of the need for a bipartisan approach. Both Labour and Conservatives recognised NATO (see page 213) as the keystone of British defence; both accepted the need for nuclear weapons (despite the involvement of the Labour left wing with the Campaign for Nuclear Disarmament), and both attempted to maintain a 'special relationship' with the United States. (And both sometimes suffered from the delusion that the Americans were equally wedded to such a relationship!)

One of the most significant controversies centred on Britain's traditional world role 'east of Suez', with its bases in the Persian Gulf, Aden, Singapore and elsewhere. Harold Wilson had come to power in 1964 proclaiming, like many a Conservative before him, that 'We are a world power and a world influence, or we are nothing'. It was believed that the bases helped to make Britain the most significant of the powers, besides the USA and USSR. But by 1968 severe financial problems meant that overseas spending had to be cut, and Wilson's government took the decision to withdraw from all bases east of Suez (except Hong Kong) by 1971. The Conservatives professed to be appalled and promised to restore some of the cuts, but it was Heath's government from 1970 which completed the process.

The European Community

Heath pinned his hopes for the future on entry into the European Community. In January 1973 Britain became a member, and two years later Wilson's third Labour administration held a referendum, which confirmed membership. Clearly the Conservatives were then keener on Europe than Labour. But was there a really significant difference between the parties?

As we saw in chapter 28, the Conservatives (in 1961–2) and Labour (in 1967) had tried, somewhat tentatively, to enter the Community. Labour's Hugh Gaitskell had been opposed to the EEC on principle, but his more flexible successor, Harold Wilson, calculated that a moderate pro-European course was most likely to keep his party together. Certainly there was no clear consensus on Europe, but divisions transcended party allegiance, both parties having their pro- and anti-marketeers.

Immigration

Another issue which seemed to divide the parties was 'New Commonwealth' immigration. The Conservative Immigrants Act of 1962, which imposed the first restrictions, was hotly opposed by Labour, and Gaitskell pledged that it would be repealed. But again Wilson avoided confrontation, especially after the shock of Gordon Walker's defeat in Smethwick (see chapters 24 and 25). Labour introduced the Race Relations Acts of 1965 and 1968, which the Conservatives opposed, but it was also Labour who rushed through Parliament in February 1968 the Bill to restrict the entry of the Kenyan Asians. Powell's speeches on immigration in the same year were condemned by both parties.

The attitudes of Labour and Conservatives towards immigration were not identical. There may have been more 'liberals' in the one and more 'anti-blacks' in the other; nevertheless, both parties contained a share of each.

Northern Ireland

Another vitally important issue in British politics, at least from 1968, was terrorism in Northern Ireland. Labour and Tory responses were not identical, but they were similar. Leading party spokesmen shared the same broad convictions:

- Northern Ireland must remain part of the United Kingdom so long as a majority of its population wished this to be so.

- Violence had to be eliminated, even at the cost of sending in British troops, of introducing internment and of direct rule.

- Blatant discrimination against the minority Catholic population had to be ended.

At the same time, both parties were willing, sometimes openly and sometimes covertly, to hold talks with the IRA and to consider 'power-sharing' and the possibility of allowing the Irish Republic a role in Ulster's affairs.

Conclusion

Does the level of agreement and bipartisanship exhibited by the two main parties warrant the use of the term 'consensus'? Remember that consensus does not demand total agreement, but only general agreement.

Party propaganda tended to emphasise the divergence of the parties. Two examples from the 1979 election can be seen in Figures 29.1 and 29.2. (There was certainly a consensus on the need to use slick advertising techniques!) Each side accused the other of economic incompetence. Labour was reminding voters of Heath's 1973–4 three-day week, while

Figure 29.1 *Conservatives reminded voters of Labour's poor employment record.*

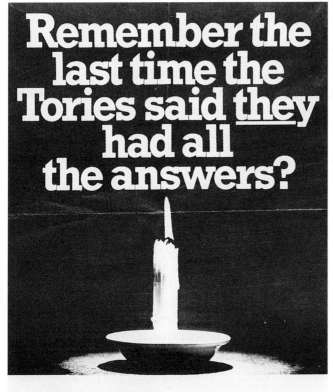

Figure 29.2 The 1979 general election: Labour reminded voters of
Conservative failures.

Figure 29.3 Jim Callaghan in the 1979 general
election. Many politicians wished to be all things to all
voters.

the Conservatives pointed to the fact that over 1.5 million people were
unemployed. (A cynic might say that it was easy to shoot at the other
side's economic record – but impossible convincingly to defend one's
own.)

However, the cartoon shown in Figure 29.3 implies that there was a consensus, in that Callaghan's moderation made him into a Tory. Similar
'turncoat' charges had been levelled at the Conservatives in the 1950s for
accepting Attlee's welfare and nationalisation reforms. Perhaps it was the
civil service, which was supposed to be politically neutral and did not lose
office as a result of elections, which was responsible for cross-party simi-
larities between governments.

Clearly the issue of consensus depends to a large extent on which issues
we stress. If we give pride of place to comprehensive schooling, then we
may be tempted to deny consensus. If, however, policy towards the trou-

bled province of Northern Ireland is high on our list of priorities, then we may insist that consensus undoubtedly existed.

Was there a consensus? Most people will answer 'Yes, but ...' or 'No, but ...'. If we think there was a consensus, we will nevertheless admit that on certain issues there was frank disagreement. In addition, we are likely to point to particular times within the 1956–79 period when consensus was either lost or wearing very thin. On the other hand, if our overall verdict is against consensus we will still point to issues or periods where there was substantial agreement.

But what is 'substantial agreement'? It is important to remember that such terms are relative, not absolute. Hence 'consensus' too is relative: it has meaning only in relation to opposing states of disagreement and dissension. The period 1956–79 may seem politically harmonious after Britons' experiences of the 1980s ('the Thatcher years'), when the Prime Minister is said to have identified consensus with woolly minded, weak conformity. On the other hand, the relative harmony of the Second World War years, when party politics were largely suspended, may make the postwar years seem a period of bitter partisan strife. And no one yet knows how 1956–79 will be perceived from the perspective of the twenty-first century.

Clearly the issue of consensus – and the parameters of the topic – will be debated again and again. Contemporary history does not allow 'final' verdicts. It is too controversial, too alive and too exciting for that.

Class discussion

The charge that there was a consensus in politics in the years 1956–79 was made most strongly by Mrs Thatcher, Prime Minister 1979–90. She saw consensus as a bad thing, which was preventing Britain from tackling serious underlying problems. In particular, she wanted to 'think the unthinkable' over issues like:

- nationalisation (where she wanted to privatise nationalised industries)
- the welfare state (which she wanted to make less all-embracing)
- protection of British industry (which she wanted to cut down).

1 What were the views of politicians in the two major parties on these three issues in the years 1956–79?

2 Do you agree with Mrs Thatcher that there was consensus on these three issues?

3 Do you agree with her that the consensus was harmful to Britain?

4 Are there any other important issues on which there was consensus between the parties from 1956 to 1979?

5 Are there any issues on which the parties strongly disagreed?

Further reading

Paul Adelman, *Britain: Domestic Politics, 1939–64* (Hodder and Stoughton, 1994) – a good starting-point.

Alan Sked and Chris Cook, *Post-War Britain* (Penguin, 1979) – a more academic text.

Bernard Porter, *Britannia's Burden* (Edward Arnold, 1994) – chapters 23–27 provide stimulating insights.

D. Kavanagh and P. Morris, *Consensus Politics from Attlee to Thatcher* (Blackwell, 1989).

Index

Pearson Education Limited
Edinburgh Gate, Harlow,
Essex CM20 2JE, England
and Associated Companies throughout the world.

First published 1996
Sixth impression 2006

Set in 10/13 Meridien Roman
Printed in Malaysia, VVP

ISBN-10: 0-582-08406-7
ISBN-13: 978-0-582-08406-3

Acknowledgements

We are grateful to the following for permission to reproduce photos and other copyright
material:

The author's agent for an extract from *Postscripts* by J. B. Priestley (Heinemann, 1940),
pages 179–180; City of Aberdeen Art Gallery and Museums Collections, page 13; *Belfast
Telegraph,* page 268; Centre for the Study of Cartoons & Caricature, University of Kent,
Canterbury, pages 52 (Sidney 'George' Strube, *Daily Express,* 19 May 1926), 102 (David
Low, *Evening Standard,* 18 July 1938), 141 (David Low, *Evening Standard,* 14 May 1940),
153 (George Whitelaw, *Daily Herald,* 2 Dec. 1942), 181 (ZEC, *Daily Mirror,* 8 May 1945),
185 (David Low, *Evening Standard,* 26 June 1945), 186 (David Low, *Evening Standard,* 30
June 1945), 195 (Vicky, *News Chronicle,* 22 May 1947), 207 (Vicky, *News Chronicle,* 23 April
1951), 209 (Vicky, *News Chronicle,* 22 May 1950), 238 (Vicky, *Evening Standard,* 19 May
1959), 250 (Nick Garland, *Daily Telegraph,* 19 Jan. 1970), 253 (TROG, *The Spectator,* 16 Oct.
1959), 272 (TROG, *The Observer,* Oct. 1969); Conservative Party, page 290; EMI Records,
page 257 below (photo: Paul Mulcahy); Mary Evans Picture Library/Jeffrey Morgan, page
31; Express Newspapers, pages 206 below (14 June 1950) and 234 (12 Jan. 1955); Hulton-
Getty Collection, pages 67, 110, 129, 171, 192 below, 216 above, 259 left; Imperial War
Museum, London, pages 21, 33, 34, 140, 158, 160, 162; International Music Publications
Ltd for an extract from the lyrics only from 'Woodstock' by Joni Mitchell © Siquomb
Publishing Corp. Warner/Chappell Music Ltd, London W1Y 3FA, page 258; National
Museum of Labour History, page 291 left; The Mansell Collection, page 35; National
Portrait Gallery, London, page 98; Popperfoto, pages 99, 116, 192 above, 193, 206 above,
216 below, 248, 279; *Punch,* pages 61, 62, 74, 82, 83, 100; *Red Star Weekly,* page 165; *Sunday
Mirror* (8 April 1979), page 291 right; Topham Picturepoint, pages 218, 257 above, 259
right; Writers & Readers Publishing Cooperative, page 270.

Cover photograph: Aerial view of the Festival of Britain; watercolour. Cover of *The Sphere,*
2 June 1951. Photo: Illustrated London News Picture Library.
Series editors: Eric Evans and Christopher Culpin
Publisher: Joan Ward
Editor: Steve Attmore
Designer: Mick Harris
Picture researcher: Louise Edgeworth
Artwork: Tony Richardson

The publisher's policy is to use paper manufactured from sustainable forests.